EatingWell®

500 CALORIE DINNERS

Easy, Delicious Recipes & Menus

BY JESSIE PRICE, NICCI MICCO & THE EATINGWELL TEST KITCHEN

JOIN US AT **WWW.EATINGWELL.COM** FOR MORE DELICIOUS RECIPES AND THE INSPIRATION AND INFORMATION YOU NEED TO MAKE HEALTHY EATING A WAY OF LIFE.

LIBRARY OF CONGRESS CATALOGING-IN-PUBLICATION DATA HAS BEEN APPLIED FOR.

ISBN 978-0-88150-846-8

AUTHORS | JESSIE PRICE (DEPUTY EDITOR: FOOD), NICCI MICCO (DEPUTY EDITOR: FEATURES & NUTRITION) & THE EDITORS OF EATINGWELL
CONTRIBUTING WRITER | JOYCE HENDLEY

ART DIRECTOR | MICHAEL J. BALZANO
PHOTOGRAPHER | KEN BURRIS
PRODUCTION DESIGNER | BETH ALESSI
PRODUCTION ASSISTANCE | AMANDA MCALLISTER

ASSOCIATE EDITOR | CAROLYN MALCOUN
TEST KITCHEN MANAGER | STACY FRASER
TEST KITCHEN | HILARY MEYER (ASSISTANT EDITOR), KATIE WEBSTER (RECIPE DEVELOPER, FOOD STYLIST), CAROLYN CASNER (RECIPE TESTER), PATSY JAMIESON (FOOD STYLIST), SUSAN HERR (FOOD STYLIST)
DIETITIAN & NUTRITION ADVISOR | SYLVIA GEIGER, M.S., R.D.

MANAGING EDITOR | WENDY S. RUOPP
ASSISTANT MANAGING EDITOR | ALESIA DEPOT
PRODUCTION MANAGER | JENNIFER B. BROWN
RESEARCH EDITOR | ANNE BLISS
INDEXER | AMY NOVICK, BACKSPACE INDEXING

EATINGWELL MEDIA GROUP
CEO | TOM WITSCHI
EDITORIAL DIRECTOR | LISA GOSSELIN

FRONT COVER PHOTOGRAPH BY KEN BURRIS | CASHEW SALMON WITH APRICOT COUSCOUS (PAGE 137)

PUBLISHED BY
THE COUNTRYMAN PRESS
P.O. BOX 748, WOODSTOCK, VT 05091
DISTRIBUTED BY
W.W. NORTON & COMPANY, INC.
500 FIFTH AVENUE, NEW YORK, NY 10110
PRINTED IN CHINA BY R.R. DONNELLEY

10 9 8 7 6 5 4 3 2 1

CONTENTS

VEGETARIAN...78

FISH & SEAFOOD...124

POULTRY...98

MEAT...148

SIDES...174

DESSERTS...194

"Any diet that's based on denying yourself the foods you really, really like is going to be temporary."

—Brian Wansink

Most of us are clueless about how many calories we're eating. We think we're eating wisely when we order General Tso's Chicken at the Chinese restaurant or the 8-ounce cut of prime rib. We don't realize that we're getting 1,200 calories in just that one entree. My research at the Cornell Food and Brand Lab shows just how bad Americans are at estimating calories. In one study, when we asked people to approximate the number of calories in a 12-inch Subway Italian BMT, the average guess was 439 calories. That sandwich packed 900!

At my lab, we look at all kinds of things that make people eat and, sometimes, eat too much. My studies have found that people tend to eat more—on average, 22 percent more—when they're offered a bigger portion of food (e.g., pasta, candy, even *stale* popcorn) and that people drink about 34 percent more from short, wide glasses than from tall, skinny ones. We've learned that giving a menu item an enticing name (e.g., "Black Forest Double Chocolate Cake" versus "Chocolate Cake") makes it more appealing. We also have discovered—through a tricky study involving an office candy dish—that the farther you have to walk to get a food, the less of it you're likely to eat. One of our most recent studies showed that people would rather have a dessert after a mediocre meal than after a really great one.

That an unsatisfying meal tends to leave you wanting dessert seems to tell us this: *Eat delicious foods and you'll feel satisfied.* It sounds like commonsense advice. But people generally don't follow it. Most of us, when we want to lose a few pounds, *give up* the great meals. Why do we insist on losing the foods we love in favor of foods we can barely tolerate? Any diet that's based on denying yourself the foods you really, really like is going to be temporary. Plus, it's likely to come back to bite you. With all that sacrificing you've been doing, there's a lot of catching up to do. And so the vicious cycle begins again.

EatingWell 500-Calorie Dinners can help break the yo-yoing weight-loss cycle once and for all. This book's flavorful recipes deliver the satisfaction we're looking for in a meal. After enjoying a great meal of Chicken, Charred Tomato & Broccoli Salad (*page 103*), wild rice with fresh herbs and a serving of Hot Fudge Pudding Cake (*page 196*), you won't want to gorge on something else—and you won't have to wander the house at night looking for supplemental snacks.

In *500-Calorie Dinners*, the recipe developers and registered dietitians at EATINGWELL marry the classic and the creative. They give us heart- and tummy-warming recipes with less grease, fewer calories and even less salt than do other contemporary cookbooks. We get more inventive combinations, more variety, more flavor and more taste complexity in easy, simple recipes.

I gave my gourmet wife, who is a graduate of Le Cordon Bleu in Paris, the book to play with in the kitchen. What she found most striking—and what was also my favorite feature—were the 500-Calorie Menus that go along with every recipe. They take the guesswork out of counting calories and show you that you can eat well and get all the nutrients you need from these meals. Having a 500-calorie ceiling allows us to just relax and enjoy dinner, without having to worry about eating too much.

For 20 years I have researched why people eat what they eat and how much they eat. For 10 of those years, I have enjoyed EATINGWELL Magazine because, as one of my lab researchers puts it, "it shows you can be a foodie without being a fatty." *EatingWell 500-Calorie Dinners* makes this even easier. This book is a tasty antidote to deprivation diets. Dig in.

—Brian Wansink, Ph.D., author of Mindless Eating: Why We Eat More Than We Think *(Bantam Books), director of the Cornell University Food and Brand Lab, former executive director of the USDA's Center for Nutrition Policy and Promotion*

LEMON CHICKEN STIR-FRY (PAGE 118)

A DELICIOUS WAY TO SLIM DOWN

BY NICCI MICCO

It used to be that dieting was all about what you *couldn't* eat: Fat. Carbohydrates. Anything that *wasn't* cabbage soup. It all depended on which plan you were pledging your allegiance to—each had a unique formula for melting away pounds. And often worked—until the inevitable day when you said, "I've had it" and went back to eating like a normal person, but with a vengeance. You made up for all of that "lost" pasta and bread and you gained the weight back. And then some.

What these gimmicky plans didn't tell you was that you could have lost the weight—and actually kept it off—eating what you love. That you didn't *have* to eat just cabbage or grapefruit or give up chocolate. That the restrictions these plans imposed simply slashed calories from your diet.

More and more, studies are proving that when it comes to losing weight, it's not really what you eat, it's how much you eat. More specifically, it's how many calories you consume. One of the latest studies to underscore this point was published in the prestigious *New England Journal of Medicine* in February 2009. Researchers from Harvard School of Public Health and the Pennington Biomedical Research Center in Louisiana recruited 811 overweight men and women and assigned them to one of four eating plans. All of the diets were focused on heart-healthy foods: healthful fats and "good carbs." All were designed to help the participants lose weight (daily calorie

targets were 750 calories less than each person was eating at the start of the study). But the plans varied in their relative proportions of fat, protein and carbohydrate. Each of the plans was either low in fat (20 percent of total calories) or high in fat (40 percent of calories), average in protein (15 percent of calories) or high in protein (25 percent). Across the four plans, carbohydrate ranged from 35 to 65 percent of total calories.

For two years, the participants followed their assigned eating plans, tracked their calories and attended regular support meetings. At the end of the study, the average weight loss was the same for all four groups: about 9 pounds. The researchers concluded, "reduced-calorie diets result in…weight loss regardless of which macronutrients they emphasize."

In other words, a calorie is a calorie is a calorie.

When you stop to think about it, the message is actually quite empowering. It means that you can eat whatever you want, so long as you limit your portions.

And there's the rub. In our modern world, where supersized foods abound, estimating portions—and calories—accurately sometimes feels next to impossible. And there's plenty of proof that, as a whole, we really are not so good at it. One study in the *American Journal of Public Health* revealed that people underestimated the calories in restaurant meals by up to 956 calories. Another showed that when registered dietitians—*nutrition experts*—were asked to estimate the calorie counts of common foods, such as lasagna and tuna-salad sandwiches, they were off (yes, they underestimated) by 200 to 600 calories.

Luckily it is getting easier to recognize reasonably sized servings and figure out calorie counts. The number of snacks offered in 100-calorie packs has skyrocketed in recent years. Since the summer of 2008, New York City restaurants with 15 or more outlets have been required by city ordinance to list the calorie counts of foods right next to their prices. The state of California passed a law requir-

ing calorie counts on menus at chain restaurants (with 20 or more outlets) by January 2011. A number of public health and medical associations are pushing for legislation that will mandate similar labeling nationwide. In 2009, major food manufacturers, including Coca-Cola and Mars (maker of M&Ms and Skittles), started listing calorie counts on the *front* of packages.

But plastering calorie content prominently on packaged goods and restaurant menus doesn't really help those of us who prefer to prepare healthy meals and snacks at home. It takes time to look up the calories of all of the whole ingredients that go into the meals you make and to create balanced, nutritious menus that won't break the calorie bank. So, we're doing the work for you. In *EatingWell 500-Calorie Dinners*, we're giving you simple, delicious recipes for appetizers, soups, salads, main courses, sides and desserts.

SECRETS OF SUCCESS

"Losing weight isn't rocket science. If you eat less and exercise more, you'll lose," says Jean Harvey-Berino, Ph.D., R.D., chair of the University of Vermont's Department of Nutrition and Food Sciences, who has made a career of teaching people to lose weight by making small daily changes. "The hardest part of losing weight is figuring out how to engineer your life so that you're able to do this." Through her research, Harvey-Berino has helped more than 1,000 people lose an average of 21 pounds in 6 months. She also co-wrote *The EatingWell Diet*, the 2008 James Beard Award-winning book that defined many of the principles—tracking calories, setting realistic goals, finding social support—outlined here in *500-Calorie Dinners*.

For more information on *The EatingWell Diet*—which provides detailed advice on customizing a weight-loss plan that works for you and more than 150 tasty weight-friendly recipes for dinners, lunches, breakfasts and snacks—visit *eatingwell.com/eatingwelldiet*.

HOW TO USE THIS BOOK

Here's how it works: we give you suggestions along with the recipes on how to round out your dinner and make it a nutritious 500-calorie meal. So, for example, with a chicken main dish we suggest vegetable sides, grain-based dishes and tasty "extras," such as dessert or a glass of wine. You choose one item from each of the categories. It's sort of like ordering from a prix fixe menu—except that instead of fixing the price in dollars, we're fixing it in calories. Each dinner menu "costs" only 500 calories. Of course our menus do give you some choices so the exact calorie count of your dinner will range depending on what you select. We can assure you that you'll end up somewhere around 500 calories, give or take a few. And you'll be shocked at how much food you get for the same number of calories you might otherwise spend on a large McDonald's fries (500 calories), a blueberry scone from Starbucks (460 calories) or an original-size fruit smoothie from Jamba Juice (450 calories).

We've focused on dinner because it's often the hardest meal to plan for: it falls during a busy time and you need recipes that are delicious enough to serve your whole family. But if you follow our menus you'll learn what the "right" number of calories looks like on your plate, and this will serve you well when you're eating out or at a friend's house and also when you're deciding what to have for breakfast or lunch.

Now. Let's get started.

Make it personal.

Cooking individual-size portions like this **Broccoli & Goat Cheese Soufflé** (*page 85*), which is made in a 10-ounce ramekin, or **Mini Meatloaves** (*page 154*), will help you control calories without even thinking about it.

1: PLAN AHEAD

What's for dinner? Rather than striking fear in your heart, this question should be a joyful one. Plan dinners that you can look forward to enjoying. How about a bowl of hearty beef and bean chili with a green salad tossed in a tangy vinaigrette (*page 159*)? Or roast chicken with gravy and a side of mashed potatoes (*page 113*)? Pasta with white clam sauce followed by a pineapple and raspberry parfait (*page 145*)?

Once you've decided what you want for dinner, plot out the rest of your day. First, you need to decide how many calories you should be eating. Most people can lose about 1 to 2 pounds per week on 1,500 calories per day—but perhaps you're not looking to lose right now, just to maintain. Or maybe you're very tall, or very short. You can calculate a daily calorie goal for yourself with the following formula: Your body weight x 12. That's the number of calories you'll need to eat each day to maintain your current weight. Subtract 500 from that number to lose a pound a week; 1,000 to lose 2. (If your result is less than 1,200 calories, bump up to that level. It's very difficult to meet your nutrient needs eating less than that.)

Now: what will you eat for breakfast? For lunch? For snacks? (Don't have an answer? See page 18 for ideas.) According to one study published in *Obesity Research*, a menu plan for the whole day really does help you lose weight. Perhaps it's because having it forces you to keep healthier foods on hand. In the study, people who had menu plans were more likely to keep nutritious low-calorie foods such as fruits and vegetables stocked at home than those who didn't. Planning ahead also helps to keep your eating on schedule: if you already know what you're having for lunch (and it's waiting for you in the fridge), you're less likely to let 6 or 7 hours pass without having something to eat—a situation that usually results in eating too much when you finally do sit down to a meal.

Try EATINGWELL's free Interactive Menu Planner at *eatingwell.com/menuplanner*—it tracks calories for you!

7³⁰ - egg (72 cal) on an English muffin w/ slice low-fat cheese (48) → This was filling !!!
- mango, ½ cup (54 cal) = (308)
+120

11ᴬᴹ strawberry yogurt -120 cal = (428)

1ᴾᴹ Greek salad —
greens & veggies - 45 cal
chicken (3oz) - 105
feta, ¼ cup - 100
Kalamata olives - 30
2 TBSP lowfat dressing -40
320
= 370 → (798)
tangelo - 50

Write what you bite.

Studies show that writing down everything you eat helps you lose weight. You might buy a pretty journal and look up calories in the back of this book. Maybe you prefer to track online. (You can do it at *eatingwell.com/ menuplanner*.) In your diary, include what you ate, how much and the calories it contained. You might also note where you ate or how you felt. Generally, the more detailed your notes are, the more they help.

2: AVOID "PORTION DISTORTION"

When you're trying to lose weight, learning to size up portions accurately is an important skill to master. Various studies show that almost everyone—heavy people and thin ones, nutrition experts and normal folks—underestimates how much they're eating a lot of the time. According to research by EATINGWELL advisor Brian Wansink, Ph.D., a professor of nutrition and marketing at Cornell University and the former executive director for the USDA's Center for Nutrition Policy and Promotion, people tend to *underestimate calorie intake by 20 to 40 percent* (see Foreword, page 7).

To combat "portion distortion," many weight-loss experts suggest using a kitchen scale or measuring cups to make sure you're getting the "right" number of calories—and not more. But whipping out measuring cups at every meal may feel, well, obsessive. It may seem "diet-y." Clinical.

There are other ways to keep an eye on portion sizes. You can take the "memorize-the-common-household items" approach. Remember that 3 ounces of meat (or other protein) looks like a deck of cards, a medium potato should be the size of a computer mouse and a quarter cup of anything is about as big as a golf ball. You might also try the "Rule of Thumb" method, which uses your hand as a reference. If you're a relatively small-framed woman, 1 teaspoon equals the tip of your thumb (to the middle joint); 1 tablespoon is the size of your thumb and 1 cup is about the size of your fist. Obviously this isn't a precise way of portioning—and the margin of error is greater the bigger your hand is—but it'll work in a pinch. It might be a good technique to try when you're eating out or at a friend's.

When you're at home, you're using the same bowls and utensils over and over again. Why not find out how much they hold? One time only, measure out the amount of soup that your ladle holds. If it's ¾ cup you'll know forever that two scoops equal a satisfying 1 ½-cup serving. On the flipside, you can measure out a given portion of a particular favorite food and serve it in the dish you'll almost always use when you eat that food. Once you know that one serving of cereal reaches only halfway up your bowl, you'll know to stop there. (This is a good trick to try with wineglasses too.)

Try it on for size.

No need to whip out measuring cups every time you want to serve up the perfect portion. Just figure out how much your ladle holds. This one, filled with **Grilled Tomato Gazpacho** (*page 40*), holds ¾ cup.

Heart-healthy monounsaturated fats (in nuts, avocados and olive oil) and polyunsaturated fats (in canola oil, plant oils and fish) infuse food with flavor. Eat 4 to 8 teaspoons per day.*

FRUITS & VEGETABLES

Fruits and vegetables are low in calories, but high in vitamins, minerals and other phytochemicals—compounds that fight disease-causing free radicals and amp up enzymes that clear toxins. Choose a rainbow of colors to get the widest variety of nutrients. Aim for 1 to 2 cups of fruits and 1 1/2 to 3 1/2 cups of vegetables per day.*

3: ENJOY A BALANCED DIET

Of course, there's more to good nutrition than counting calories. When you're cutting down portions, you're also reducing your intake of helpful nutrients, too, so it's even more important to make healthful choices. (In fact, it's probably a good idea to take a multivitamin that provides 100 percent of the Daily Values, just to cover your bases). Eating in balance also is likely to help you feel fuller on fewer calories.

*Daily intake guides are those recommended by the USDA's My Pyramid. For more information on what counts as a serving, see page 213.

LEAN PROTEINS

Some studies show that, gram for gram, protein may keep you feeling fuller than carbohydrates or fats do. For overall health, choose sources that are low in saturated fat: seafood, poultry, lean meat and tofu. Eat: 3 to 6½ ounce-equivalents per day.*

WHOLE GRAINS

Whole grains provide fiber, trace minerals and antioxidants and slow-release carbohydrates that keep your body and brain fueled. Aim for 4 to 9 ounce-equivalents per day.*

LOW-FAT DAIRY

Nonfat (or low-fat) milk and yogurt provide a satisfying combination of carbohydrate and protein. They're also good sources of calcium, which dieters often fall short on. Cheeses contain calcium, too, but pack in calories. Choose cheese with bold tastes so you don't need a lot to get great flavor. Eat: 2 to 3 cups of dairy daily.*

4: SHARE DELICIOUS MEALS

No one wants to nibble on carrots sticks and eat cottage cheese with a baby spoon while others at the table load up on pasta smothered in cream sauce. So if parceling out portions of bland, boring foods day after day is the approach you're taking, you're going to have one heck of a time trying to drum up the "social support" that is helpful in losing weight and keeping it off. Research in the *Journal of Consulting and Clinical Psychology* showed that when friends joined and participated in a group weight-loss program together, they lost more weight and kept it off more successfully than people who did the program on their own.

So tempt your family and friends to join you on your quest for better health (and a slimmer shape) by preparing them delicious meals. Who would refuse an invitation to a dinner of crab cakes (*page 126*) with a spinach salad, a spicy corn-and-pepper sauté and peach popsicles for dessert? And do Seared Steaks with Caramelized Onions & Gorgonzola (*page 150*) sound like a "diet-friendly" supper? *Exactly.* Once you've biased your loved ones with a few delectable meals, *then* reveal what you're up to.

Then, suggest that you jog together twice a week. *Then*, challenge them to a weight-loss competition. After all, as the saying goes, "you can catch more flies with honey..." Or, we'd add, Banana Pudding Pops (*page 202*).

> Researchers have shown that people who consistently eat a healthful diet have an easier time controlling their weight than people who go "all out" on weekends and holidays and diet strictly the rest of the time.

5: MOVE ON FROM SLIP-UPS

You planned out your meals; snacks, treats too. So you "shouldn't" have felt deprived and you "shouldn't" have binged on the brownies but—guess what?—you did. It happens. And what you *really* shouldn't do is throw in the towel for the day and go on an eating free-for-all. The key to overcoming slip-ups is to forgive, forget it and get right back on track. Acknowledge the fact that you just ate your weight in pizza or ice cream, and then forget about it. Guilt begets more bingeing. Don't succumb to that. Don't fall into the splurge-and-then-skimp cycle that derails so many dieters. Researchers at Brown Medical School's Weight Control and Diabetes Research Center have shown that people who consistently eat a healthful diet have an easier time controlling their weight than people who go "all out" on weekends and holidays and diet strictly the rest of the time.

Besides, punishing yourself with Spartan meals doesn't exactly inspire healthy habits that you can keep—and enjoy—for a lifetime. Planning out a week's worth of delicious calorie-controlled dinners (and breakfasts and lunches and snacks, *page 18*) will.

3 WEIGHT-LOSS MYTHS DEBUNKED

MYTH: You can lose 10 pounds in 2 weeks. You probably *can* lose 10 pounds in two weeks if you crash diet but you'll feel terrible—and most of the weight will return once you start eating normally. To *truly* lose 1 pound, you need to "eliminate" 3,500 calories—the amount stored in a pound of fat—by eating less and moving more. If you cut 500 calories (or cut 300 and burn 200 through exercise) every single day of the week, you'll lose about a pound a week. And that's real weight loss.

MYTH: If you exercise, you can eat as much as you want. Unless you're working out like an Olympic athlete, to lose weight you'll still need to keep an eye on how many calories you're eating. "Calories in" add up much more quickly than "calories out." Consider this: two medium cookies cost you about 400 calories. To burn 400 calories, the average person needs to run or walk 4 miles.

MYTH: You should expect to be hungry while dieting. If you cut calories randomly, you're probably going to feel hungry. On the other hand, if you plan out your day so that you're replenishing yourself with nutritious foods every three or four hours, you'll likely feel quite satisfied on significantly fewer calories. Aim to include a source of lean protein (e.g., skim milk, turkey) and fiber (e.g., hummus, carrots) in every meal and snack.

6: TREAT YOURSELF

You love chocolate. You *live* for chocolate. But when you're trying to lose weight, you aim for eating perfection: yogurt and berries—with just a sprinkle of chopped almonds—for breakfast. A colorful salad and a whole-grain roll for lunch. Wild-caught salmon, green beans and brown rice for dinner. Plenty of water, fruit for snacks and a cup or two of green tea in between. "Picture perfect" eating sure does feel virtuous. But, for most people, it's impossible to achieve every minute of every day. Recognizing realistic expectations is key to succeeding at slimming down. Why?

Aiming to be "too good" sets you up to fail. For example, if your favorite treat is chocolate but then you suddenly ban it entirely, you're likely to binge big-time the next time someone marches through the office with a tray of brownies for a co-worker's birthday. Don't let yourself feel deprived. If you have a sweet tooth, plan to have a low-calorie sweet treat every day. Choose those that come in discrete units, such as our recipe for Chocolate-Dipped Gingersnaps (157 calories for two cookies). If you like to have a glass of wine with dinner, do it. Just make room for the calories by passing on something else—perhaps the bread. In other words, *prioritize*.

Indulge a little.

Believe it or not, treats like **Chocolate-Dipped Gingersnaps** (*page 200*) may be the secret to losing weight— for good.

WHAT DOES A 1,500-CALORIE DAY LOOK LIKE?

Most people will lose weight on a daily diet of 1,500 calories, which is the total calorie count for all the food pictured here.* To create your own 1,500-calorie day, start with one of the dinner menus in this book and select one of the breakfasts, one of the lunches and a couple of the snacks we suggest.

FOR BREAKFAST, CHOOSE ONE OF THESE 300- TO 350-CALORIE OPTIONS:

Egg and Cheese Sandwich (1 egg on a whole-wheat English muffin with 1-oz. slice low-fat cheese) + ½ cup diced mango= **308 calories**

Breakfast Taco (1 scrambled egg, ¼ cup salsa, ¼ cup shredded low-fat Cheddar on a 6-inch corn tortilla) + 12 oz. nonfat latte = **319 calories**

½ whole-wheat bagel with 1 Tbsp. reduced-fat cream

cheese and 1 oz. ham + 1 cup honeydew melon + 1 cup nonfat milk = **337 calories**

1 ½ cups whole-grain cereal with 1 cup nonfat milk + 1 medium banana = **345 calories**

Whole-wheat English muffin with 1 Tbsp. peanut butter + 6 oz. nonfat plain yogurt + ½ cup diced papaya = **350 calories**

1 cup oatmeal topped with ¼ cup non-fat plain yogurt and ½ cup berries + 12 oz. nonfat latte = 349 calories

BREAKFAST
349
calories

1 cup baby carrots + ¼ cup hummus = 157 calories

SNACK
157
calories

One slice whole-wheat bread, toasted with ½ oz. Cheddar and 2 slices tomatoes + 1 ½ cups black bean soup = 362 calories

LUNCH
362
calories

AIM TO MAKE LUNCH 325 TO 400 CALORIES. TRY:

Tuna Sandwich (2 slices multigrain bread, ½ cup tuna salad made with 2 tsp. low-fat mayonnaise; lettuce, tomato) + 1 peach = **327 calories**

Grilled Chicken Sandwich (whole-wheat roll + 3 oz. grilled chicken breast + 1-oz. slice reduced-fat Swiss cheese, lettuce, tomato, 2 tsp. low-fat mayonnaise) + ½ cup diced watermelon = **373 calories**

Bean Burrito (8-inch whole-wheat tortilla, ¼ cup nonfat refried beans, ¼ cup salsa, 2 oz. low-fat Cheddar cheese)

+ small salad (1 cup lettuce, ½ cup veggies, 2 Tbsp. reduced-fat ranch dressing) = **393 calories**

Grilled Salmon Caesar Wrap (8-inch whole-wheat tortilla + 3 oz. grilled salmon, ¾ cup shredded romaine, 2 tsp. low-calorie Caesar dressing) + ½ cup grapes = **393 calories**

Greek Salad with chicken (2 cups greens + ⅓ cup each diced bell peppers, tomatoes and onions + ¼ cup feta + 3 oz. cooked chicken breast, 4 kalamata olives + 2 Tbsp. low-calorie vinaigrette) = **400 calories**

ADD IN A COUPLE OF HEALTHY SNACKS. HOW ABOUT...

1 cup strawberries + 2 Tbsp. nonfat plain yogurt = **70 calories**

1 cup cantaloupe + 2 small gingersnaps = **113 calories**

½ cup nonfat cottage cheese + ½ cup fresh mandarin oranges = **122 calories**

1 oz. string cheese + 2 oz. sliced deli turkey = **140 calories**

Hard-boiled egg, sliced, on 1 slice whole-wheat toast with 2 tsp. Dijon mustard = **141 calories**

1 small apple + 1 Tbsp. natural creamy peanut butter = **172 calories**

1 small apple, 12 almonds + ice water with lemon = 170 calories

Tuna Steaks Provençal (*page 142*) with Sicilian-Style Broccoli (*page 183*), ½ cup pearl barley + Baby Tiramisù (*page 200*) = 481 calories

DINNER
481
calories

SNACK
170
calories

*Notice there aren't any juices or soft drinks here. Why? Studies show that sweet beverages don't satisfy us the way solids do, so do you really want to spend 150 calories on a drink?

APPETIZERS

Done right, appetizers can be a dieter's best friend. They are, after all, *small*. And you get a big bang of flavor in just a bite or two. Plus they allow you to sample little tastes of lots of different things, rather than committing to a big plate of just one.

Problem is, we often encounter these powerful little palate-pleasers at parties where they're hard to avoid. It's too tempting to resist second and third trips to that buffet table packed with creamy dips. The pastry puffs stuffed with savory meats look and smell so delicious that you help yourself to just one more, overlooking the fact that dinner will be served soon.

But with a little planning it's actually easy to incorporate an appetizer or two into a dinner that still weighs in under 500 calories. The healthy appetizer recipes in this chapter, such as garlicky marinated mushrooms or roasted eggplant-and-feta dip, won't break the bank calorie-wise. And we've even included a lightened-up version of one of those appetizer-buffet staples—creamy spinach dip. But with this version, you can feel free to indulge and still have room for Garlic & Herb Pita Chips (*page 186*) to scoop up the dip, Linguine with Escarole & Shrimp (*page 127*) and Chunky Peach Popsicles (*page 202*) for dessert.

Serve Salmon & Cucumber Mini Smørrebrød (*page 22*), 91 calories, or Watercress & Roquefort Eggs (*page 24*), 30 calories, or Mississippi Spiced Pecans (*page 23*), 107 calories, as a starter to your dinner.

PER SERVING: **91 calories**; 2 g fat (1 g sat, 1 g mono); 8 mg cholesterol; 10 g carbohydrate; 7 g protein; 1 g fiber; 288 mg sodium; 62 mg potassium.

H✷W L↓C H♥H

THE 500-CALORIE MENU

SERVE WITH ONE FROM EACH GROUP

Pork Chops with Orange & Fennel Salad, page 166 (257 cal.)
OR
Lemon-Garlic Shrimp & Vegetables, page 128 (227 cal.)

Shredded Root Vegetable Pancakes, page 176 (106 cal.)
OR
Whole-Grain Rice Pilaf, page 186 (97 cal.)

Creamy Chopped Cauliflower Salad, page 59 (49 cal.)
OR
Tangerine (1 medium, 47 cal.)

DIET TIP

Get into the open-faced sandwich habit and you'll automatically cut bread calories in half and barely notice. An average regular-size piece of bread is about 100 calories.

SALMON & CUCUMBER MINI SMØRREBRØD

ACTIVE TIME: **15 MINUTES** | TOTAL: **15 MINUTES**
TO MAKE AHEAD: Cover and refrigerate for up to 8 hours.

Denmark is famous for creative open-faced sandwiches like these. Here, crunchy cucumber, fresh dill and cured salmon top thinly sliced rye bread for a simply spectacular appetizer—or a great light lunch with a salad on the side. (Photograph: page 20.)

  ¼ cup reduced-fat sour cream
  3 tablespoons nonfat plain yogurt (preferably Greek-style; *see Note, page 209*)
 16 slices cocktail-size thin rye *or* pumpernickel bread
 16 slices cucumber
 16 small sprigs fresh dill
 16 slices Scandinavian-style cured salmon (*gravad lax*) *or* smoked salmon

Combine sour cream and yogurt in a small bowl. Top each slice of bread with a slice of cucumber, 1 teaspoon of the sour cream mixture, a sprig of dill and a slice of salmon.

MAKES 8 SERVINGS, 2 PIECES EACH.

MISSISSIPPI SPICED PECANS

ACTIVE TIME: **20 MINUTES** | TOTAL: **20 MINUTES**
TO MAKE AHEAD: Store in an airtight container for up to 2 weeks.

These mildly sweet and salty nuts are great to have on hand over the holidays. Rather than eating them by the handful, savor them in moderation by sprinkling a few onto salads or stir-fries. (Photograph: page 20.)

1 pound pecan halves
1 tablespoon packed dark brown sugar
1½ teaspoons kosher salt
1 teaspoon chopped fresh thyme
1 teaspoon chopped fresh rosemary
½ teaspoon freshly ground pepper
½ teaspoon *piment d'Espelette* (*see Note, page 207*) *or* a pinch of cayenne pepper
2 tablespoons extra-virgin olive oil

1. Preheat oven to 350°F.

2. Spread pecans on a large baking sheet. Bake until fragrant, about 12 minutes. Watch carefully so they don't burn.

3. Combine brown sugar, salt, thyme, rosemary, pepper and *piment d'Espelette* (or cayenne) in a small bowl. Transfer the toasted pecans to a large bowl, drizzle with oil and toss well to coat completely. Sprinkle with the spice mixture and toss again. Serve warm or let cool completely and store in an airtight container.

MAKES 4 CUPS.

PER 2-TABLESPOON SERVING: **107 calories**; 11 g fat (1 g sat, 6 g mono); 0 mg cholesterol; 2 g carbohydrate; 1 g protein; 1 g fiber; 53 mg sodium; 58 mg potassium.

THE 500-CALORIE MENU

SERVE WITH ONE FROM EACH GROUP

Cornmeal-Crusted Chicken with Pepián Sauce, page 101 (314 cal.)
OR
Black-Eyed Peas with Pork & Greens, page 165 (279 cal.)

Basic Sautéed Kale, page 178 (102 cal.)
OR
Mixed greens (1½ cups) with 2 Tbsp. Cucumber Herb Vinaigrette, page 74 (70 cal.)

DIET TIP

Chew your nuts well. One study found that people who chewed almonds thoroughly (up to 40 chews) felt full longer than those who chewed the same amount of nuts fewer times.

PER SERVING: **30 calories**; 2 g fat (1 g sat, 1 g mono); 54 mg cholesterol; 1 g carbohydrate; 3 g protein; 0 g fiber; 68 mg sodium; 40 mg potassium.

THE 500-CALORIE MENU

SERVE WITH ONE FROM EACH GROUP

Seared Steaks with Caramelized Onions & Gorgonzola, page 150 (306 cal.)
OR
Seared Chicken with Apricot Sauce, page 100 (252 cal.)

Baby spinach (1½ cups) with 2 Tbsp. Garlic-Yogurt Dressing, page 79 (39 cal.)
OR
Steamed broccoli (½ cup) with fresh chopped herbs and a squeeze of lemon (see Guide, page 191; 22 cal.)

Orange Crisps with Citrus Fruit Salad, page 198 (128 cal.)
OR
Red wine (5-ounce glass, 120 cal.)

DIET TIP

Egg yolks may pack more calories and fat than the whites, but they're full of nutrients—vitamins A and D as well as the antioxidants zeaxanthin and lutein, which help to protect vision. Use the extras from this recipe judiciously: crumble and sprinkle over steamed vegetables or toss into a spinach salad.

WATERCRESS & ROQUEFORT EGGS

ACTIVE TIME: **20 MINUTES** | TOTAL: **20 MINUTES**
TO MAKE AHEAD: Cover and refrigerate for up to 2 days.

Peppery watercress and tangy Roquefort are a sophisticated addition to deviled eggs. We cut the amount of yolks in this recipe by half, saving an ample amount of calories and fat (about 54 calories and 5 grams of fat per yolk). (Photograph: page 20.)

- 12 hard-boiled eggs (*see Note, page 209*)
- ½ cup fresh breadcrumbs (*see Note, page 207*), preferably whole-wheat
- ¼ cup reduced-fat sour cream
- 2 tablespoons chopped fresh watercress, plus 24 sprigs for garnish
- 1½ tablespoons crumbled Roquefort cheese *or* other blue cheese
- 2 teaspoons lemon juice
- ¼ teaspoon salt
  Freshly ground pepper to taste

Halve eggs. Scoop out yolks, reserving 6 for another use. Mash the remaining 6 yolks in a small bowl. Mix in breadcrumbs, sour cream, chopped watercress, cheese and lemon juice. Season with salt and pepper. Spoon the yolk mixture into the egg white halves and garnish each with a sprig of watercress.

MAKES 24 SERVINGS, ½ EGG EACH.

SHERRIED MUSHROOMS

ACTIVE TIME: **40 MINUTES** | TOTAL: **40 MINUTES**

TO MAKE AHEAD: Cover and refrigerate for up to 1 day. Bring to room temperature before serving.

These tender, juicy mushrooms work with just about any menu—and they're a terrific low-cal nibble. Place a dish of toothpicks next to the serving dish and let guests help themselves.

3	pounds white mushrooms, trimmed
1	tablespoon extra-virgin olive oil
¾	cup cream sherry (*see Note, page 208*)
8	cloves garlic, minced
2	tablespoons lemon juice
½	teaspoon kosher salt
	Freshly ground pepper to taste
2	tablespoons minced fresh parsley

Clean mushrooms and cut in half (or quarters if large). Heat oil in a large skillet or Dutch oven over medium-high heat. Add mushrooms and cook, stirring, for 10 minutes. Stir in sherry and garlic and continue cooking, stirring occasionally, until most of the juices have evaporated, 10 to 14 minutes more. Stir in lemon juice and season with salt and pepper. Stir in parsley just before serving.

MAKES 12 SERVINGS, ½ CUP EACH.

PER SERVING: **49 calories**; 1 g fat (0 g sat, 1 g mono); 0 mg cholesterol; 5 g carbohydrate; 2 g protein; 0 g fiber; 56 mg sodium; 495 mg potassium.

H)(W   L↓C   H♥H

THE 500-CALORIE MENU
SERVE WITH ONE FROM EACH GROUP

Smoky Corn & Black Bean Pizza, page 80 (303 cal.)
OR
Skillet Gnocchi with Chard & White Beans, page 83 (327 cal.)

Pineapple-Raspberry Parfaits, page 201 (112 cal.)
OR
Red wine (5-ounce glass, 120 cal.)

PER SERVING: **73 calories**; 3 g fat (0 g sat, 2 g mono); 92 mg cholesterol; 1 g carbohydrate; 10 g protein; 0 g fiber; 154 mg sodium; 108 mg potassium.

H✂W   L⬇C   H♥H

THE 500-CALORIE MENU

SERVE WITH ONE FROM EACH GROUP

Salmon Burgers with Green Goddess Sauce, page 138 (187 cal.)
OR
Pan-Roasted Chicken & Gravy, page 113 (177 cal.)

Brussels Sprouts with Bacon-Horseradish Cream, page 181 (80 cal.)
OR
Basic Sautéed Kale, page 178 (102 cal.)

Hot Fudge Pudding Cake, page 196 (142 cal.)
OR
White wine (5-ounce glass, 116 cal.)

DIET TIP

Keep shrimp in your freezer for diet-friendly meals: a 3-ounce serving—about 15 large shrimp—provides only 84 calories and 1 gram of fat.

LEMON-GARLIC MARINATED SHRIMP

ACTIVE TIME: **10 MINUTES** | TOTAL: **10 MINUTES**
TO MAKE AHEAD: Cover and refrigerate for up to 2 hours.

Marinating precooked shrimp in garlic- and lemon-infused oil makes a simple, elegant appetizer. If you have leftovers, turn them into a protein-packed, satisfying lunch by tossing with an equal amount of drained canned white beans and chopped celery.

1¼ pounds cooked shrimp
3 tablespoons minced garlic
2 tablespoons extra-virgin olive oil
¼ cup lemon juice
¼ cup minced fresh parsley
½ teaspoon kosher salt
½ teaspoon freshly ground pepper

Place shrimp in a large bowl. Cook garlic and oil in a small skillet over medium heat until fragrant, about 1 minute. Add lemon juice, parsley, salt and pepper. Pour the lemon-garlic mixture over the shrimp and toss to coat. Chill until ready to serve.

MAKES 12 SERVINGS.

THE 500-CALORIE MENU

SERVE WITH ONE FROM EACH GROUP

Toasted whole-grain baguette (2 inches, 132 cal.)
OR
Garlic & Herb Pita Chips, page 186 (117 cal.)

Linguine with Escarole & Shrimp, page 127 (271 cal.)
OR
Broccoli & Goat Cheese Soufflé, page 85 (254 cal.)

Chunky Peach Popsicles, page 202 (33 cal.)
OR
Sliced fresh strawberries (½ cup, 27 cal.)

DIET TIP

Try replacing full-fat sour cream and mayonnaise in creamy dips and salad dressings with a combination of reduced-fat cream cheese, cottage cheese and/or nonfat plain yogurt. You'll cut calories and the layers of flavors will still taste rich.

CREAMY SPINACH DIP

ACTIVE TIME: **15 MINUTES** | TOTAL: **15 MINUTES**
TO MAKE AHEAD: Cover and refrigerate for up to 3 days. Stir before serving.

This light spinach dip is made healthier with reduced-fat cream cheese, nonfat yogurt and low-fat cottage cheese instead of full-fat cheese, mayonnaise and sour cream. You'll save a whopping 84 calories and 10 grams of fat per serving compared to traditional versions. Serve it with pita chips and crunchy vegetables or spread it on a sandwich.

  1 small shallot, peeled
  1 5- to 8-ounce can water chestnuts, rinsed
  ½ cup reduced-fat cream cheese (Neufchâtel)
  ½ cup low-fat cottage cheese
  ¼ cup nonfat plain yogurt
  1 tablespoon lemon juice
  ½ teaspoon salt
     Freshly ground pepper to taste
  6 ounces baby spinach
  2 tablespoons chopped fresh chives

Pulse shallot and water chestnuts in a food processor until coarsely chopped. Add cream cheese, cottage cheese, yogurt, lemon juice, salt and pepper and pulse until just combined. Add spinach and chives and pulse until incorporated.

MAKES 10 SERVINGS, ABOUT ¼ CUP EACH.

ROASTED EGGPLANT & FETA DIP

ACTIVE TIME: **40 MINUTES** | TOTAL: **40 MINUTES**
TO MAKE AHEAD: Cover and refrigerate for up to 2 days.

There are countless variations on this classic meze *(appetizer) in Greece; our version gets a kick from fresh chile and cayenne pepper.*

1	medium eggplant (about 1 pound)
2	tablespoons lemon juice
¼	cup extra-virgin olive oil
½	cup crumbled feta cheese, preferably Greek
½	cup finely chopped red onion
1	small red bell pepper, finely chopped
1	small chile pepper, such as jalapeño, seeded and minced (optional)
2	tablespoons chopped fresh basil
1	tablespoon finely chopped flat-leaf parsley
¼	teaspoon cayenne pepper, or to taste
¼	teaspoon salt
	Pinch of sugar (optional)

1. Position oven rack about 6 inches from the heat source; preheat broiler.

2. Line a baking pan with foil. Place eggplant in the pan and poke a few holes all over it to vent steam. Broil the eggplant, turning with tongs every 5 minutes, until the skin is charred and a knife inserted into the dense flesh near the stem goes in easily, 14 to 18 minutes. Transfer to a cutting board until cool enough to handle.

3. Put lemon juice in a medium bowl. Cut the eggplant in half lengthwise and scrape the flesh into the bowl, tossing with the lemon juice to help prevent discoloring. Add oil and stir with a fork until it is absorbed. (The eggplant should be a little chunky.) Stir in feta, onion, bell pepper, chile pepper (if using), basil, parsley, cayenne and salt. Taste and add sugar if desired.

MAKES 12 SERVINGS, ABOUT ¼ CUP EACH.

PER SERVING: **75 calories**; 6 g fat (2 g sat, 4 g mono); 6 mg cholesterol; 4 g carbohydrate; 2 g protein; 2 g fiber; 129 mg sodium; 121 mg potassium.

H✖W L⬇C

THE 500-CALORIE MENU
SERVE WITH ONE FROM EACH GROUP

Toasted whole-grain baguette (2 inches, 132 cal.)
OR
Garlic & Herb Pita Chips, page 186 (117 cal.)

Provençal-Style Edamame Sauté, page 96 (318 cal.)
OR
Grapefruit Chicken Satay Salad, page 68 (313 cal.)

SOUPS

If you're trying to feel full on fewer calories, learn to love soups. Research conducted at Penn State University has shown that starting a meal with vegetable-based soup (like Curried Carrot Soup (*page 32*), Grilled Tomato Gazpacho (*page 40*) or one of the many others featured in this chapter) resulted in people eating 20 percent fewer calories over the course of their entire meal. Why is soup so satisfying? It's mostly water (which is, of course, calorie-free!)—but our bodies register it as "food" so it fills us up.

Don't think of soups as just starters. Hearty recipes that include beans, chicken, fish or lean beef are usually substantial enough to serve as a main course—but they're low enough in calories that you can round them out with a couple of side dishes. A bowl of Black Bean Soup with a salad, a slice of whole-grain baguette *and* dessert feels like a feast. Who'd ever guess that it "costs" less than 500 calories?

A 494-Calorie Dinner (*left*): Black Bean Soup (*page 42*), 191 calories; 1½ cups mixed greens with 2 tablespoons Goat Cheese & Tomato Dressing (*page 76*), 102 calories; toasted whole-grain baguette, 132 calories; 1½ cups diced watermelon, 69 calories.

THE 500-CALORIE MENU

SERVE WITH ONE FROM EACH GROUP

Sugar Snap Pea & Barley Salad, page 184 (152 cal.)
OR
Baby spinach (1½ cups) with 2 Tbsp. Roasted Garlic Dressing, page 75 (169 cal.)

Tuna Steaks Provençal, page 142 (214 cal.)
OR
Grilled wild Pacific salmon fillet (3 ounces, 184 cal.)

CURRIED CARROT SOUP

ACTIVE TIME: **40 MINUTES** | TOTAL: **1 HOUR**
TO MAKE AHEAD: Cover and refrigerate for up to 1 day.

This hearty soup only sounds complex: you probably have the ingredients in your pantry and refrigerator already (see "The Healthy Pantry," page 207). If you like a bit of heat, use hot Madras curry powder. (Photograph: page 51.)

3	tablespoons canola oil
2	teaspoons curry powder
8	medium carrots, peeled and thinly sliced
4	medium stalks celery, thinly sliced
1	medium onion, coarsely chopped
5	cups reduced-sodium chicken broth
1	tablespoon lemon juice
¼	teaspoon salt
	Freshly ground pepper to taste

1. Cook oil and curry powder in a large saucepan over medium heat, stirring, until fragrant, 1 to 2 minutes. Stir in carrots, celery and onion; toss to coat in oil. Cook, stirring frequently, for 10 minutes. Stir in broth. Bring to a boil. Reduce heat and simmer until the vegetables are very tender, about 10 minutes. Remove from the heat; let stand for 10 minutes. Use a paper towel to blot away any oil that has risen to the top.

2. Working in batches of no more than 2 cups at a time, transfer the soup to a blender and puree (use caution when pureeing hot liquids). Return the pureed soup to the pan, place over medium heat and heat through. Season with lemon juice, salt and pepper.

MAKES 6 SERVINGS, 1⅓ CUPS EACH.

GOLDEN SUMMER SQUASH & CORN SOUP

ACTIVE TIME: 30 MINUTES | TOTAL: 30 MINUTES
TO MAKE AHEAD: Cover and refrigerate for up to 2 days.

Use this easy summer soup as a start to your meal or enjoy it as a light lunch. We love the way fresh thyme elevates the flavor, but any herb you have on hand will work well. Try goat cheese in place of the feta too.

1	tablespoon extra-virgin olive oil
1	medium shallot, chopped
2	medium summer squash (about 1 pound), diced
3	teaspoons chopped fresh herbs, such as thyme *or* oregano, divided
1	14-ounce can reduced-sodium chicken broth *or* vegetable broth
¼	teaspoon salt
1	cup fresh corn kernels (from 1 large ear; *see Note, page 209*) *or* frozen
1	teaspoon lemon juice
¼	cup crumbled feta cheese

1. Heat oil in a large saucepan over medium heat. Add shallot and cook, stirring, 1 minute. Add squash and 1 teaspoon herbs and cook, stirring occasionally, until the squash starts to soften, 3 to 5 minutes. Add broth and salt; bring to a boil. Reduce heat to a simmer and cook until the squash is soft and mostly translucent, about 5 minutes more.

2. Transfer the soup to a blender and puree until smooth (use caution when pureeing hot liquids). Return the soup to the pan and stir in corn. Bring to a simmer over medium heat and cook, stirring occasionally, until the corn is tender, 3 to 5 minutes. Remove from the heat; stir in lemon juice. Serve garnished with feta and the remaining 2 teaspoons herbs.

MAKES 4 SERVINGS, ABOUT 1 CUP EACH.

PER SERVING: **111 calories**; 6 g fat (2 g sat, 3 g mono); 6 mg cholesterol; 13 g carbohydrate; 5 g protein; 2 g fiber; 462 mg sodium; 497 mg potassium.
NUTRITION BONUS: Vitamin C (40% daily value).

H✖W L⬇C H♥H

THE 500-CALORIE MENU
SERVE WITH

Spinach & Beet Salad with Chicken, page 69 (379 cal.)
OR
Spaghetti with Tuna & Tomato Sauce, page 144 (360 cal.)

DIET TIP

Zucchini or any summer squash is an awesome calorie bargain—under 20 calories per cupful. Snack on it raw, shred it into salads, soups and casseroles or toss it into stir-fries.

PER SERVING: **60 calories**; 1 g fat (0 g sat, 0 g mono); 0 mg cholesterol; 12 g carbohydrate; 2 g protein; 3 g fiber; 532 mg sodium; 249 mg potassium. NUTRITION BONUS: Vitamin A (160% daily value), Vitamin A (17% dv).

H✂W   L↓C   H♥H

THE 500-CALORIE MENU

SERVE WITH ONE FROM EACH GROUP

Southwestern Tofu Scramble, page 88 (202 cal.)
OR
Salmon with Pepita-Lime Butter, page 139 (185 cal.)

Quinoa with Latin Flavors, page 186 (181 cal.)
OR
Warm corn tortillas (two 6-inch, 140 cal.)

Glazed Mini Carrots, page 179 (74 cal.)
OR
Chilled Snap Peas with Creamy Tarragon Dressing, page 179 (61 cal.)

BAJA BUTTERNUT SQUASH SOUP

ACTIVE TIME: **45 MINUTES** | TOTAL: **1 HOUR 20 MINUTES**
TO MAKE AHEAD: Cover and refrigerate for up to 3 days.

This silky-smooth butternut soup gets a hit of spice from chipotle, cloves and cumin. It's perfect when you're craving something warm and creamy (and you'll swear it's made with real cream, though there's nary a drop). Adapted from Chef Jesús González, La Cocina Que Canta at Rancho La Puerta.

1½	pounds (1 small to medium) butternut *or* other winter squash
1	teaspoon canola oil
2	stalks celery, chopped
1	small onion, diced
1	carrot, chopped
1	teaspoon ground cumin
¼-½	teaspoon ground chipotle pepper (*see Note, page 207*)
⅛	teaspoon ground cloves
6	cups vegetable broth
1	teaspoon sea salt
¼	teaspoon freshly ground pepper
½	cup nonfat plain yogurt
2	tablespoons snipped fresh chives *or* chopped parsley

1. Preheat oven to 350°F.

2. Cut squash in half and seed. Place the halves on a baking sheet, cut-side down. Bake until tender when pierced with a knife, 45 minutes to 1 hour. When cool enough to handle, scoop out the flesh.

3. Heat oil in a large saucepan over medium heat. Add celery, onion and carrot and stir to coat. Cover, reduce heat to medium-low and cook, stirring frequently, until soft, 8 to 10 minutes. Stir in the squash flesh, cumin, chipotle to taste and cloves. Add broth and simmer, covered, until the vegetables are very tender, 20 to 25 minutes.

4. Puree the soup with an immersion blender or in batches in a blender until smooth (use caution when pureeing hot liquids). Season with salt and pepper. Garnish with a drizzle of yogurt and sprinkle of chives (or parsley).

MAKES 10 SERVINGS, ABOUT ¾ CUP EACH.

PER SERVING: **160 calories**; 7 g fat (3 g sat, 2 g mono); 18 mg cholesterol; 18 g carbohydrate; 8 g protein; 1 g fiber; 446 mg sodium; 555 mg potassium. NUTRITION BONUS: Potassium (16% daily value).

H ❋ W   L ↓ C

THE 500-CALORIE MENU

SERVE WITH ONE FROM EACH GROUP

Baby spinach (1½ cups) with 2 Tbsp. Roasted Garlic Dressing, page 75 (169 cal.)

OR

Claire's Mixed Green Salad with Feta Vinaigrette, page 53 (165 cal.)

Pan-Roasted Chicken & Gravy, page 113 (177 cal.)

OR

Sautéed shrimp (3 ounces) with 1 tsp. olive oil and a squeeze of lemon (126 cal.)

DIET TIP

Use meaty, rich mushrooms to help make a meal more satisfying. Research reports that when people ate mushroom-based entrees, they felt just as satisfied as when they'd eaten those same dishes made with beef—though they'd taken in a fraction of the calories and fat.

CREAMY CREMINI MUSHROOM SOUP

ACTIVE TIME: **40 MINUTES** | TOTAL: **40 MINUTES**

Reduced-fat sour cream and low-fat milk make this soup creamy without all the fat. The pudgy brown mushrooms called cremini are actually baby portobello mushrooms and are sometimes called baby bellas. They're firmer and richer-tasting than common white mushrooms.

1½	teaspoons extra-virgin olive oil
1	large onion, chopped
1½	teaspoons chopped fresh thyme *or* ½ teaspoon dried
1	pound cremini mushrooms, sliced
½	cup all-purpose flour
2	14-ounce cans reduced-sodium chicken broth
1	cup reduced-fat sour cream
1	cup low-fat milk
¼	teaspoon salt
	Freshly ground pepper to taste
	Lemon juice to taste
	Dry sherry to taste (*see Note, page 208*), optional

1. Heat oil in a Dutch oven or soup pot over low heat. Add onion and cook, stirring, until soft and translucent, 5 to 7 minutes. Add thyme and cook for 1 minute more. Stir in mushrooms, cover and steam until the mushrooms exude their moisture, about 5 minutes.

2. Sprinkle flour over the mushrooms. Increase heat to medium and cook, stirring, for 3 to 4 minutes. Gradually whisk in broth, scraping up any flour that clings to the pan. Simmer, stirring occasionally, until thickened and smooth, 5 to 7 minutes.

3. Combine sour cream and milk; whisk into the mushrooms. Season with salt and pepper. Gently heat until the soup is hot but not boiling. Just before serving, stir in lemon juice and sherry (if using).

MAKES 6 SERVINGS, 1¼ CUPS EACH.

ROASTED ONION SOUP

ACTIVE TIME: **20 MINUTES** | TOTAL: **1 HOUR 10 MINUTES**

Sweet caramelized onions, bolstered by roasted shallots and garlic, combine in a luscious but not overpowering soup.

  3   Spanish onions, cut in half lengthwise and thinly sliced
  3   large shallots, cut in half lengthwise and thinly sliced
  1   large head garlic, cloves separated, peeled and cut in half
  2   teaspoons extra-virgin olive oil
  4   cups reduced-sodium chicken broth, divided
¼   cup brandy
  1   tablespoon chopped fresh thyme *or* 1 teaspoon dried
     Freshly ground pepper to taste
¼   cup freshly grated Parmesan cheese, preferably Parmigiano-Reggiano

1. Position rack in lower third of oven; preheat to 450°F.

2. Combine onions, shallots, garlic and oil in a large shallow roasting pan. Roast, stirring every 5 minutes, until the onions are golden, 20 to 25 minutes. Remove from the oven and pour in 1 cup broth; stir, scraping the bottom of the pan to loosen and dissolve any caramelized bits. (The liquid will become quite dark.)

3. Transfer the onion mixture to a soup pot and add the remaining 3 cups broth, brandy and thyme. Bring to a boil; reduce heat to low and simmer, covered, for 30 minutes. Season with pepper. Sprinkle each serving with Parmesan.

MAKES 4 SERVINGS, ABOUT 1¼ CUPS EACH.

PER SERVING: **171 calories**; 4 g fat (1 g sat, 2 g mono); 4 mg cholesterol; 20 g carbohydrate; 8 g protein; 2 g fiber; 641 mg sodium; 515 mg potassium.
NUTRITION BONUS: Vitamin C (25% daily value).

H❌W L⬇C H❤H

THE 500-CALORIE MENU
SERVE WITH ONE FROM EACH GROUP

Broccoli & Goat Cheese Soufflé, page 85 (254 cal.)
OR
Tuna Steaks Provençal, page 142 (214 cal.)

Simple Sautéed Spinach, page 178 (68 cal.)
OR
Chilled Snap Peas with Creamy Tarragon Dressing, page 179 (61 cal.)

DIET TIP

Skip the blanket of melted cheese that typically tops French onion soup and use a sprinkle of flavorful aged Parmesan for just 22 calories per tablespoon.

BORSCHT

ACTIVE TIME: **30 MINUTES** | TOTAL: **30 MINUTES**

Looking for a hearty start to a meal? Try this rich borscht made with beef broth and garnished with sour cream. We give it extra kick with a little horseradish. For a vegetarian soup, use vegetable broth instead.

2	tablespoons extra-virgin olive oil
1	medium onion, chopped
2	cups reduced-sodium beef broth *or* vegetable broth
1	medium russet potato, peeled and diced
½	teaspoon salt
¼	teaspoon freshly ground pepper
1½	cups steamed cubed beets, ½-inch cubes (*see Note, page 209*)
2	teaspoons red-wine vinegar
¼	cup reduced-fat sour cream
1	tablespoon prepared horseradish
1	tablespoon chopped fresh parsley

1. Heat oil in a large saucepan over medium heat. Add onion and cook, stirring, until beginning to brown, about 4 minutes. Add broth, potato, salt and pepper; bring to a boil. Reduce heat to a simmer, cover and cook until the potato is just tender, about 8 minutes. Add beets and vinegar; return to a boil. Cover and continue cooking until the broth is deep red and the potato is very soft, 2 to 3 minutes more.

2. Combine sour cream and horseradish in a small bowl. Serve the soup with a dollop of the horseradish-sour cream and a sprinkle of parsley.

MAKES 4 SERVINGS, ABOUT 1 CUP EACH.

PER SERVING: **160 calories**; 9 g fat (2 g sat, 6 g mono); 8 mg cholesterol; 18 g carbohydrate; 4 g protein; 3 g fiber; 579 mg sodium; 495 mg potassium. NUTRITION BONUS: Vitamin C (25% daily value), Potassium (15% dv).

H✂W   L↓C   H♥H

THE 500-CALORIE MENU
SERVE WITH ONE FROM EACH GROUP

Bistro Flank Steak Sandwich, page 152 (294 cal.)
OR
Turkey & Tomato Panini, page 105 (285 cal.)

Fresh blueberries (½ cup, 42 cal.)
OR
Carrot sticks (½ cup, 26 cal.)

PER SERVING: **84 calories**; 5 g fat (1 g sat, 4 g mono); 0 mg cholesterol; 9 g carbohydrate; 2 g protein; 2 g fiber; 219 mg sodium; 405 mg potassium. NUTRITION BONUS: Vitamin C (60% daily value), Vitamin A (35% dv).

H✄W   L↓C   H♥H

THE 500-CALORIE MENU

SERVE WITH ONE FROM EACH GROUP

Smoky Corn & Black Bean Pizza, page 80 (303 cal.)
OR
Mozzarella-Stuffed Turkey Burgers, page 108 (300 cal.)

Lemon-Dill Green Beans, page 180 (74 cal.)
OR
Banana Pudding Pops, page 202 (82 cal.)

GRILLED TOMATO GAZPACHO

ACTIVE TIME: **35 MINUTES** | TOTAL: **1 HOUR 35 MINUTES**
TO MAKE AHEAD: Cover and refrigerate for up to 1 day. Stir to recombine and garnish just before serving.

Grill the vegetables for this refreshing soup earlier in the day or even the night before. Serve in wineglasses or tumblers to show off the rich color. (Photograph: page 13.)

2	pounds ripe plum tomatoes
1	small red bell pepper
1	English cucumber, peeled and seeded, divided
½	cup torn fresh *or* day-old country bread (crust removed)
1	small clove garlic
2-3	tablespoons red-wine vinegar
1	tablespoon chopped fresh parsley
¼	teaspoon *piment d'Espelette* (*see Note, page 207*) *or* hot Spanish paprika *or* a pinch of cayenne pepper
½	teaspoon salt
¼	teaspoon freshly ground pepper
2	tablespoons extra-virgin olive oil

1. Preheat grill to medium-high.

2. Grill tomatoes and bell pepper, turning a few times, until they soften and the skins are blistered and charred in spots, about 8 minutes. Transfer the pepper to a plastic bag and let it steam until cool enough to handle. Peel off the skin; cut the pepper in half and discard the stem and seeds. Place one half in a blender (reserve the other half for garnish). When the tomatoes are cool enough to handle, core and roughly chop. Add the tomatoes, skins and all, to the blender.

3. Add half the cucumber to the blender along with bread, garlic, vinegar to taste, parsley, *piment d'Espelette* (or paprika or cayenne), salt and pepper. Blend until smooth. Add oil and blend until well combined. Refrigerate until room temperature or chilled, at least 1 hour.

4. Before serving, finely dice the remaining cucumber and bell pepper; stir half of each into the gazpacho and garnish with the rest.

MAKES 6 SERVINGS, ABOUT 1 CUP EACH.

QUICK TOMATO SOUP

ACTIVE TIME: **15 MINUTES** | TOTAL: **30 MINUTES**
TO MAKE AHEAD: Cover and refrigerate for up to 3 days.

This is a great "pantry soup"—that is, it comes together in minutes from ingredients that you can keep on hand all the time (see "The Healthy Pantry," page 207).

1	tablespoon extra-virgin olive oil
3	cloves garlic, minced
1	teaspoon dried herbs, such as thyme, oregano, rosemary *or* basil
¼	teaspoon crushed red pepper (optional)
2	28-ounce cans crushed tomatoes
1	cup water
2	teaspoons sugar
2	cups nonfat *or* low-fat milk

Heat oil in a large saucepan over medium heat. Add garlic, herbs and crushed red pepper (if using); cook, stirring, until fragrant, about 30 seconds. Add tomatoes, water and sugar. Bring to a boil; reduce heat and simmer for 10 minutes. Stir in milk and heat through, about 1 minute.

MAKES 6 SERVINGS, ABOUT 1½ CUPS EACH.

PER SERVING: **142 calories**; 3 g fat (1 g sat, 2 g mono); 2 mg cholesterol; 25 g carbohydrate; 7 g protein; 5 g fiber; 393 mg sodium; 920 mg potassium.
NUTRITION BONUS: Vitamin C (45% daily value), Vitamin A (35% dv), Potassium (26% dv), Calcium & Iron (20% dv).

H✂W   H⬆F   H♥H

THE 500-CALORIE MENU

SERVE WITH ONE FROM EACH GROUP

Smoky Ham & Corn Salad, page 71 (182 cal.)
OR
Claire's Mixed Green Salad with Feta Vinaigrette, page 53 (165 cal.)

Toasted whole-grain baguette (2 inches, 132 cal.)
OR
Small whole-wheat crackers (about 15, 130 cal.)

Chunky Peach Popsicles, page 202 (33 cal.)
OR
Sliced fresh strawberries (½ cup, 27 cal.)

PER SERVING: **191 calories**; 4 g fat (0 g sat, 2 g mono); 0 mg cholesterol; 31 g carbohydrate; 9 g protein; 9 g fiber; 408 mg sodium; 535 mg potassium. NUTRITION BONUS: Folate (22% daily value), Iron, Potassium & Vitamin C (15% dv).

H✶W H⬆F H♥H

THE 500-CALORIE MENU

SERVE WITH ONE FROM EACH GROUP

Mixed greens (1½ cups) with 2 Tbsp. Goat Cheese & Tomato Dressing, page 76 (102 cal.)
OR
Baby spinach (1½ cups) with 2 Tbsp. Cucumber Herb Vinaigrette, page 74 (71 cal.)

Warm corn tortillas (two 6-inch, 140 cal.)
OR
Toasted whole-grain baguette (2 inches, 132 cal.)

Diced watermelon (1½ cups, 69 cal.)
OR
Chewy Chocolate Cookies, page 197 (68 cal.)

BLACK BEAN SOUP

ACTIVE TIME: **15 MINUTES** | TOTAL: **25 MINUTES**
TO MAKE AHEAD: Cover and refrigerate for up to 3 days. Garnish with sour cream and cilantro, if desired, just before serving.

This is a zippy Southwestern-flavored black bean soup. We make it with canned beans so it comes together in minutes. If you have leftovers, pack them up in individual serving containers for lunch the next day. (Photograph: page 30.)

1	tablespoon canola oil
1	small onion, chopped
1	tablespoon chili powder
1	teaspoon ground cumin
2	15-ounce cans black beans, rinsed
3	cups water
½	cup prepared salsa
¼	teaspoon salt
1	tablespoon lime juice
4	tablespoons reduced-fat sour cream (optional)
2	tablespoons chopped fresh cilantro (optional)

1. Heat oil in a large saucepan over medium heat. Add onion and cook, stirring, until beginning to soften, 2 to 3 minutes. Add chili powder and cumin and cook, stirring, 1 minute more. Add beans, water, salsa and salt. Bring to a boil; reduce heat and simmer for 10 minutes. Remove from the heat and stir in lime juice.

2. Transfer half the soup to a blender and puree (use caution when pureeing hot liquids). Stir the puree back into the saucepan. Serve garnished with sour cream and cilantro, if desired.

MAKES 4 SERVINGS, ABOUT 1¼ CUPS EACH.

CHICKEN & RICE SOUP

ACTIVE TIME: **35 MINUTES** | TOTAL: **35 MINUTES**

This is a great, easy chicken-and-rice soup. We like to use instant brown rice because it cooks so quickly, but you could substitute cooked brown rice (stirred in at the end) if you have it on hand. Try the recipe with other herbs if you like, such as dill or tarragon.

1	tablespoon extra-virgin olive oil
2	medium carrots, diced
1	medium onion, diced
1	stalk celery, diced
7	cups reduced-sodium chicken broth
1	cup instant brown rice
8	ounces boneless, skinless chicken breast, trimmed and cut into ¾-inch pieces
1	cup frozen peas, thawed
¼	cup chopped fresh parsley
2	teaspoons cider vinegar
¼	teaspoon freshly ground pepper

Heat oil in a large saucepan over medium heat. Add carrots, onion and celery and cook, stirring, until beginning to soften, 3 to 5 minutes. Add broth and bring to a boil. Add rice, reduce heat and simmer for 5 minutes. Add chicken and peas and gently simmer until the chicken is just cooked through, about 5 minutes. Stir in parsley, vinegar and pepper.

MAKES 6 SERVINGS, 1½ CUPS EACH.

PER SERVING: **175 calories**; 4 g fat (1 g sat, 2 g mono); 21 mg cholesterol; 21 g carbohydrate; 15 g protein; 3 g fiber; 709 mg sodium; 473 mg potassium. NUTRITION BONUS: Vitamin A (80% daily value), Vitamin C (15% dv).

THE 500-CALORIE MENU
SERVE WITH ONE FROM EACH GROUP

Baby spinach (1½ cups) with 2 Tbsp. Roasted Garlic Dressing, page 75 (169 cal.)

OR

Claire's Mixed Green Salad with Feta Vinaigrette, page 53 (165 cal.)

Hot Fudge Pudding Cake, page 196 (142 cal.)

OR

White wine (5-ounce glass, 116 cal.)

THE 500-CALORIE MENU

SERVE WITH ONE FROM EACH GROUP

Mixed Lettuce Salad with Cucumber Herb Vinaigrette, page 52 (83 cal.)

OR

Warm corn tortilla (6-inch, 70 cal.)

Fast Strawberry Frozen Yogurt, page 201 (100 cal.)

OR

Indoor S'mores, page 203 (98 cal.)

DIET TIP

In one study, consuming a little hot pepper (in tomato juice or in capsules) 30 minutes before a meal helped study participants feel less hungry and eat about 10 percent less.

CALDO TLALPEÑO

ACTIVE TIME: **30 MINUTES** | TOTAL: **40 MINUTES**

Although there are many variations of this classic Mexican chicken soup, spicy chipotle chile peppers are always part of the broth. Garlic, cooked in broth and then pureed, gives the soup complex flavor and creaminess for almost zero calories.

- 6 cups reduced-sodium chicken broth
- ½ cup water
- 1 head garlic, cloves separated and peeled
- 8 ounces boneless, skinless chicken breast, trimmed
- 2 teaspoons canola oil
- 1 medium onion, chopped
- 1 poblano *or* Anaheim chile pepper, chopped
- 1 chipotle pepper in adobo sauce (*see Note, page 207*)
- 1 cup instant brown rice
- 4 radishes, sliced
- 1 small avocado, chopped
- ¼ cup chopped fresh cilantro
- 1 lime, quartered

1. Bring broth, water, garlic and chicken to a boil in a large saucepan over medium-high heat. Reduce heat to a simmer and cook, skimming any foam that rises to the top, until the garlic is tender and the chicken is cooked through, 12 to 15 minutes. Remove from the heat. Use a slotted spoon to transfer the garlic to a blender and the chicken to a clean cutting board.

2. Meanwhile, heat oil in a medium skillet over medium heat. Add onion and poblano (or Anaheim) chile and cook, stirring, until beginning to brown, 8 to 10 minutes. Add to the broth in the pan.

3. Add chipotle pepper and ½ cup of the broth to the blender and process until smooth (use caution when pureeing hot liquids). Pour the mixture back into the pan. Stir in rice. Bring to a boil, reduce to a simmer and cook until the rice is tender, about 10 minutes.

4. Shred the chicken and divide among 4 bowls. Ladle the soup over the chicken and top with equal portions of radishes, avocado and cilantro. Serve with a wedge of lime.

MAKES 4 SERVINGS, 1¾ CUPS EACH.

FRAGRANT FISH SOUP

ACTIVE TIME: 30 MINUTES | TOTAL: 30 MINUTES

Here, lemony rice, delicately flavored broth and gently poached tilapia are topped with a colorful blend of vegetables and herbs. A pleasure for all your senses that's surprisingly easy to make.

- 1 cup jasmine rice
- 2 cups water
  Zest and juice of 1 lemon
- 4 cups reduced-sodium chicken broth *or* vegetable broth
- 1 pound tilapia fillets (*see Note, page 210*) *or* other firm white fish
- 4 cups bite-size pieces arugula *or* watercress (about 1 bunch), tough stems removed
- 1 cup finely shredded carrots
- ¼ cup very thinly sliced fresh mint
- 2 scallions, finely chopped

1. Combine rice and water in a medium saucepan. Bring to a simmer over medium heat; cover and cook until the water is absorbed, about 20 minutes. Stir in lemon zest and juice.

2. Meanwhile, bring broth to a simmer in another medium saucepan over medium-high heat. Reduce the heat so the broth remains steaming, but not simmering. Add fish and cook until just tender, about 5 minutes. Remove and break into bite-size chunks.

3. Divide the lemony rice among 4 bowls. Top with equal portions of the fish, arugula (or watercress), carrot, mint and scallions. Ladle 1 cup of the warm broth into each bowl and serve.

MAKES 4 SERVINGS, ABOUT 1¼ CUPS EACH.

PER SERVING: **229 calories**; 2 g fat (1 g sat, 1 g mono); 57 mg cholesterol; 25 g carbohydrate; 29 g protein; 2 g fiber; 644 mg sodium; 776 mg potassium. NUTRITION BONUS: Vitamin A (110% daily value), Vitamin C (25% dv), Folate (16% dv).

THE 500-CALORIE MENU
SERVE WITH ONE FROM EACH GROUP

Toasted whole-grain baguette (2 inches, 132 cal.)
OR
Garlic & Herb Pita Chips, page 186 (117 cal.)

Orange Crisps with Citrus Fruit Salad, page 198 (128 cal.)
OR
White wine (5-ounce glass, 116 cal.)

PER SERVING: **237 calories**; 8 g fat (2 g sat, 5 g mono); 37 mg cholesterol; 19 g carbohydrate; 21 g protein; 4 g fiber; 713 mg sodium; 767 mg potassium. NUTRITION BONUS: Vitamin A (80% daily value), Vitamin C (35% dv), Zinc (26% dv), Potassium (20% dv), Iron (15% dv).

H✖W L↓C H♥H

THE 500-CALORIE MENU

SERVE WITH ONE FROM EACH GROUP

Garlic & Herb Pita Chips, page 186 (117 cal.)
OR
Whole-Grain Rice Pilaf, page 186 (97 cal.)

Mixed Lettuce Salad with Cucumber Herb Vinaigrette, page 52 (83 cal.)
OR
Creamy Chopped Cauliflower Salad, page 59 (48 cal.)

Raspberry Applesauce, page 201 (67 cal.)
OR
Chewy Chocolate Cookies, page 197 (68 cal.)

MOROCCAN VEGETABLE SOUP

ACTIVE TIME: **35 MINUTES** | TOTAL: **1½ HOURS** | EQUIPMENT: Kitchen string

Hearty with chunks of beef or lamb, plenty of vegetables and a bit of pasta, this Moroccan soup gets its rich, golden-orange color from turmeric.

2	tablespoons extra-virgin olive oil
1	medium onion, finely diced
2	teaspoons ground turmeric
1	pound beef stew meat (such as chuck) *or* lamb stew meat (shoulder or leg), trimmed and cut into ½-inch cubes
6	cups reduced-sodium beef broth *or* water
1	14-ounce can diced tomatoes
2	small turnips, peeled and diced
2	carrots, diced
2	stalks celery with leaves, thinly sliced
	Pinch of saffron threads (*see Note, page 207*)
12	sprigs flat-leaf parsley, plus more leaves for garnish
8	sprigs fresh cilantro, plus more leaves for garnish
1	large zucchini, peeled and cut into ¼-inch dice
2	ounces angel hair pasta (capellini), broken into small pieces (about ½ cup), *or* orzo, preferably whole-wheat
¼-2	teaspoons salt
½	teaspoon freshly ground pepper

1. Heat oil in a Dutch oven over medium-high heat. Add onion and turmeric; stir to coat. Add meat and cook, stirring occasionally, until the onion is tender, 4 to 5 minutes. Add broth (or water), tomatoes and their juice, turnips, carrots, celery and saffron. Tie parsley and cilantro sprigs together with kitchen string and add to the pot. Bring the soup to a boil. Cover and reduce to a simmer. Cook until the meat is tender, 45 to 50 minutes.

2. Stir in zucchini and cook, covered, until soft, 8 to 10 minutes. Add pasta and cook until soft, 4 to 10 minutes, depending on the type of pasta. Discard the parsley and cilantro sprigs. Season with salt (start with ¼ teaspoon if you're using beef broth; add more if you're using water) and pepper. Serve sprinkled with parsley and/or cilantro leaves, if desired.

MAKES 6 SERVINGS, ABOUT 2 CUPS EACH.

SALADS

Salads are synonymous with dieting and not necessarily in a good way. Often people hear "salad" and think "rabbit." It makes sense—if your idea of a salad is a couple of pieces of iceberg lettuce peppered with a few shreds of carrot. But that's certainly not how we see salads.

Sure, having a salad is an easy way to minimize calories at a meal—but it's also an opportunity to maximize nutrients. Whether you start with leafy greens (rich in beta carotene and folate), cabbage (a source of cancer-fighting isothiocyanates) or tomatoes (vitamin C and lycopene), you'll be getting plenty of nutrients, including fiber. That's why a side salad is a great add-on to any entree.

Speaking of entrees, we love topping greens with chicken or lean beef to give the salad center-stage status. When you think about it, an entree salad is basically the best parts of a sandwich turned out into a bowl. And we bet you won't miss the bread because by skipping it you'll save about 200 calories, which you can spend on something else—like dessert.

A 469-Calorie Dinner (*left*): Thai Beef Salad (*page 72*), 226 calories; Curried Carrot Soup (*page 32*), 123 calories; 5-ounce glass of red wine, 120 calories.

PER SERVING: **83 calories**; 6 g fat (1 g sat, 3 g mono); 106 mg cholesterol; 4 g carbohydrate; 5 g protein; 2 g fiber; 152 mg sodium; 297 mg potassium. NUTRITION BONUS: Vitamin A (35% daily value), Vitamin C (25% dv), Folate (22% dv).

H✳W   L↓C   H♥H

THE 500-CALORIE MENU

SERVE WITH ONE FROM EACH GROUP

Southwestern Rice & Pinto Bean Salad, page 89 (304 cal.)

OR

Turkey & Tomato Panini, page 105 (285 cal.)

Fast Strawberry Frozen Yogurt, page 201 (100 cal.)

OR

White wine (5-ounce glass, 116 cal.)

DIET TIP

Eggs boost this salad's staying power, and maybe your weight loss, too: in one study, dieters who ate eggs for breakfast felt full for longer and lost more than twice as much weight as those who got the same amount of calories from a bagel for breakfast.

MIXED LETTUCE SALAD WITH CUCUMBER HERB VINAIGRETTE

ACTIVE TIME: **30 MINUTES** | TOTAL: **30 MINUTES** (including making vinaigrette)

Keep your salads interesting by experimenting with different types of greens. Here, mild and delicate oak leaf and baby romaine lettuces pair wonderfully with peppery radishes and chopped hard-boiled eggs.

½ small clove garlic
    Pinch of salt
2 cups Red Oak *or* other red leaf lettuce
2 cups Freckles *or* other baby romaine lettuce
¼ cup Cucumber Herb Vinaigrette (*page 74*)
½ cup sliced radishes
4 scallions, sliced
2 hard-boiled eggs (*see Note, page 209*), peeled and chopped

Season a wooden salad bowl by rubbing it with garlic and salt. Chop the garlic and add to the bowl along with all the lettuce. Pour Cucumber Herb Vinaigrette over the greens; toss to coat. Serve the salad garnished with radishes, scallions and hard-boiled egg.

MAKES 4 SERVINGS, ABOUT 1 CUP EACH.

CLAIRE'S MIXED GREEN SALAD WITH FETA VINAIGRETTE

ACTIVE TIME: **15 MINUTES** | TOTAL: **15 MINUTES**

Sweet cherry tomatoes make a satisfying "pop" in your mouth. Pair them with salty feta vinaigrette and spicy arugula and you have a winning combination. Adapted from Chef Steven Obranovich of Claire's Restaurant in Hardwick, Vermont.

FETA VINAIGRETTE

3	tablespoons sunflower oil *or* canola oil
3	tablespoons extra-virgin olive oil, preferably mild-flavored
¼	cup finely crumbled feta cheese
1	tablespoon cider vinegar
1	tablespoon red-wine vinegar
2	teaspoons lemon juice, or to taste
1	teaspoon freshly ground pepper, or to taste
¼	teaspoon salt, or to taste

SALAD

8	cups lightly packed mixed salad greens *or* arugula, any tough stems removed
2	cups sliced cucumbers
1½	cups cherry tomatoes, halved
5	radishes, thinly sliced
¼	cup very thinly sliced red onion

1. **To prepare vinaigrette:** Place sunflower (or canola) oil, olive oil, feta, cider vinegar, red-wine vinegar, lemon juice, pepper and salt in a blender and puree until combined. Adjust seasoning with additional lemon juice, salt or pepper, if desired.

2. **To prepare salad:** Toss greens (or arugula) in a large bowl with half the vinaigrette. Mound on a large platter. Arrange cucumbers, tomatoes, radishes and onion on top of the greens. Drizzle the remaining vinaigrette over the salad.

MAKES 6 SERVINGS, ABOUT 1½ CUPS EACH.

PER SERVING: **165 calories**; 16 g fat (3 g sat, 7 g mono); 6 mg cholesterol; 6 g carbohydrate; 3 g protein; 3 g fiber; 189 mg sodium; 415 mg potassium. NUTRITION BONUS: Vitamin A (50% daily value), Vitamin C (35% dv), Folate (23% dv).

H✱W L↓C H↑F

THE 500-CALORIE MENU

SERVE WITH

Penne in Spicy Tomato Sauce, page 81 (315 cal.)
OR
Indian-Spiced Chicken Pitas, page 107 (333 cal.)

DIET TIP

Work a little cheese into your salad dressing instead of crumbling it on top of the salad. You'll use less cheese and its flavor will coat every leaf instead of just a few.

PER SERVING: **183 calories**; 11 g fat (2 g sat, 7 g mono); 5 mg cholesterol; 19 g carbohydrate; 4 g protein; 2 g fiber; 242 mg sodium; 173 mg potassium. NUTRITION BONUS: Vitamin A (50% daily value).

H✳W   L↓C   H♥H

THE 500-CALORIE MENU

SERVE WITH ONE FROM EACH GROUP

Black Bean Soup, page 42 (191 cal.)
OR
Creamy Cremini Mushroom Soup, page 36 (160 cal.)

Garlic & Herb Pita Chips, page 186 (117 cal.)
OR
Toasted whole-grain baguette (2 inches, 132 cal.)

DIET TIP

Whenever you have leftover whole-grain bread, make croutons using this easy recipe. Freeze them to have on hand for when you need them. Adding croutons to soups and salads makes them feel more substantial and helps you get some whole grains into your day.

BABY GREENS WITH SPICY MEDITERRANEAN VINAIGRETTE

ACTIVE TIME: **35 MINUTES** | TOTAL: **50 MINUTES** (including making vinaigrette)

Watching your weight doesn't mean you're stuck with Spartan salads. This one feels positively indulgent, with sweet-tart cranberries, smoky cheese, crunchy croutons and a spicy-sweet dressing.

CROUTONS
1½   cups cubed whole-wheat *or* multigrain bread
  1   tablespoon extra-virgin olive oil
SALAD
½   small clove garlic
     Pinch of salt
  4   cups baby beet greens, baby chard *or* baby spinach
¼   cup Spicy Mediterranean Vinaigrette (*page 75*)
¼   cup dried cranberries
¼   cup shredded smoked cheese, such as Cheddar

1. **To prepare croutons:** Preheat oven to 375°F.

2. Toss bread and oil in a medium bowl until well combined. Spread in a single layer on a large baking sheet. Bake, stirring once, until golden and crisp, 12 to 15 minutes.

3. **To prepare salad:** Season a wooden salad bowl by rubbing it with garlic and salt. Chop the garlic and add to the bowl along with greens. Pour Spicy Mediterranean Vinaigrette over the greens. Sprinkle the salad with cranberries, cheese and the croutons; toss and serve.

MAKES 4 SERVINGS, ABOUT 1 CUP EACH.

PER SERVING: **135 calories**; 11 g fat (2 g sat, 5 g mono); 0 mg cholesterol; 8 g carbohydrate; 3 g protein; 3 g fiber; 355 mg sodium; 561 mg potassium. NUTRITION BONUS: Vitamin A (210% daily value), Vitamin C (100% dv), Folate (39% dv), Magnesium & Potassium (16% dv).

H✖W L↓C H♥H

THE 500-CALORIE MENU

SERVE WITH ONE FROM EACH GROUP

Japanese Chicken-Scallion Rice Bowl, page 119 (258 cal.)

OR

Lemon-Garlic Shrimp & Vegetables, page 128 (227 cal.)

Pineapple-Raspberry Parfaits, page 201 (112 cal.)

OR

Nonfat vanilla frozen yogurt (1/2 cup, 95 cal.)

DIET TIP

Add spinach to soups, stews and casseroles. It pumps up the volume—so you feel like you're getting more—for virtually no additional calories.

SPINACH SALAD WITH JAPANESE GINGER DRESSING

ACTIVE TIME: **20 MINUTES** | TOTAL: **20 MINUTES** | TO MAKE AHEAD: Cover and refrigerate the dressing (Step 1) for up to 5 days.

This spinach salad tossed with spunky ginger dressing was inspired by the iceberg salads served at Japanese steakhouses across the U.S. Try topping it with cooked shrimp and you've got a healthy one-bowl lunch.

  3 tablespoons minced onion
  3 tablespoons peanut oil *or* canola oil
  2 tablespoons distilled white vinegar
  1½ tablespoons finely grated fresh ginger
  1 tablespoon ketchup
  1 tablespoon reduced-sodium soy sauce
  ¼ teaspoon minced garlic
  ¼ teaspoon salt
     Freshly ground pepper to taste
 10 ounces baby spinach
  1 large carrot, grated
  1 medium red bell pepper, very thinly sliced

1. Combine onion, oil, vinegar, ginger, ketchup, soy sauce, garlic, salt and pepper in a blender. Process until combined.

2. Toss spinach, carrot and bell pepper with the dressing in a large bowl until evenly coated.

MAKES 4 SERVINGS, ABOUT 1½ CUPS EACH.

JAPANESE CUCUMBER SALAD

ACTIVE TIME: **15 MINUTES** | TOTAL: **15 MINUTES**

This Japanese-inspired, cool, crisp salad is as elegant and well balanced as it is simple. Sesame seeds add appealing crunch, but if you don't have any handy a light drizzle of toasted sesame oil will work instead.

2	medium cucumbers *or* 1 large English cucumber
¼	cup rice vinegar
1	teaspoon sugar
¼	teaspoon salt
2	tablespoons sesame seeds, toasted (*see Note, page 208*)

1. Peel cucumbers to leave alternating long green stripes. Slice the cucumbers in half lengthwise; scrape the seeds out with a spoon. Using a food processor or sharp knife, cut into very thin slices. Place in a double layer of paper towel and squeeze gently to remove any excess moisture.

2. Combine vinegar, sugar and salt in a medium bowl, stirring to dissolve. Add the cucumber slices and sesame seeds; toss well to combine. Serve immediately.

MAKES 4 SERVINGS, ABOUT 1 CUP EACH.

PER SERVING: **46 calories**; 2 g fat (0 g sat, 0 g mono); 0 mg cholesterol; 4 g carbohydrate; 1 g protein; 1 g fiber; 147 mg sodium; 137 mg potassium.
NUTRITION BONUS: Iron (35% daily value).

H✖W   L⬇C   H❤H

THE 500-CALORIE MENU
SERVE WITH ONE FROM EACH GROUP

Toasted Quinoa with Scallops & Snow Peas, page 132 (326 cal.)
OR
Ginger-Steamed Fish with Troy's Hana-Style Sauce, page 135 (298 cal.)

Orange Crisps with Citrus Fruit Salad, page 198 (128 cal.)
OR
White wine (5-ounce glass, 116 cal.)

CREAMY CHOPPED CAULIFLOWER SALAD

ACTIVE TIME: **15 MINUTES** | TOTAL: **15 MINUTES**

This caraway-flavored salad with crunchy cauliflower and apple is perfect in the fall or winter. Try it with Honeycrisp apples while they're in season.

  5 tablespoons low-fat mayonnaise
  2 tablespoons cider vinegar
  1 small shallot, finely chopped
½ teaspoon caraway seeds
¼ teaspoon freshly ground pepper
  3 cups chopped cauliflower florets (about ½ large head)
  2 cups chopped hearts of romaine
  1 tart-sweet red apple, chopped

Whisk mayonnaise, vinegar, shallot, caraway seeds and pepper in a large bowl until smooth. Add cauliflower, romaine and apple; toss to coat.

MAKES 6 SERVINGS, ABOUT 1 CUP EACH.

PER SERVING: **48 calories**; 1 g fat (0 g sat, 0 g mono); 0 mg cholesterol; 10 g carbohydrate; 1 g protein; 3 g fiber; 127 mg sodium; 255 mg potassium. NUTRITION BONUS: Vitamin C (50% daily value), Vitamin A (30% dv), Folate (15% dv).

H✼W   L↓C   H♥H

THE 500-CALORIE MENU
SERVE WITH ONE FROM EACH GROUP

Barbecue Portobello Quesadillas, page 86 (378 cal.)
OR
Grilled Whole Trout with Lemon-Tarragon Bean Salad, page 136 (341 cal.)

Simple Sautéed Spinach, page 178 (68 cal.)
OR
Sliced strawberries (½ cup) with ¼ cup low-fat plain yogurt (66 cal.)

DIET TIP

Adding color and a little bit of sweetness to a savory salad—here, with apple—means you can probably use a little less dressing. Try using half as much dressing as you think you want, taste, then add more if needed.

PER SERVING: **64 calories**; 4 g fat (1 g sat, 1 g mono); 0 mg cholesterol; 7 g carbohydrate; 2 g protein; 3 g fiber; 112 mg sodium; 189 mg potassium. NUTRITION BONUS: Vitamin C (80% daily value), Vitamin A (20% dv).

THE 500-CALORIE MENU

SERVE WITH ONE FROM EACH GROUP

Chinese Braised Mushrooms & Tofu, page 90 (181 cal.)
OR
Honey-Soy Broiled Salmon, page 140 (161 cal.)

Wild Rice with Shiitakes & Toasted Almonds, page 185 (158 cal.)
OR
Brown rice with 1 tsp. sesame oil and a squeeze of lime (*see Guide, page 190*; ½ cup, 149 cal.)

Papaya-Lime Sorbet, page 199 (110 cal.)
OR
White wine (5-ounce glass, 116 cal.)

DIET TIP

Toasted sesame oil brims with rich, nutty flavor. Even a tiny 1-teaspoon drizzle (about 40 calories) can have a huge impact on a dish, keeping calories down without sacrificing taste. Try adding it to brown rice or steamed vegetables, such as broccoli, snow peas or carrots.

HOT & SOUR SLAW

ACTIVE TIME: **20 MINUTES** | TOTAL: **20 MINUTES**

This creative combination of thinly sliced vegetables is tossed with a dressing full of the classic flavors of Chinese hot-and-sour soup—vinegar, soy sauce, sesame, ginger and white pepper.

3	tablespoons rice vinegar
1	tablespoon reduced-sodium soy sauce
1	tablespoon toasted sesame oil
1	teaspoon grated fresh ginger
¼	teaspoon ground white pepper
¼	teaspoon crushed red pepper, or to taste
3	cups shredded napa *or* green cabbage
1	cup thinly sliced red bell pepper
⅓	cup sliced scallions
1	8-ounce can bamboo shoots, drained and thinly sliced

Whisk vinegar, soy sauce, oil, ginger, white pepper and crushed red pepper in a large bowl. Add cabbage, bell pepper, scallions and bamboo shoots; toss to coat.

MAKES 4 SERVINGS, GENEROUS 1 CUP EACH.

MELON, TOMATO & ONION SALAD WITH GOAT CHEESE

ACTIVE TIME: 30 MINUTES | TOTAL: 30 MINUTES

This riff on the traditional tomato, mozzarella and basil salad is gorgeous and refreshing. Any variety of pale green- or orange-fleshed melon will work well. Compose the salad on a large platter for a crowd or assemble it on individual plates.

1 cup very thinly sliced sweet white onion, separated into rings
1 small firm ripe melon
2 large tomatoes, very thinly sliced
1 small cucumber, very thinly sliced
1/2 teaspoon kosher salt
1/4 teaspoon freshly ground pepper
1 cup crumbled goat cheese
1/4 cup extra-virgin olive oil
4 teaspoons balsamic vinegar
1/3 cup very thinly sliced fresh basil

1. Place onion rings in a medium bowl, add cold water to cover and a handful of ice cubes. Set aside for about 20 minutes. Drain and pat dry.

2. Meanwhile, cut melon in half lengthwise and scoop out the seeds. Remove the rind with a sharp knife. Place each melon half cut-side down and slice crosswise into 1/8-inch-thick slices.

3. Make the salad on a large platter or 8 individual salad plates. Begin by arranging a ring of melon slices around the edge. Top with a layer of over-lapping tomato slices. Arrange a second ring of melon slices toward the center. Top with the remaining tomato slices. Tuck cucumber slices between the layers of tomato and melon. Sprinkle with salt and pepper. Top with goat cheese and the onion rings. Drizzle with oil and vinegar. Sprinkle with basil.

MAKES 8 SERVINGS.

PER SERVING: **192 calories**; 12 g fat (4 g sat, 6 g mono); 11 mg cholesterol; 19 g carbohydrate; 5 g protein; 2 g fiber; 176 mg sodium; 541 mg potassium.
NUTRITION BONUS: Vitamin C (61% daily value), Potassium & Vitamin A (15% dv).

L ↓ C

THE 500-CALORIE MENU

SERVE WITH ONE FROM EACH GROUP

Salmon with Pepita-Lime Butter, page 139 (185 cal.)
OR
Grilled chicken breast (3 ounces, 140 cal.)

Grilled whole-grain baguette (2 inches, 132 cal.)
OR
Quinoa with 2 tsp. chives and a squeeze of lemon (*see Guide, page 190*; 1/2 cup, 111 cal.)

PER SERVING: **196 calories**; 14 g fat (4 g sat, 5 g mono); 13 mg cholesterol; 15 g carbohydrate; 4 g protein; 3 g fiber; 173 mg sodium; 237 mg potassium. NUTRITION BONUS: Vitamin A (40% daily value), Folate (15% dv).

H✴W   L↓C

THE 500-CALORIE MENU

SERVE WITH ONE FROM EACH GROUP

Tuna Steaks Provençal, page 142 (214 cal.)

OR

Pan-Roasted Chicken & Gravy, page 113 (177 cal.)

Steamed brown rice (see Guide, page 190; 1/2 cup, 109 cal.)

OR

Shredded Root Vegetable Pancakes, page 176 (106 cal.)

ROASTED APPLE & CHEDDAR SALAD

ACTIVE TIME: **20 MINUTES** | TOTAL: **40 MINUTES**
TO MAKE AHEAD: Cover and refrigerate dressing (Step 2) for up to 1 week.

Roasted apples and Cheddar cheese turn an ordinary mixed green salad into something extra-special. You can use pears for this recipe as well.

DRESSING

- 3 tablespoons red-wine vinegar
- 2 tablespoons apple juice *or* cider
- 1 tablespoon extra-virgin olive oil
- 1 tablespoon honey
- 2 teaspoons Dijon mustard
- 1/8 teaspoon salt
    Freshly ground pepper to taste

ROASTED APPLES & SALAD

- 2 apples, preferably Fuji, peeled and cut into wedges
- 2 teaspoons plus 1 tablespoon extra-virgin olive oil, divided
- 4 sprigs fresh thyme *or* 1/4 teaspoon dried
- 1/4 cup chopped walnuts
- 3 cups baby spinach *or* torn spinach leaves
- 3 cups torn Boston lettuce
- 3 cups torn curly endive
- 2/3 cup grated sharp Cheddar cheese

1. Preheat oven to 400°F.

2. **To prepare dressing:** Whisk vinegar, apple juice (or cider), oil, honey, mustard, salt and pepper in a small bowl.

3. **To roast apples & prepare salad:** Toss apples with 2 teaspoons oil and thyme in a medium bowl; spread evenly on a baking sheet. Roast, turning once or twice, until the apples are soft and golden, 25 to 30 minutes. Discard fresh thyme, if using. Let cool. (While the apples are roasting, toast walnuts in a small baking pan until fragrant, about 5 minutes. Let cool.)

4. Combine spinach, lettuce and endive in a large bowl; toss gently to mix. Divide the greens among 6 plates, drizzle with the dressing and top with cheese, the roasted apples and the toasted walnuts. Serve immediately.

MAKES 6 SERVINGS, 1 1/2 CUPS EACH.

PER SERVING: **343 calories**; 18 g fat (5 g sat, 7 g mono); 89 mg cholesterol; 11 g carbohydrate; 31 g protein; 3 g fiber; 618 mg sodium; 656 mg potassium.
NUTRITION BONUS: Vitamin A (140% daily value), Vitamin C (45% dv), Folate (31% dv), Potassium (19% dv), Calcium (15% dv).

H✖W   L⬇C   H♥H

THE 500-CALORIE MENU

SERVE WITH

Toasted pita breads (two 4-inch, 148 cal.)

OR

Hot Fudge Pudding Cake, page 196 (142 cal.)

DIET TIP

Between the cheese, olives and gobs of dressing, a Greek salad at a restaurant can load you up with 30 grams of fat. Keep an eye on portions and ask for dressing on the side when eating out.

CHOPPED GREEK SALAD WITH CHICKEN

ACTIVE TIME: 25 MINUTES | TOTAL: 25 MINUTES

This super-fast salad is a great way to get dinner on the table in a hurry. You can use whatever vegetables you have on hand—try substituting other chopped fresh vegetables, such as broccoli or bell peppers, for the tomatoes or cucumber. Use leftover chicken or quickly poach a couple of boneless, skinless chicken breasts while you prepare the rest of the salad.

> 1/3 cup red-wine vinegar
> 2 tablespoons extra-virgin olive oil
> 1 tablespoon chopped fresh dill *or* oregano *or* 1 teaspoon dried
> 1 teaspoon garlic powder
> 1/4 teaspoon salt
> 1/4 teaspoon freshly ground pepper
> 6 cups chopped romaine lettuce
> 2 1/2 cups chopped cooked chicken (about 12 ounces; *see Note, page 209*)
> 2 medium tomatoes, chopped
> 1 medium cucumber, peeled, seeded and chopped
> 1/2 cup finely chopped red onion
> 1/2 cup sliced ripe black olives
> 1/2 cup crumbled feta cheese

Whisk vinegar, oil, dill (or oregano), garlic powder, salt and pepper in a large bowl. Add lettuce, chicken, tomatoes, cucumber, onion, olives and feta; toss to coat.

MAKES 4 SERVINGS, ABOUT 3 CUPS EACH.

PER SERVING: **313 calories**; 11 g fat (2 g sat, 1 g mono); 63 mg cholesterol; 24 g carbohydrate; 30 g protein; 6 g fiber; 627 mg sodium; 692 mg potassium.
NUTRITION BONUS: Vitamin A (190% daily value), Vitamin C (110% dv), Folate (39% dv), Potassium (20% dv), Iron (16% dv).

H❊W   H⬆F   H♥H

THE 500-CALORIE MENU

SERVE WITH ONE FROM EACH GROUP

Quinoa with 1 tsp. each olive oil and chopped fresh mint (*see Guide, page 190*; ½ cup, 153 cal.)
OR
Garlic & Herb Pita Chips, page 186 (117 cal.)

Chunky Peach Popsicles, page 202 (33 cal.)
OR
Sliced strawberries (½ cup, 27 cal.)

DIET TIP

Grapefruit's "diet food" rep might be justified: one study found that when people simply ate grapefruit with each meal, they lost up to 3½ pounds over three months. Grapefruit may help manage appetite by lowering insulin levels, say researchers.

GRAPEFRUIT CHICKEN SATAY SALAD

ACTIVE TIME: **40 MINUTES** | TOTAL: **50 MINUTES**

This salad has a delicious dressing inspired by the peanut sauce served with Thai satays.

2   large pink *or* ruby-red grapefruit
1   pound boneless, skinless chicken breasts, trimmed and cut into ¼-inch-thick strips
1   teaspoon dry mustard
1   teaspoon garlic powder
1   teaspoon ground cinnamon
1   teaspoon ground coriander
1   teaspoon ground ginger
1   teaspoon freshly ground pepper
½   teaspoon salt
¼   cup smooth natural peanut butter
2   tablespoons reduced-sodium soy sauce
1   teaspoon sugar
¼   teaspoon hot sauce, or to taste
8   cups roughly chopped romaine lettuce (about 2 hearts)
1   cup sliced radishes (about 8 radishes)

1. Peel grapefruit and cut the segments from the surrounding membranes, letting them drop into a small bowl. Squeeze the remaining membranes over a large bowl to extract the juice. Set the segments and juice aside separately.

2. Position rack in upper third of oven; preheat broiler. Line a broiler pan or baking sheet with foil.

3. Toss chicken, dry mustard, garlic powder, cinnamon, coriander, ginger, pepper and salt in a large bowl until the chicken is well coated. Place on the prepared pan in a single layer. Broil the chicken until cooked through, about 5 minutes.

4. Meanwhile, whisk peanut butter, soy sauce, sugar and hot sauce into the reserved grapefruit juice until smooth. Add the chicken and lettuce; toss to combine. Serve the salad topped with radishes and the grapefruit segments.

MAKES 4 SERVINGS, ABOUT 2 CUPS EACH.

SPINACH & BEET SALAD WITH CHICKEN

ACTIVE TIME: 30 MINUTES | TOTAL: 30 MINUTES

Real maple syrup is the key to the richly flavored dressing on this elegant salad. The darker the syrup the better, for its deeper flavor goes a long way.

1 pound boneless, skinless chicken breast, trimmed
3 tablespoons walnut oil *or* canola oil
2 tablespoons pure maple syrup
2 tablespoons cider vinegar
1 tablespoon whole-grain mustard
1 tablespoon reduced-sodium soy sauce
¼ teaspoon salt
¼ teaspoon freshly ground pepper
8 cups baby spinach
1 15-ounce can whole beets, drained and quartered
½ cup crumbled goat cheese
¼ cup chopped pecans, toasted (*see Note, page 208*)

1. Place chicken in a medium skillet or saucepan and add enough water to cover; bring to a simmer over high heat. Cover, reduce heat and simmer gently until the chicken is cooked through and no longer pink in the middle, 10 to 12 minutes. Transfer the chicken to a cutting board. When cool enough to handle, cut into ¼-inch-thick slices.

2. Meanwhile, whisk oil, syrup, vinegar, mustard, soy sauce, salt and pepper in a large bowl. Reserve ¼ cup dressing in a small bowl. Add spinach to the large bowl and toss to coat with the dressing. Divide the spinach among 4 plates and top with the chicken, beets, goat cheese and pecans. Drizzle with the reserved dressing.

MAKES 4 SERVINGS.

PER SERVING: **379 calories**; 21 g fat (4 g sat, 7 g mono); 69 mg cholesterol; 19 g carbohydrate; 29 g protein; 4 g fiber; 681 mg sodium; 755 mg potassium.
NUTRITION BONUS: Vitamin A (116% daily value), Folate (39% dv), Vitamin C (36% dv), Iron (28% dv), Magnesium (25% dv), Potassium (22% dv).

H❋W   L⬇C   H♥H

THE 500-CALORIE MENU

SERVE WITH

Toasted whole-grain baguette (2 inches, 132 cal.)
OR
White wine (5-ounce glass, 116 cal.)

SMOKY HAM & CORN SALAD

ACTIVE TIME: **15 MINUTES** | TOTAL: **15 MINUTES**

Look for frisée, a light-green chicory with frilly leaves, for this dinner salad. Its sturdy texture and slightly bitter flavor hold up well when tossed with the smoky, creamy tomato dressing. This is a great salad for summer, when fresh corn is at its best. We call for store-bought croutons in this recipe to keep it quick, but if you have the time and extra bread try making your own with the recipe on page 54.

- ⅓ cup reduced-fat sour cream
- 2 tablespoons distilled white vinegar
- 1 teaspoon paprika, preferably smoked (*see Note, page 207*)
- ¼ teaspoon salt
- 8 cups trimmed frisée (about 1 large head) *or* mixed salad greens
- 1 medium tomato, diced
- 1 cup fresh corn kernels (from 1 large ear; *see Note, page 209*)
- 1 cup croutons, preferably whole-grain
- ¾ cup diced ham (about 4 ounces)

Whisk sour cream, vinegar, paprika and salt in a large bowl. Add frisée (or salad greens), tomato, corn, croutons and ham; toss to coat.

MAKES 4 SERVINGS, ABOUT 2 CUPS EACH.

PER SERVING: **182 calories**; 7 g fat (2 g sat, 2 g mono); 23 mg cholesterol; 20 g carbohydrate; 13 g protein; 6 g fiber; 679 mg sodium; 707 mg potassium. NUTRITION BONUS: Vitamin A (70% daily value), Folate (52% dv), Vitamin C (25% dv), Potassium (20% dv).

H✳W L↓C H↑F H♥H

THE 500-CALORIE MENU
SERVE WITH ONE FROM EACH GROUP

Roasted Eggplant & Feta Dip, page 29 (75 cal.)
OR
Lemon-Garlic Marinated Shrimp, page 26 (73 cal.)

Garlic & Herb Pita Chips, page 186 (117 cal.)
OR
Toasted whole-grain baguette (2 inches, 132 cal.)

Nonfat vanilla frozen yogurt (½ cup, 95 cal.)
OR
White wine (5-ounce glass, 116 cal.)

DIET TIP

Choose frisée or other robust greens, such as escarole, curly endive or romaine, for salads. They contain more nutrients than iceberg.

PER SERVING: **226 calories**; 12 g fat (3 g sat, 5 g mono); 42 mg cholesterol; 6 g carbohydrate; 24 g protein; 2 g fiber; 607 mg sodium; 529 mg potassium. NUTRITION BONUS: Vitamin A (50% daily value), Zinc (31% dv), Folate (24% dv), Iron, Potassium & Vitamin C (15% dv).

H✴W   L↓C

THE 500-CALORIE MENU

SERVE WITH ONE FROM EACH GROUP

Curried Carrot Soup, page 32 (123 cal.)
OR
Quinoa with chopped fresh mint and lime zest (*see Guide, page 190;* ½ cup, 111 cal.)

Orange Crisps with Citrus Fruit Salad, page 198 (128 cal.)
OR
Red wine (5-ounce glass, 120 cal.)

THAI BEEF SALAD

ACTIVE TIME: **45 MINUTES** | TOTAL: **45 MINUTES** (plus overnight marinating)

The steak for a Thai salad is often marinated before it's broiled and that's a shame, because most of those flavorings simply drip off. For the best taste, first sear the steak, then let it sit overnight in the marinade before tossing it with the greens. (Photograph: page 50.)

1	pound sirloin steak, trimmed
1	tablespoon reduced-sodium soy sauce
½	teaspoon freshly ground pepper
2	scallions, cut into 1-inch pieces
	Zest of 1 lime
3	tablespoons lime juice
1½	tablespoons fish sauce
½	teaspoon sugar
¼	teaspoon crushed red pepper
4	cups torn frisée *or* curly endive
2	cups torn red leaf lettuce
2	tablespoons chopped fresh mint
2	tablespoons untoasted sesame oil *or* canola oil

1. Position rack in upper third of oven; preheat broiler. Rub steak all over with soy sauce and black pepper. Place on a baking sheet; broil, turning once, 14 to 16 minutes for medium-rare to medium, respectively. Let rest on a cutting board for 5 minutes.

2. Meanwhile, mix scallions, lime zest and juice, fish sauce, sugar and crushed red pepper in a shallow dish. Slice the steak against the grain into thin strips and cut each strip into bite-size pieces. Add the steak to the marinade, along with any accumulated juices, and toss well. Cover and refrigerate overnight.

3. Place frisée (or endive), lettuce and mint in a salad bowl. Add the steak and marinade, drizzle with oil, gently toss, and serve.

MAKES 4 SERVINGS, 2 CUPS EACH.

ASIAN-STYLE GRILLED TOFU WITH GREENS

ACTIVE TIME: 45 MINUTES | TOTAL: 45 MINUTES

Here's a dish that will turn you into a tofu-and-greens lover! Try Asian greens (tatsoi, mizuna and/or pea shoots) packaged as a salad mix; their slightly bitter flavors stand up well to this aromatic, vinegary dressing. We use carrot juice in the dressing for a touch of sweetness—look for it in the produce section of the supermarket.

DRESSING

1	small carrot, peeled and coarsely chopped
½	cup prepared carrot juice
2	tablespoons white *or* yellow miso (*see Note, page 207*)
2	tablespoons rice vinegar
2	tablespoons canola oil
1	tablespoon coarsely chopped fresh ginger
½	teaspoon minced garlic

TOFU & GREENS

28	ounces water-packed firm tofu, drained and rinsed
2	tablespoons honey
2	tablespoons canola oil
2	tablespoons reduced-sodium soy sauce
1	tablespoon black bean-garlic sauce (*see Note, page 207*)
2	teaspoons minced garlic
10	ounces mixed Asian greens *or* baby spinach

1. **To prepare dressing:** Puree carrot, carrot juice, miso, vinegar, oil, ginger and ½ teaspoon garlic in a blender or food processor until smooth.

2. **To prepare tofu:** Slice each tofu block crosswise into 5 slices; pat dry with paper towels. Combine honey, oil, soy sauce, black bean-garlic sauce and 2 teaspoons garlic in a small bowl. Spread half the marinade in a large baking dish and top with the tofu slices. Spread the remaining marinade over the tofu, covering completely.

3. Preheat grill to medium-high. Oil the grill rack (*see Note, page 210*). Grill the tofu until heated through, 2 to 3 minutes per side. To serve, toss greens (or spinach) with the dressing. Divide among 6 plates and top with the tofu.

MAKES 6 SERVINGS.

PER SERVING: **242** calories; 16 g fat (2 g sat, 4 g mono); 0 mg cholesterol; 12 g carbohydrate; 17 g protein; 4 g fiber; 383 mg sodium; 70 mg potassium.
NUTRITION BONUS: Vitamin A (150% daily value), Iron & Vitamin C (25% dv), Calcium (20% dv).

H✣W   L↓C   H♥H

THE 500-CALORIE MENU
SERVE WITH ONE FROM EACH GROUP

Wild Rice with Shiitakes & Toasted Almonds, page 185 (158 cal.)
OR
Small whole-wheat crackers (about 15, 130 cal.)

Apple Cider Granita, page 203 (103 cal.)
OR
Fast Strawberry Frozen Yogurt, page 201 (100 cal.)

CHAMPAGNE VINAIGRETTE

ACTIVE TIME: **5 MINUTES** | TOTAL: **5 MINUTES**
TO MAKE AHEAD: Cover and refrigerate for up to 1 week.

Whirring this vinaigrette in the blender gives it a creamy consistency (without any fatty cream, of course). If you don't have a blender, mince the shallots and whisk the ingredients in a bowl.

- 1   shallot, peeled and quartered
- ¼   cup champagne vinegar *or* white-wine vinegar
- ¼   cup extra-virgin olive oil
- 1   tablespoon Dijon mustard
- ¾   teaspoon salt
      Freshly ground pepper to taste

Combine shallot, champagne (or white-wine) vinegar, oil, mustard, salt and pepper in a blender. Puree until smooth.

MAKES ²/₃ CUP.
PER TABLESPOON: **53 calories**; 5 g fat (1 g sat, 4 g mono); 0 mg cholesterol; 1 g carbohydrate; 0 g protein; 0 g fiber; 182 mg sodium; 4 mg potassium.

CUCUMBER HERB VINAIGRETTE

ACTIVE TIME: **10 MINUTES** | TOTAL: **10 MINUTES**
TO MAKE AHEAD: Cover and refrigerate for up to 3 days.

As the base of this herb-spiked dressing, pureed cucumber provides a mellow grassy flavor and a luxurious texture. Pureeing vegetables into a salad dressing is a great way to give it body (and to sneak in more low-cal vegetables). Experiment with tomatoes, arugula and/or roasted garlic to create your own dressing magic.

CUCUMBER HERB VINAIGRETTE

SPICY MEDITERRANEAN VINAIGRETTE

1   small cucumber, peeled, seeded and chopped
¼   cup extra-virgin olive oil
2   tablespoons red-wine vinegar
2   tablespoons chopped fresh chives
2   tablespoons chopped fresh parsley
1   tablespoon nonfat *or* low-fat plain yogurt
1   teaspoon Dijon mustard
1   teaspoon prepared horseradish
1   teaspoon sugar
½   teaspoon salt

Puree cucumber, oil, vinegar, chives, parsley, yogurt, mustard, horseradish, sugar and salt in a blender until smooth.

MAKES ABOUT 1¼ CUPS.
PER TABLESPOON: **28 calories**; 3 g fat (0 g sat, 2 g mono);
0 mg cholesterol; 1 g carbohydrate; 0 g protein; 0 g fiber;
63 mg sodium; 14 mg potassium.

SPICY MEDITERRANEAN VINAIGRETTE

ACTIVE TIME: **20 MINUTES** | TOTAL: **20 MINUTES**
TO MAKE AHEAD: Cover and refrigerate for up to 3 days.

Sweet raisins, honey and carrot juice balance the heat of crushed red pepper in this brightly colored vinaigrette.

½   teaspoon black mustard seeds
¼   teaspoon ground coriander
⅛   teaspoon ground cumin
½   cup prepared carrot juice
2   tablespoons golden raisins
2   tablespoons red-wine vinegar
4   sprigs fresh cilantro
1   tablespoon nonfat plain yogurt
1   teaspoon honey
1½   teaspoons crushed red pepper
¼   teaspoon salt
     Freshly ground pepper to taste
¼   cup extra-virgin olive oil

1. Heat mustard seeds, coriander and cumin in a small dry skillet over medium heat until fragrant, 2 to 3 minutes. Add carrot juice and simmer over medium heat until reduced by half, about 3 minutes.
2. Place raisins in a blender and add the hot juice. Let stand for 5 minutes to plump the raisins. Then add vinegar, cilantro, yogurt, honey, crushed red pepper, salt and pepper and blend until combined. Pour in oil and blend until smooth, about 1 minute.

MAKES ABOUT ¾ CUP.
PER TABLESPOON: **55 calories**; 5 g fat (1 g sat, 4 g mono);
0 mg cholesterol; 3 g carbohydrate; 0 g protein; 0 g fiber;
53 mg sodium; 50 mg potassium.
NUTRITION BONUS: Vitamin A (40% daily value).

ROASTED GARLIC DRESSING

ACTIVE TIME: **10 MINUTES** | TOTAL: **1¼ HOURS**
TO MAKE AHEAD: Cover and refrigerate for up to 3 days.

Rich roasted garlic makes an incomparably flavored dressing. Try this on any salad with bold-flavored greens or ingredients. You may want to roast an extra head of garlic when you make this dressing. The roasted cloves are great to spread on a sandwich (instead of mayo) or add faux creaminess to other dressings or sauces.

1   large head *or* 2 small heads garlic
4   tablespoons extra-virgin olive oil, divided
2   tablespoons balsamic vinegar *or* red-wine vinegar
1   tablespoon lime juice
⅛   teaspoon salt
     Freshly ground pepper to taste

1. Preheat oven to 400°F.
2. Rub off the excess papery skin from garlic without separating the cloves. Slice the tips off the head (or heads), exposing the ends of the cloves. Place the garlic on a piece

of foil, drizzle with 1 tablespoon oil and wrap into a package. Put in a baking dish and bake until the garlic is very soft, 40 minutes to 1 hour. Unwrap and let cool slightly.

3. Squeeze the garlic pulp into a blender or food processor (discard the skins). Add the remaining 3 tablespoons oil, vinegar, lime juice, salt and pepper and blend or process until smooth.

MAKES A SCANT ½ CUP.

PER TABLESPOON: **77 calories**; 7 g fat (1 g sat, 5 g mono); 0 mg cholesterol; 3 g carbohydrate; 1 g protein; 0 g fiber; 39 mg sodium; 35 mg potassium.

GOAT CHEESE & TOMATO DRESSING

ACTIVE TIME: **10 MINUTES** | TOTAL: **10 MINUTES**
TO MAKE AHEAD: Cover and refrigerate for up to 3 days.

GOAT CHEESE & TOMATO DRESSING

Tomatoes and goat cheese pair deliciously in this dressing. If you don't have tarragon, try this with another fresh herb, such as basil or thyme. Soft goat cheese and other fresh cheeses, such as farmer cheese, usually contain more water than firmer, concentrated cheeses—and tend to have fewer calories per ounce.

¼	cup crumbled goat cheese
2	tablespoons white-wine vinegar
2	teaspoons pure maple syrup
¼	cup extra-virgin olive oil
2	plum tomatoes, seeded and chopped
½	teaspoon salt
	Freshly ground pepper to taste
1	tablespoon chopped fresh tarragon

Blend goat cheese, vinegar and maple syrup in a blender or food processor until combined. Add oil and tomatoes and blend until smooth. Season with salt and pepper. Stir in tarragon.

MAKES ABOUT 1 CUP.

PER TABLESPOON: **44 calories**; 4 g fat (1 g sat, 3 g mono); 2 mg cholesterol; 1 g carbohydrate; 1 g protein; 0 g fiber; 85 mg sodium; 24 mg potassium.

BUTTERMILK DRESSING

ACTIVE TIME: **10 MINUTES** | TOTAL: **10 MINUTES**
TO MAKE AHEAD: Cover and refrigerate for up to 2 days.

Homemade ranch dressing is so easy, you'll never go back to the bottled stuff again (especially those "light" versions with strange-sounding ingredients). Here, lemon, dill and onion balance tangy buttermilk. Buttermilk sounds fattening and feels rich in the mouth, but it's lean dairy at its best—usually 1 percent fat or less. Keep some handy to make easy dressings, cold vegetable or fruit soups—or just for sipping.

| ½ | cup nonfat buttermilk |
| ¼ | cup nonfat plain yogurt |

¼ cup low-fat mayonnaise
1 tablespoon lemon juice
2 teaspoons dried minced onion
½ teaspoon dill seed, crushed
½ teaspoon sugar
½ teaspoon salt
¼ teaspoon freshly ground pepper

Whisk buttermilk, yogurt, mayonnaise, lemon juice, onion, dill, sugar, salt and pepper in a small bowl until blended.

MAKES ABOUT 1 CUP.
PER TABLESPOON: **10 calories**; 0 g fat (0 g sat, 0 g mono); 1 mg cholesterol; 2 g carbohydrate; 0 g protein; 0 g fiber; 114 mg sodium; 6 mg potassium.

PARMESAN-PEPPER DRESSING

ACTIVE TIME: **10 MINUTES** | TOTAL: **10 MINUTES**
TO MAKE AHEAD: Cover and refrigerate for up to 2 days.

An assertive dressing like this one needs vegetables with heft and flavor. Toss with crisp greens, such as romaine and curly endive, tomatoes and slivers of red onion.

⅓ cup nonfat buttermilk
⅓ cup nonfat cottage cheese
⅓ cup freshly grated Parmesan cheese
4 teaspoons white-wine vinegar
1 small clove garlic, minced
½ teaspoon cracked black pepper, or to taste

Combine buttermilk, cottage cheese, Parmesan, vinegar and garlic in a food processor or blender; blend until smooth. Stir in pepper.

MAKES 1 CUP.
PER TABLESPOON: **12 calories**; 0 g fat (0 g sat, 0 g mono); 2 mg cholesterol; 1 g carbohydrate; 1 g protein; 0 g fiber; 47 mg sodium; 4 mg potassium.

GARLIC-YOGURT DRESSING

ACTIVE TIME: **10 MINUTES** | TOTAL: **10 MINUTES**

Garlic and fresh herbs star in this creamy yogurt-based dressing that comes together in just minutes. If you make more than you need, store the extra dressing for a couple of days. Place it—along with some cut-up raw veggies—front and center in the fridge. That way when you're craving a snack it's even easier than opening a bag of chips.

½ cup nonfat plain yogurt
2 tablespoons low-fat milk
1½ tablespoons lemon juice
1 teaspoon honey
1 teaspoon extra-virgin olive oil
½ teaspoon dried oregano
½ teaspoon minced garlic
½ teaspoon salt
Freshly ground pepper to taste

Combine yogurt, milk, lemon juice, honey, oil, oregano and garlic in a small bowl. Season with salt and pepper.

MAKES ¾ CUP.
PER TABLESPOON: **12 calories**; 0 g fat (0 g sat, 0 g mono); 0 mg cholesterol; 2 g carbohydrate; 1 g protein; 0 g fiber; 104 mg sodium; 4 mg potassium.

VEGETARIAN

It used to be that a "proper" dinner centered around meat: a piece of steak, a chicken breast, pork chops. Vegetarian meals were for, well, *vegetarians*. But more and more, people are realizing that going meatless even once or twice a week can have real health benefits, including weight loss and reduced risk for heart disease. Why? Plant-based foods, such as vegetables, beans and lentils, are low in saturated fat and full of fiber, which helps you feel satisfied on fewer calories. (Most Americans eat only about half the 25 to 38 grams of fiber that's recommended each day.)

Plus, when you plan more vegetarian dinners you'll save on grocery bills *and* reduce your carbon footprint: the worldwide meat industry generates nearly one-fifth of manmade greenhouse-gas emissions, according to the United Nations. These vegetarian recipes are packed with flavor, such as the curry on page 94 that's spiced with chiles, cumin and turmeric or the black bean pizza (*left*) that gets a touch of smokiness from smoked mozzarella and the grill. With meals like these, who needs meat?

A 461-Calorie Dinner (*left*): Smoky Corn & Black Bean Pizza (*page 80*), 303 calories; Creamy Chopped Cauliflower Salad (*page 59*), 48 calories; Papaya-Lime Sorbet (*page 199*), 110 calories.

PER SERVING: **303 calories**; 6 g fat (3 g sat, 0 g mono); 13 mg cholesterol; 48 g carbohydrate; 14 g protein; 4 g fiber; 530 mg sodium; 94 mg potassium. NUTRITION BONUS: Calcium (15% daily value).

THE 500-CALORIE MENU

SERVE WITH ONE FROM EACH GROUP

Baja Butternut Squash Soup, page 34 (60 cal.)
OR
Creamy Chopped Cauliflower Salad, page 59 (48 cal.)

Low-fat plain yogurt (½ cup) with ½ cup blueberries (118 cal.)
OR
Papaya-Lime Sorbet, page 199 (110 cal.)

DIET TIP

Try whole-wheat pizza dough—not only does it make a slightly sturdier crust that holds up better on the grill, but you'll also get a little more fiber and trace minerals, such as selenium and magnesium.

SMOKY CORN & BLACK BEAN PIZZA

ACTIVE TIME: **30 MINUTES** | TOTAL: **30 MINUTES**

The secret to a grilled pizza is having all your ingredients ready to go before you head out to the grill. (Photograph: page 78.)

1	cup canned black beans, rinsed
1	cup fresh corn kernels (about 2 ears; *see Note, page 209*)
1	plum tomato, diced
2	tablespoons cornmeal
1	pound prepared whole-wheat pizza dough
⅓	cup barbecue sauce
1	cup shredded mozzarella cheese, preferably smoked

1. Preheat grill to medium.

2. Combine beans, corn and tomato in a medium bowl. Sprinkle cornmeal on a large baking sheet. Stretch dough into about a 12-inch circle and lay it on the cornmeal, coating the entire underside of the dough.

3. Transfer the crust from the baking sheet to the grill. Close the lid and cook until the crust is puffed and lightly browned on the bottom, 4 to 5 minutes.

4. Using a large spatula, flip the crust. Spread barbecue sauce on it and quickly sprinkle with the bean mixture and cheese. Close the lid; grill the pizza until the cheese is melted and the bottom of the crust is browned, 4 to 5 minutes.

MAKES 6 SERVINGS.

PENNE IN SPICY TOMATO SAUCE

ACTIVE TIME: 30 MINUTES | TOTAL: 30 MINUTES

This easy pasta favorite comes together in 30 minutes. The heat level of the spicy tomato sauce can be adjusted to your taste.

1	pound whole-wheat penne
1	tablespoon extra-virgin olive oil
3	cloves garlic, finely chopped
¼	teaspoon crushed red pepper, or to taste
1	28-ounce can plum tomatoes, drained
½	cup freshly grated Pecorino Romano cheese
¼	cup finely chopped flat-leaf parsley
¼	teaspoon salt
	Freshly ground pepper to taste

1. Cook pasta in a large pot of boiling water until just tender, 8 to 10 minutes or according to package directions.

2. Meanwhile, heat oil in a large nonstick skillet over low heat. Add garlic and crushed red pepper; cook, stirring, until the garlic is golden, about 1 minute. Add tomatoes, crushing them roughly with the back of a wooden spoon. Bring to a simmer over low heat and cook until slightly reduced, about 5 minutes.

3. When the pasta is ready, drain and return to the pot. Stir in the sauce and place the pot over high heat. Stir until the mixture sizzles. Remove from the heat. Add cheese and parsley; toss well. Season with salt and pepper; serve immediately.

MAKES 6 SERVINGS.

PER SERVING: **315 calories**; 4 g fat (2 g sat, 2 g mono); 8 mg cholesterol; 59 g carbohydrate; 10 g protein; 7 g fiber; 257 mg sodium; 21 mg potassium.

H✖W   H⬆F   H❤H

THE 500-CALORIE MENU

SERVE WITH ONE FROM EACH GROUP

Simple Sautéed Spinach, page 178 (68 cal.)
OR
Sicilian-Style Broccoli, page 183 (63 cal.)

Baby Tiramisù, page 200 (107 cal.)
OR
Red wine (5-ounce glass, 120 cal.)

SKILLET GNOCCHI WITH CHARD & WHITE BEANS

ACTIVE TIME: 30 MINUTES | TOTAL: 30 MINUTES

In this one-skillet supper, we toss dark leafy greens, diced tomatoes and white beans with gnocchi and top it all with gooey mozzarella. Look for shelf-stable gnocchi near other pasta in the Italian section of most supermarkets.

1	tablespoon plus 1 teaspoon extra-virgin olive oil, divided
1	16-ounce package shelf-stable gnocchi
1	medium yellow onion, thinly sliced
4	cloves garlic, minced
½	cup water
6	cups chopped chard leaves (about 1 small bunch) *or* spinach
1	15-ounce can diced tomatoes with Italian seasonings
1	15-ounce can white beans, rinsed
¼	teaspoon freshly ground pepper
½	cup shredded part-skim mozzarella cheese
¼	cup finely shredded Parmesan cheese

1. Heat 1 tablespoon oil in a large nonstick skillet over medium heat. Add gnocchi and cook, stirring often, until plumped and starting to brown, 5 to 7 minutes. Transfer to a bowl.

2. Add the remaining 1 teaspoon oil and onion to the pan and cook over medium heat, stirring, for 2 minutes. Stir in garlic and water. Cover and cook until the onion is soft, 4 to 6 minutes. Add chard (or spinach) and cook, stirring, until starting to wilt, 1 to 2 minutes. Stir in tomatoes, beans and pepper and bring to a simmer. Stir in the gnocchi and sprinkle with mozzarella and Parmesan. Cover and cook until the cheese is melted and the sauce is bubbling, about 3 minutes more.

MAKES 6 SERVINGS.

PER SERVING: **327 calories**; 7 g fat (2 g sat, 3 g mono); 8 mg cholesterol; 56 g carbohydrate; 14 g protein; 6 g fiber; 587 mg sodium; 360 mg potassium.
NUTRITION BONUS: Vitamin A (50% daily value), Vitamin C (40% dv), Calcium & Iron (19% dv).

H✴W   H⬆F   H♥H

THE 500-CALORIE MENU
SERVE WITH ONE FROM EACH GROUP

Golden Summer Squash & Corn Soup, page 33 (111 cal.)
OR
Mixed greens (1½ cups) with 2 Tbsp. Goat Cheese & Tomato Dressing, page 76 (102 cal.)

Chunky Peach Popsicles, page 202 (33 cal.)
OR
Sliced strawberries (½ cup, 27 cal.)

THE 500-CALORIE MENU

SERVE WITH ONE FROM EACH GROUP

Quick Tomato Soup, page 41 (1½ cups, 142 cal.)

OR

Mixed greens (1½ cups) with 2 Tbsp. Champagne Vinaigrette, page 74 (120 cal.)

Apple Cider Granita, page 203 (103 cal.)

OR

White wine (5-ounce glass, 116 cal.)

RISOTTO WITH BROCCOLI RABE & RED PEPPER

ACTIVE TIME: **45 MINUTES** | TOTAL: **45 MINUTES**

Sweet red bell pepper balances the bitterness of broccoli rabe in this earthy risotto. If you can't find broccoli rabe, use chard instead and shorten the cooking time slightly. We like the rich, hearty flavor of vegetarian, chicken-flavored broth instead of vegetable broth in this risotto.

4   cups "no-chicken" broth
1   cup water
2   teaspoons extra-virgin olive oil
1   red bell pepper, diced
1   onion, finely chopped
2   cloves garlic, minced
2   teaspoons chopped fresh rosemary *or* ¾ teaspoon dried
¼   teaspoon crushed red pepper
1   cup arborio rice
1   bunch broccoli rabe *or* chard, stemmed and coarsely chopped
⅔   cup freshly grated Parmesan cheese
    Freshly ground pepper to taste

1. Combine broth and water in a large saucepan and bring to a simmer. Reduce heat to low to maintain a simmer.

2. Heat oil in a large skillet over medium heat; add bell pepper and onion and cook, stirring, until softened, 4 to 6 minutes. Add garlic, rosemary and crushed red pepper and cook, stirring, until fragrant, about 1 minute. Stir in rice and cook, stirring, for 1 minute more.

3. Ladle ½ cup of the simmering liquid into the skillet and cook, stirring frequently, until most of it has been absorbed, about 1 minute. Continue stirring and adding liquid as it is absorbed, ½ cup at a time, until you've added 4 cups, about 15 minutes total.

4. Stir in broccoli rabe (or chard) and the remaining liquid. Cook, stirring, until the rice is just tender and the mixture is creamy, 5 to 7 minutes. Remove from the heat and stir in Parmesan. Season with pepper.

MAKES 4 SERVINGS, ABOUT 1½ CUPS EACH.

BROCCOLI & GOAT CHEESE SOUFFLÉ

ACTIVE TIME: 25 MINUTES | TOTAL: 45 MINUTES

These elegant broccoli and goat cheese mini soufflés will wow your family and friends, and they're surprisingly easy. The only trick is getting them on the table before they deflate, so be ready. (Photograph: page 11.)

1½	cups finely chopped broccoli florets
1	tablespoon butter
1	tablespoon extra-virgin olive oil
2	tablespoons all-purpose flour
1¼	cups low-fat milk
1	teaspoon Dijon mustard
¼	teaspoon dried rosemary
¼	teaspoon salt
½	cup crumbled goat cheese
3	large eggs, separated
2	large egg whites
¼	teaspoon cream of tartar

1. Preheat oven to 375°F. Coat four 10-ounce ramekins (or a 2- to 2½-quart soufflé dish) with cooking spray and place on a baking sheet.

2. Microwave broccoli, covered, until tender-crisp, 1 to 2 minutes. Set aside.

3. Melt butter and oil in a large saucepan over medium-high heat. Whisk in flour and cook, whisking, for 1 minute. The mixture should be the color of caramel. Add milk, mustard, rosemary and salt; cook, whisking constantly, until thickened, 1 to 2 minutes. Remove from heat and whisk in goat cheese and 3 egg yolks until well combined. Transfer to a large bowl.

4. Beat the 5 egg whites in a medium bowl with an electric mixer on high speed until soft peaks form. Add cream of tartar and beat until stiff peaks form. Using a rubber spatula, gently fold half the whites into the milk mixture. Gently fold in the remaining whites and the reserved broccoli just until no streaks remain. Transfer to the prepared ramekins or soufflé dish.

5. Bake until puffed and an instant-read thermometer registers 160°F, about 20 minutes in ramekins or 30 minutes in a soufflé dish.

MAKES 4 SERVINGS.

PER SERVING: **254 calories**; 17 g fat (8 g sat, 6 g mono); 184 mg cholesterol; 10 g carbohydrate; 16 g protein; 1 g fiber; 398 mg sodium; 199 mg potassium.
NUTRITION BONUS: Vitamin C (30% daily value), Vitamin A (25% dv), Calcium (15% dv).

L ⬇ C

THE 500-CALORIE MENU

SERVE WITH ONE FROM EACH GROUP

Baby spinach (1½ cups) with 2 Tbsp. Champagne Vinaigrette, page 74 (120 cal.)
OR
Roasted Asparagus with Garlic-Lemon Sauce, page 182 (89 cal.)

Whole-Grain Rice Pilaf, page 186 (97 cal.)
OR
Crushed Red Potatoes with Buttermilk, page 188 (85 cal.)

Chunky Peach Popsicles, page 202 (33 cal.)
OR
Apple slices (½ cup, 28 cal.)

PER SERVING: **378 calories**; 15 g fat (5 g sat, 6 g mono); 19 mg cholesterol; 48 g carbohydrate; 12 g protein; 5 g fiber; 879 mg sodium; 689 mg potassium. NUTRITION BONUS: Potassium (22% daily value), Calcium (19% dv).

H✕W H↑F

THE 500-CALORIE MENU

SERVE WITH

Southwestern Calico Corn, page 184 (98 cal.)

OR

Basic Sautéed Kale, page 178 (102 cal.)

DIET TIP

Read the label when you choose whole-wheat tortillas—they vary widely. Look for ones supplying at least 3 grams of fiber apiece. More fiber means your meal will be absorbed more slowly, and may help you stay satiated longer.

BARBECUE PORTOBELLO QUESADILLAS

ACTIVE TIME: **45 MINUTES** | TOTAL: **45 MINUTES**

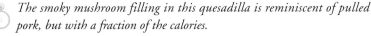

The smoky mushroom filling in this quesadilla is reminiscent of pulled pork, but with a fraction of the calories.

½   cup barbecue sauce
1   tablespoon tomato paste
1   tablespoon cider vinegar
1   chipotle pepper in adobo sauce (*see Note, page 207*), minced, *or* ¼ teaspoon ground chipotle pepper
1   pound portobello mushroom caps (about 5 medium)
1   tablespoon plus 2 teaspoons canola oil, divided
1   medium onion, finely diced
4   8- to 10-inch whole-wheat tortillas
¾   cup shredded Monterey Jack cheese

1. Combine barbecue sauce, tomato paste, vinegar and chipotle in a medium bowl. Gently scrape off and discard the gills from the underside of the mushroom caps; dice the caps.

2. Heat 1 tablespoon oil in a large nonstick skillet over medium heat. Add the mushrooms and cook, stirring occasionally, for 5 minutes. Add onion and cook, stirring, until the onion and mushrooms are beginning to brown, 5 to 7 minutes more. Transfer to the bowl with the barbecue sauce; stir to combine. Wipe out the pan.

3. Place tortillas on a work surface. Spread 3 tablespoons cheese on half of each tortilla and top with one-fourth (about ½ cup) of the filling. Fold tortillas in half, pressing gently to flatten.

4. Heat 1 teaspoon oil in the pan over medium heat. Add 2 quesadillas and cook, turning once, until golden on both sides, 3 to 4 minutes total. Transfer to a cutting board and tent with foil to keep warm. Repeat with the remaining 1 teaspoon oil and quesadillas. Cut each quesadilla into wedges and serve.

MAKES 4 SERVINGS.

PER SERVING: **202 calories**; 12 g fat (4 g sat, 5 g mono); 13 mg cholesterol; 12 g carbohydrate; 13 g protein; 3 g fiber; 501 mg sodium; 422 mg potassium. NUTRITION BONUS: Calcium (35% daily value), Vitamin C (20% dv), Iron & Vitamin A (15% dv).

H✖W L⬇C

THE 500-CALORIE MENU

SERVE WITH ONE FROM EACH GROUP

Southwestern Calico Corn, page 184 (98 cal.)

OR

Warm corn tortilla (6-inch, 70 cal.)

Black beans (½ cup) with 1 Tbsp. reduced-fat sour cream (134 cal.)

OR

Mixed greens (1½ cups) with 2 Tbsp. Spicy Mediterranean Vinaigrette, page 75 (124 cal.)

Chewy Chocolate Cookies, page 197 (68 cal.)

OR

Low-fat plain yogurt (¼ cup) with ½ cup sliced strawberries (66 cal.)

DIET TIP

Stock up on salsa. The low-cal condiment is long on flavor and fiber—and it packs a whole vegetable serving in every ½ cup.

SOUTHWESTERN TOFU SCRAMBLE

ACTIVE TIME: 30 MINUTES | TOTAL: 30 MINUTES

Cooking crumbled firm tofu in a skillet approximates the fluffy texture of scrambled eggs in this vegetable-studded, vegetarian main dish. It's also great for breakfast or lunch.

- 3 teaspoons canola oil, divided
- 1 14-ounce package water-packed firm tofu, rinsed and crumbled
- 1½ teaspoons chili powder
- 1 teaspoon ground cumin
- ½ teaspoon salt, divided
- 1 small zucchini, diced
- ¾ cup frozen corn, thawed
- 4 scallions, sliced
- ½ cup shredded Monterey Jack cheese
- ½ cup prepared salsa
- ¼ cup chopped fresh cilantro

1. Heat 1½ teaspoons oil in a large nonstick skillet over medium heat. Add tofu, chili powder, cumin and ¼ teaspoon salt and cook, stirring, until the tofu begins to brown, 4 to 6 minutes. Transfer to a bowl.

2. Add the remaining 1½ teaspoons oil to the pan. Add zucchini, corn, scallions and the remaining ¼ teaspoon salt. Cook, stirring, until the vegetables are just tender, about 3 minutes. Return the tofu to the pan and cook, stirring, until heated through, about 2 minutes more. Remove from the heat and stir in cheese until just melted. Top each serving with 2 tablespoons salsa and 1 tablespoon cilantro.

MAKES 4 SERVINGS, ABOUT ¾ CUP EACH.

SOUTHWESTERN RICE & PINTO BEAN SALAD

ACTIVE TIME: **20 MINUTES** | TOTAL: **1 HOUR** | TO MAKE AHEAD: Cover and refrigerate for up to 2 days.

Brown rice doesn't have to be boring. The slightly chewy texture of ruddy-red Wehani rice makes it perfect for salads; seek it out in larger supermarkets and natural-foods stores.

1	cup Wehani brown rice *or* brown basmati rice
2½	cups water
2	teaspoons cumin seeds *or* 1 teaspoon ground cumin
¼	cup extra-virgin olive oil
¼	cup sherry vinegar
1	tablespoon chopped fresh oregano *or* 1 teaspoon dried
1	large clove garlic, crushed and peeled
¼	teaspoon salt
½	teaspoon freshly ground pepper
2	15-ounce cans pinto beans, rinsed
8	scallions, trimmed and sliced (about 1½ cups)
1	medium bell pepper (any color), chopped (about 1 cup)

1. Combine rice and water (use just 2 cups water if using brown basmati) in a 3-quart saucepan; bring to a boil. Reduce heat to low, cover and cook until all the water has been absorbed, 40 to 45 minutes. Remove from heat; let rest, covered, for 10 minutes. Spread the rice out on a large baking sheet until cooled to room temperature, about 15 minutes.

2. Meanwhile, toast cumin in a small skillet over medium-high heat until fragrant and lightly toasted, 1 to 2 minutes for seeds, 1 minute for ground cumin. Transfer to a blender or food processor and let cool for several minutes. Add oil, vinegar, oregano, garlic, salt and pepper and process until the garlic is finely chopped.

3. Transfer the rice to a large bowl and toss with beans, scallions and bell pepper. Pour the dressing over the salad and toss well to combine.

MAKES 6 SERVINGS, 1⅓ CUPS EACH.

PER SERVING: **304 calories**; 11 g fat (2 g sat, 8 g mono); 0 mg cholesterol; 45 g carbohydrate; 9 g protein; 8 g fiber; 121 mg sodium; 442 mg potassium. NUTRITION BONUS: Vitamin C (40% daily value), Iron (16% dv).

H↑F   H♥H

THE 500-CALORIE MENU
SERVE WITH ONE FROM EACH GROUP

Sliced avocado (one-fourth), lime wedge, shredded romaine lettuce (1 cup) with 2 Tbsp. reduced-fat sour cream (128 cal.)
OR
Golden Summer Squash & Corn Soup, page 33 (111 cal.)

Banana Pudding Pops, page 202 (82 cal.)
OR
Raspberry Applesauce, page 201 (67 cal.)

DIET TIP

Combining rice and beans in a dish gives you high-quality protein—and an ample dose of satisfying fiber.

PER SERVING: **181 calories**; 8 g fat (1 g sat, 3 g mono); 0 mg cholesterol; 17 g carbohydrate; 11 g protein; 5 g fiber; 545 mg sodium; 599 mg potassium. NUTRITION BONUS: Calcium (22% daily value), Potassium (17% dv), Iron (15% dv).

H❋W L⬇C H⬆F H♥H

THE 500-CALORIE MENU

SERVE WITH ONE FROM EACH GROUP

Sesame Snap Peas with Carrots & Peppers, page 183 (78 cal.)
OR
Sautéed bok choy with 1 tsp. olive oil and a dash of reduced-sodium soy sauce (1 cup, 62 cal.)

Quinoa (see Guide, page 190; ½ cup, 111 cal.)
OR
Brown rice (see Guide, page 190; ½ cup, 109 cal.)

Orange Crisps with Citrus Fruit Salad, page 198 (128 cal.)
OR
Papaya-Lime Sorbet, page 199 (110 cal.)

DIET TIP

Try chopped mushrooms to stand in for some or all of the ground meat in dishes like chili, meatloaf or meatballs. You'll cut calories and fat without sacrificing texture or flavor.

CHINESE BRAISED MUSHROOMS & TOFU

ACTIVE TIME: 40 MINUTES | TOTAL: 40 MINUTES

Ma Po Tofu, a classic dish from the Szechuan province of China, inspired this recipe. The original is made with fatty ground pork or beef—but portobello mushrooms are a tasty, much leaner stand-in.

  1 tablespoon canola oil
  4 cloves garlic, minced
  2 teaspoons minced fresh ginger
  4 portobello mushroom caps, gills removed, chopped
  1 tablespoon chile-garlic sauce (see Note, page 207)
1¼ cups mushroom broth *or* vegetable broth
  2 tablespoons dry sherry (see Note, page 208)
  2 tablespoons reduced-sodium soy sauce
  2 teaspoons brown sugar
  1 14-ounce package water-packed firm tofu, cut into ½-inch cubes
  1 8-ounce can water chestnuts, rinsed and coarsely chopped
  1 tablespoon water
1½ teaspoons cornstarch

1. Heat oil in a large saucepan over medium heat. Add garlic and ginger and cook, stirring, until fragrant, about 30 seconds. Add mushrooms and chile-garlic sauce and cook, stirring occasionally, until most of the mushroom liquid has evaporated, 4 to 6 minutes.

2. Add broth, sherry, soy sauce, brown sugar, tofu and water chestnuts and bring to a simmer. Cook, stirring occasionally and adjusting the heat as necessary to maintain a simmer, for 10 minutes to blend flavors.

3. Combine water and cornstarch in a small bowl. Stir the mixture into the saucepan and simmer until the sauce is thickened, about 2 minutes.

MAKES 4 SERVINGS, ABOUT 1 CUP EACH.

MOO SHU VEGETABLES

ACTIVE TIME: **20 MINUTES** | TOTAL: **20 MINUTES**

This vegetarian version of the classic Chinese stir-fry, Moo Shu, uses already-shredded vegetables to cut down on the prep time.

- 3 teaspoons toasted sesame oil, divided
- 4 large eggs, lightly beaten
- 2 teaspoons minced fresh ginger
- 2 cloves garlic, minced
- 1 12-ounce bag shredded mixed vegetables, such as "rainbow salad" *or* "broccoli slaw"
- 2 cups mung bean sprouts
- 1 bunch scallions, sliced, divided
- 1 tablespoon reduced-sodium soy sauce
- 1 tablespoon rice vinegar
- 2 tablespoons hoisin sauce (*see Note, page 207*)

1. Heat 1 teaspoon oil in a large nonstick skillet over medium heat. Add eggs; cook, stirring gently, until set, 2 to 3 minutes. Remove to a plate.

2. Wipe out the pan and heat the remaining 2 teaspoons oil over medium heat. Add ginger and garlic and cook, stirring, until softened and fragrant, 1 minute. Add shredded vegetables, bean sprouts, half the sliced scallions, soy sauce and vinegar. Stir to combine. Cover and cook, stirring once or twice, until the vegetables are just tender, about 3 minutes. Add hoisin and the reserved eggs; cook, uncovered, stirring and breaking up the scrambled eggs, until heated through, 1 to 2 minutes. Stir in the remaining scallions and remove from the heat.

MAKES 4 SERVINGS, ABOUT 1¼ CUPS EACH.

PER SERVING: **171 calories**; 9 g fat (2 g sat, 4 g mono); 212 mg cholesterol; 14 g carbohydrate; 11 g protein; 4 g fiber; 328 mg sodium; 226 mg potassium. NUTRITION BONUS: Vitamin C (20% daily value), Folate (17% dv).

H✱W   L↓C   H♥H

THE 500-CALORIE MENU
SERVE WITH ONE FROM EACH GROUP

Glazed Mini Carrots, page 179 (74 cal.)
OR
Steamed snap peas with a drizzle (1 tsp.) of olive oil (½ cup, 77 cal.)

Warm whole-wheat tortilla (8-inch, 140 cal.)
OR
Brown rice (*see Guide, page 190*; ½ cup, 109 cal.)

Low-fat vanilla ice cream (½ cup, 104 cal.)
OR
White wine (5-ounce glass, 116 cal.)

PER SERVING: **161 calories**; 3 g fat (0 g sat, 2 g mono); 0 mg cholesterol; 30 g carbohydrate; 6 g protein; 6 g fiber; 700 mg sodium; 663 mg potassium. NUTRITION BONUS: Vitamin A (40% daily value), Vitamin A (35% dv), Folate (28% dv), Potassium (19% dv).

THE 500-CALORIE MENU
SERVE WITH ONE FROM EACH GROUP

Baby spinach (1½ cups) with 2 Tbsp. Buttermilk Dressing, page 76 (35 cal.)
OR
Mixed greens (1½ cups) with 2 Tbsp. Garlic-Yogurt Dressing, page 77 (38 cal.)

Toasted whole-grain baguette (2 inches, 132 cal.)
OR
Quinoa (see Guide, page 190; ½ cup, 111 cal.)

Hot Fudge Pudding Cake, page 196 (142 cal.)
OR
Orange Crisps with Citrus Fruit Salad, page 198 (128 cal.)

DIET TIP

Add split peas to soups and stews to make them heartier. Their fiber and protein help to slow digestion, prolonging the release of hormones that trigger the "I'm satisfied" feeling.

GINGER, SPLIT PEA & VEGETABLE CURRY

ACTIVE TIME: **50 MINUTES** | TOTAL: **50 MINUTES**

This hearty, stewlike curry works well with nearly any vegetable; sweet potatoes, winter squash and spinach create a sweeter offering. Don't be alarmed by the number of chiles—the vegetables and split peas bring the heat level down.

1	large russet *or* Yukon Gold potato, peeled and cut into ½-inch cubes
½	cup yellow split peas
1	cup cauliflower florets (1-inch pieces)
1	cup green bean pieces, frozen *or* fresh (1-inch pieces)
1	small eggplant (8 ounces), cut into ½-inch cubes
1	medium carrot, cut into ¼-inch-thick slices
1¾	teaspoons salt
½	teaspoon ground turmeric
1	tablespoon canola oil
1	teaspoon cumin seeds
4	large cloves garlic, cut into thin slivers
1-3	fresh green chiles, such as Thai *or* serrano chiles, stemmed and thinly sliced crosswise (do not seed)
1	tablespoon cornstarch
¼	cup finely chopped fresh cilantro
4	long thin slices fresh ginger, cut into matchsticks Juice of 1 medium lime
1	teaspoon ghee (*see Note, page 209*) *or* butter (optional)

1. Place potato in a small bowl and cover with cold water. Place split peas in a large saucepan. Fill the pan halfway with water and rinse the peas by rubbing them between your fingers. (The water will become cloudy.) Drain. Repeat three or four times, until the water remains relatively clear; drain. Add 4 cups water to the split peas and bring to a boil over medium-high heat. Skim off any foam that rises to the surface. Drain the potato and add to the peas. Return to a boil, reduce heat to medium and simmer, un-covered, for 5 minutes.

2. Stir in cauliflower, green beans, eggplant, carrot, salt and turmeric. Return to a boil; cover, reduce to a gentle simmer and cook, stirring occasionally, until the vegetables are fork-tender and the peas are soft but firm-looking, 7 to 10 minutes more.

3. Meanwhile, heat oil in a small skillet over medium-high heat. Add cumin seeds and cook until they sizzle and smell fragrant, 15 to 20 seconds. Stir in garlic and chiles to taste; cook, stirring, until the garlic is light brown and the chiles are fragrant, 1 to 2 minutes. Stir the garlic-chile mixture into the cooked vegetables. Scoop a ladleful of cooking liquid from the saucepan to the skillet; swish it around and pour the "washings" back into the saucepan.

4. Whisk cornstarch with 3 tablespoons of the cooking liquid in a small bowl until smooth. Stir it into the curry along with cilantro and ginger. Increase heat to medium-high and simmer the curry, uncovered, stirring occasionally, until it thickens, about 2 minutes. Stir in lime juice and ghee (or butter), if using.

MAKES 6 SERVINGS, GENEROUS 1 CUP EACH.

THE 500-CALORIE MENU

SERVE WITH ONE FROM EACH GROUP

Quinoa (see *Guide, page 190*; ½ cup, 111 cal.)

OR

Polenta (see *Guide, page 190*; ½ cup, 74 cal.)

Raspberry Applesauce, page 201 (67 cal.)

OR

Chewy Chocolate Cookies, page 197 (68 cal.)

DIET TIP

Get edamame—green soybeans—into your diet. They have satisfying protein and fiber. Try adding them to salads, stir-fries or soups.

PROVENÇAL-STYLE EDAMAME SAUTÉ

ACTIVE TIME: **35 MINUTES** | TOTAL: **35 MINUTES**

Provence, in southeast France, is justly famous for dishes prepared with plenty of garlic, olive oil and olives. We've kept the "á la Provençal" spirit and flavor while easing up on the calorie-rich olives and oil in this quick and hearty one-skillet supper.

2 tablespoons extra-virgin olive oil
1 large fennel bulb, trimmed, cored and thinly sliced
2 tablespoons minced garlic
½ teaspoon herbes de Provence (see *Note, page 207*)
¾ cup dry white wine
1 10-ounce package frozen shelled edamame (about 2 cups), thawed
1 9-ounce package frozen artichoke hearts, thawed
¼ cup vegetable broth or reduced-sodium chicken broth
1 teaspoon freshly grated lemon zest
¼ cup lemon juice
½ teaspoon salt
½ cup crumbled feta cheese
2 tablespoons chopped cured olives

Heat oil in a large skillet over medium heat. Add fennel and cook, stirring, until starting to soften and brown, 3 to 5 minutes. Add garlic and herbes de Provence; cook, stirring, until fragrant, about 30 seconds. Add wine; increase heat to high and bring to a boil. Boil until the wine is almost evaporated, about 3 minutes. Stir in edamame, artichoke hearts and broth; cover and cook, stirring occasionally, until hot, about 5 minutes. Remove from the heat; stir in lemon zest, lemon juice and salt. Serve sprinkled with feta and olives.

MAKES 4 SERVINGS, ABOUT 1½ CUPS EACH.

POULTRY

America's most popular meat, by a long shot, is chicken. In 2006, the average American ate 86.5 pounds of chicken versus 65 pounds of beef and about 50 pounds of pork, according to the USDA. And lean boneless, skinless chicken breast has always ranked as a favorite, especially for anyone watching their weight. With only 140 calories and 3 grams of fat per 3-ounce cooked serving, it's a real diet bargain. Chicken breast also owes some of its popularity to its convenience—it's super-easy to prep and cooks up in minutes.

While we're huge fans of the boneless, skinless chicken breast, we also love rich, dark chicken and turkey meat because its flavor is so intense and it stays moister than white meat. So although dark meat is slightly higher in calories and fat (174 calories and 8 grams of fat for chicken, 159 calories and 6 grams of fat for turkey), we're OK with the tradeoff. When it comes to ground turkey or chicken we usually skip the 99%-lean and go for 93%-lean instead. Why? Two words: taste and texture. The less-lean grind is just more juicy and delicious. Try the mozzarella-stuffed turkey burgers on page 108 for proof. Sure, we could make a leaner, lower-calorie burger, but it wouldn't taste as good as this one!

A 508-Calorie Dinner (*left*): Seared Chicken with Apricot Sauce (*page 100*), 252 calories; 1/2 cup steamed spinach, 21 calories; Cheesy Broccoli-Potato Mash (*page 188*), 135 calories; Fast Strawberry Frozen Yogurt (*page 201*), 100 calories.

PER SERVING: **252 calories**; 5 g fat (1 g sat, 3 g mono); 66 mg cholesterol; 15 g carbohydrate; 27 g protein; 1 g fiber; 517 mg sodium; 444 mg potassium. NUTRITION BONUS: Vitamin A (15% daily value).

THE 500-CALORIE MENU

SERVE WITH ONE FROM EACH GROUP

Steamed broccoli with a squeeze of lemon (see *Guide, page 191*; ½ cup, 22 cal.)
OR
Steamed spinach with a squeeze of lemon (½ cup, 21 cal.)

Cheesy Broccoli-Potato Mash, page 188 (135 cal.)
OR
Quinoa tossed with chopped fresh herbs (see *Guide, page 190*; ½ cup, 111 cal.)

Fast Strawberry Frozen Yogurt, page 201 (100 cal.)
OR
Banana Pudding Pops, page 202 (82 cal.)

SEARED CHICKEN WITH APRICOT SAUCE

ACTIVE TIME: **30 MINUTES** | TOTAL: **30 MINUTES**

Fresh apricots, white wine, apricot preserves and tarragon combine in a quick sauce that's delicious on chicken. Try different combinations of wine (or even fruit juice with a touch of vinegar) and other fruits and preserves. (Photograph: page 98.)

4	boneless, skinless chicken breasts (about 1¼ pounds), trimmed and tenders removed (*see Note, page 209*)
¾	teaspoon salt, divided
¼	teaspoon freshly ground pepper
¼	cup all-purpose flour
1	tablespoon canola oil
¾	cup dry white wine
1	medium shallot, minced
4	fresh apricots, pitted and chopped
2	tablespoons apricot preserves
2	teaspoons chopped fresh tarragon *or* ½ teaspoon dried

1. Flatten one piece of chicken at a time between sheets of plastic wrap with a rolling pin, meat mallet or heavy skillet to an even ½-inch thickness. Sprinkle with ¼ teaspoon salt and pepper. Place flour in a shallow dish. Dredge the chicken in the flour, shaking off excess. (Discard any leftover flour.)

2. Heat oil in a large skillet over medium heat. Add the chicken and cook until browned and no longer pink in the center, 3 to 5 minutes per side. Transfer to a plate, cover and keep warm. (If necessary, cook the chicken in two batches with an additional 1 tablespoon oil.)

3. Off the heat, add wine and shallot to the pan. Return to medium heat and cook, scraping up any browned bits, until slightly reduced, about 3 minutes. Add apricots and cook until the fruit begins to break down, 2 to 3 minutes. Stir in preserves, tarragon and the remaining ½ teaspoon salt. Return the chicken to the pan and cook until heated through, 1 to 2 minutes. Serve the chicken with the sauce.

MAKES 4 SERVINGS.

CORNMEAL-CRUSTED CHICKEN WITH PEPIÁN SAUCE

ACTIVE TIME: 40 MINUTES | TOTAL: 40 MINUTES

Tomatillos and pepitas (hulled pumpkin seeds) form the basis for this rich-tasting pepián sauce.

- 4 tomatillos, husked and rinsed
- ¼ cup diced onion
- 4 tablespoons pepitas (*see Note, page 208*), divided
- 3 tablespoons chopped fresh cilantro, divided
- 1 clove garlic, peeled
- ½ cup reduced-sodium chicken broth
- ½ teaspoon salt, divided
- 2 tablespoons reduced-fat sour cream
- 4 boneless, skinless chicken breasts (about 1¼ pounds), trimmed and tenders removed (*see Note, page 209*)
- 1 large egg white
- 2 tablespoons water
- ½ cup yellow cornmeal
- 3 teaspoons canola oil, divided

1. Place tomatillos, onion, 3 tablespoons pepitas, 2 tablespoons cilantro, garlic, broth and ¼ teaspoon salt in a blender or food processor; process until smooth. Transfer to a saucepan and cook over medium-high heat, stirring occasionally, until reduced to about ¾ cup, 12 to 15 minutes. The mixture will resemble a thick paste. Off the heat, stir in sour cream. Set aside.

2. Meanwhile, flatten one piece of chicken at a time between sheets of plastic wrap with a rolling pin, meat mallet or heavy skillet to an even ¼-inch thickness. Whisk egg white and water in a shallow dish. Whisk cornmeal and the remaining ¼ teaspoon salt in another shallow dish. Dip each chicken breast in egg white, then dredge in cornmeal, coating evenly.

3. Cook the chicken in two batches in a large nonstick skillet over medium heat, using 1½ teaspoons oil for each batch. Cook until browned and no longer pink in the middle, 2 to 4 minutes per side. Serve with the reserved sauce and the remaining 1 tablespoon each pepitas and cilantro.

MAKES 4 SERVINGS.

PER SERVING: **314 calories**; 14 g fat (3 g sat, 5 g mono); 66 mg cholesterol; 17 g carbohydrate; 31 g protein; 2 g fiber; 519 mg sodium; 464 mg potassium. NUTRITION BONUS: Magnesium (27% daily value), Iron (20% dv).

H✖W L⬇C H❤H

THE 500-CALORIE MENU

SERVE WITH ONE FROM EACH GROUP

Baja Butternut Squash Soup, page 34 (60 cal.)
OR
Steamed broccoli with a squeeze of lime and a dash of hot sauce (*see Guide, page 191*; 1 cup, 44 cal.)

Black beans (½ cup, 114 cal.)
OR
Brown rice with a pinch of chili powder (*see Guide, page 190*; ½ cup, 109 cal.)

CHICKEN, CHARRED TOMATO & BROCCOLI SALAD

ACTIVE TIME: 40 MINUTES | TOTAL: 1 HOUR | TO MAKE AHEAD: Cover and refrigerate for up to 2 days.

This simple but substantial main-course salad gets its goodness from smoky skillet-blackened tomatoes and a dressing prepared right in the pan—maximizing all the flavor from the tomatoes.

4	cups broccoli florets
1½	pounds medium tomatoes
2	teaspoons plus 3 tablespoons extra-virgin olive oil, divided
1	teaspoon salt
1	teaspoon freshly ground pepper
½	teaspoon chili powder
¼	cup lemon juice
3	cups shredded cooked chicken breast (*see Note, page 209*)

1. Bring a large pot of water to a boil. Add broccoli and cook until tender, 3 to 5 minutes. Drain and rinse with cold water until cool. Set aside.

2. Core tomatoes and cut in half crosswise. Gently squeeze out seeds and discard. Drain cut-side down on paper towels for about 5 minutes.

3. Place a large heavy skillet, such as cast iron, over high heat until very hot. Brush the cut sides of the tomatoes with 1 teaspoon oil and place cut-side down in the pan. Cook until charred and beginning to soften, 4 to 5 minutes. Brush the tops lightly with another 1 teaspoon oil, turn and cook until the skin is charred, 1 to 2 minutes more. Transfer to a plate to cool. Do not clean the pan.

4. Heat the remaining 3 tablespoons oil in the pan over medium heat. Stir in salt, pepper and chili powder and cook, stirring constantly, until fragrant, about 45 seconds. Slowly pour in lemon juice (it may splatter), then remove the pan from the heat. Stir to scrape up any browned bits.

5. Coarsely chop the tomatoes and combine them in a large bowl with shredded chicken, the reserved broccoli and the pan dressing; toss to coat.

MAKES 6 SERVINGS, 1⅓ CUPS EACH.

PER SERVING: **231 calories**; 11 g fat (2 g sat, 8 g mono); 60 mg cholesterol; 8 g carbohydrate; 24 g protein; 3 g fiber; 460 mg sodium; 619 mg potassium.
NUTRITION BONUS: Vitamin C (110% daily value), Vitamin A (50% dv), Potassium (18% dv).

H❋W L↓C H♥H

THE 500-CALORIE MENU

SERVE WITH ONE FROM EACH GROUP

Wild rice tossed with chopped fresh chives and a squeeze of lime (*see Guide, page 190; ½ cup, 83 cal.*)
OR
Warm whole-wheat pita bread (74 cal.)

Claire's Mixed Green Salad with Feta Vinaigrette, page 53 (165 cal.)
OR
Hot Fudge Pudding Cake, page 196 (142 cal.)

DIET TIP

Try cast-iron pans, which are virtually nonstick when they're well-seasoned, to cut down on the amount of oil you use. They're a great option because you can safely apply plenty of heat and get a tasty browned crust on your food.

PER SERVING: **240 calories**; 4 g fat (1 g sat, 1 g mono); 63 mg cholesterol; 27 g carbohydrate; 24 g protein; 1 g fiber; 574 mg sodium; 281 mg potassium.

THE 500-CALORIE MENU

SERVE WITH ONE FROM EACH GROUP

Toasted whole-grain baguette (2 inches, 132 cal.)
OR
Garlic & Herb Pita Chips, page 186 (117 cal.)

Baby spinach (1 ½ cups) with 2 Tbsp. Spicy Mediterranean Vinaigrette, page 75 (125 cal.)
OR
Roasted Asparagus with Garlic-Lemon Sauce, page 182 (89 cal.)

DIET TIP

In recipes that call for mayonnaise, use the low-fat version, which has just 15 calories and 1 gram of fat compared with 90 calories and 10 grams of fat in the traditional kind.

CURRIED CHICKEN SALAD

ACTIVE TIME: **30 MINUTES** | TOTAL: 1 ½ **HOURS** (including chilling time)
TO MAKE AHEAD: Prepare through Step 1; cover and refrigerate overnight.

Chilling the poached chicken breasts in the cooking liquid makes the meat so moist and flavorful, you don't need much creamy dressing to make it succulent.

2	cups reduced-sodium chicken broth
2	cups water
1 ½	pounds boneless, skinless chicken breasts, trimmed
½	cup low-fat mayonnaise
½	cup nonfat plain yogurt
½	cup mango chutney
2	teaspoons curry powder, or to taste
1	tart apple, such as Granny Smith, chopped
¼	cup currants *or* raisins

1. Bring broth and water to a boil in a large shallow pan. Add chicken and reduce heat to low. Simmer, partially covered, until the chicken is no longer pink inside, 10 to 15 minutes. Transfer the chicken to a shallow dish and pour the cooking liquid over the top. Refrigerate until chilled, at least 1 hour or overnight.

2. Remove the chicken from the cooking liquid and dice. (Discard the cooking liquid.) Stir mayonnaise, yogurt, chutney and curry powder in a medium bowl until well blended. Add the diced chicken, apple and currants (or raisins) and toss until thoroughly coated.

MAKES 6 SERVINGS.

TURKEY & TOMATO PANINI

ACTIVE TIME: 25 MINUTES | TOTAL: 25 MINUTES

Turn a plain sandwich dinner into something special by preparing it panini-style (which doesn't, by the way, require a fancy panini maker). They're best served hot out of the pan. If you do have a panini maker, prepare the sandwiches (Step 2) and toast them in a preheated panini maker instead of in the skillet.

    3 tablespoons low-fat mayonnaise
    2 tablespoons nonfat plain yogurt
    2 tablespoons shredded Parmesan cheese
    2 tablespoons chopped fresh basil
    1 teaspoon lemon juice
       Freshly ground pepper to taste
    8 slices whole-wheat bread
    8 ounces thinly sliced reduced-sodium deli turkey
    8 slices tomato
    2 teaspoons canola oil

1. Have four 15-ounce cans and a medium skillet (not nonstick) ready by the stove.

2. Combine mayonnaise, yogurt, Parmesan, basil, lemon juice and pepper in a small bowl. Spread about 2 teaspoons of the mixture on each slice of bread. Divide turkey and tomato slices among 4 slices of bread; top with the remaining bread.

3. Heat 1 teaspoon oil in a large nonstick skillet over medium heat. Place 2 panini in the pan. Place the medium skillet on top of the panini, then weigh it down with the cans. Cook the panini until golden on one side, about 2 minutes. Reduce the heat to medium-low, flip the panini, replace the top skillet and cans, and cook until the second side is golden, 1 to 3 minutes more. Repeat with another 1 teaspoon oil and the remaining panini.

MAKES 4 SERVINGS.

PER SERVING: **285 calories**; 6 g fat (1 g sat, 3 g mono); 27 mg cholesterol; 36 g carbohydrate; 10 g protein; 5 g fiber; 680 mg sodium; 116 mg potassium.
NUTRITION BONUS: Fiber (20% daily value), Calcium & Iron (15% dv).

H✖W   H⬆F   H♥H

THE 500-CALORIE MENU

SERVE WITH ONE FROM EACH GROUP

Baby spinach (1½ cups) with 2 Tbsp. Goat Cheese & Tomato Dressing, page 76 (103 cal.)
OR
Simple Sautéed Spinach, page 178 (68 cal.)

Roasted cauliflower (*see Guide, page 193*; 71 cal.)
OR
Quick Pickled Beets, page 182 (44 cal.)

Tangerine (1 medium, 47 cal.)
OR
Cubed watermelon (1 cup, 46 cal.)

DIET TIP

Make your own panini so you can keep the ingredients healthy and the portion size reasonable. Restaurant panini are typically made with big slabs of focaccia bread and can weigh in at over 800 calories apiece.

INDIAN-SPICED CHICKEN PITAS

ACTIVE TIME: 30 MINUTES | TOTAL: 30 MINUTES
TO MAKE AHEAD: Prepare through Step 2. Refrigerate the chicken in an airtight container for up to 2 days.

Tuck grilled spice-rubbed chicken breasts into whole-wheat pitas with fresh vegetables and a tangy yogurt sauce for an easy supper. Garam masala is a blend of spices used in Indian cooking. Look for it in the spice section of most supermarkets.

1	pound boneless, skinless chicken breasts, trimmed
1½	teaspoons garam masala, divided
¾	teaspoon kosher salt, divided
1	cup thinly sliced seeded cucumber
¾	cup nonfat plain yogurt
1	tablespoon chopped fresh cilantro *or* mint
2	teaspoons lemon juice
	Freshly ground pepper to taste
4	6-inch whole-wheat pitas, warmed
1	cup shredded romaine lettuce
2	small *or* 1 large tomato, sliced
¼	cup thinly sliced red onion

1. Preheat grill to medium-high or position rack in upper third of oven and preheat broiler. If grilling, oil the grill rack (*see Note, page 210*). If broiling, coat a broiler pan with cooking spray.

2. Sprinkle chicken with 1 teaspoon garam masala and ½ teaspoon salt. Place the chicken on the grill rack or prepared pan and cook until no longer pink in the center and an instant-read thermometer inserted into the thickest part registers 165°F, 4 to 8 minutes per side, depending on the size of the breast. Transfer the chicken to a clean cutting board and let rest for 5 minutes.

3. Meanwhile, combine cucumber, yogurt, cilantro (or mint), lemon juice, the remaining ½ teaspoon garam masala and ¼ teaspoon salt and pepper in a small bowl. Thinly slice the chicken. Split open the warm pitas and fill with the chicken, yogurt sauce, lettuce, tomato and onion.

MAKES 4 SERVINGS.

PER SERVING: **333 calories**; 5 g fat (1 g sat, 1 g mono); 64 mg cholesterol; 44 g carbohydrate; 32 g protein; 6 g fiber; 637 mg sodium; 485 mg potassium.
NUTRITION BONUS: Vitamin C (35% daily value), Vitamin A (25% dv), Magnesium (21% dv), Iron (20% dv).

THE 500-CALORIE MENU

SERVE WITH ONE FROM EACH GROUP

Crushed Red Potatoes with Buttermilk, page 188 (85 cal.)
OR
Roasted Eggplant & Feta Dip, page 29 (75 cal.)

Glazed Mini Carrots, page 179 (74 cal.)
OR
Mixed greens (1½ cups) with 2 Tbsp. Parmesan-Pepper Dressing, page 77 (38 cal.)

DIET TIP

Use spices to add calorie-free flavor to food. Your spices should be fresh to get maximum impact, so buy them in small amounts, label with a date, and discard and replace after one year.

PER SERVING: **300 calories**; 15 g fat (4 g sat, 5 g mono); 74 mg cholesterol; 14 g carbohydrate; 28 g protein; 2 g fiber; 706 mg sodium; 386 mg potassium. NUTRITION BONUS: Vitamin C (35% daily value), Vitamin A (20% dv), Calcium & Iron (16% dv).

H✳W L⬇C

THE 500-CALORIE MENU

SERVE WITH ONE FROM EACH GROUP

Cheesy Broccoli-Potato Mash, page 188 (135 cal.)
OR
Zesty Dill Potato Salad, page 189 (123 cal.)

Mixed greens (1½ cups) with 2 Tbsp. Buttermilk Dressing, page 76 (34 cal.)
OR
Steamed broccoli tossed with lemon pepper (*see Guide, page 191*; 1 cup, 44 cal.)

DIET TIP

Try lean ground turkey instead of beef to cut fat and calories by more than half. Mix ground turkey with finely chopped onions and/or cooked greens, herbs and plenty of seasonings to keep leaner burgers moist and full of flavor.

MOZZARELLA-STUFFED TURKEY BURGERS

ACTIVE TIME: **50 MINUTES** | TOTAL: **50 MINUTES**
TO MAKE AHEAD: Cover and refrigerate the marinara sauce (Step 1) for up to 5 days.

Craving a sausage pizza but not the calories? Try these tasty turkey burgers, served on a piece of toasted focaccia and dressed with marinara sauce. Shredded mozzarella combined with fresh basil melts beautifully inside these gems.

MARINARA SAUCE

- 2 teaspoons extra-virgin olive oil
- 1 small onion, finely chopped
- 4 cloves garlic, minced
- 2 cups chopped plum tomatoes, with juices
- 6 oil-packed sun-dried tomatoes, drained and finely chopped
- ½ teaspoon salt
- ½ teaspoon freshly ground pepper
- 2 tablespoons chopped fresh basil

BURGERS

- 1 pound 93%-lean ground turkey
- ¼ cup finely chopped scallions
- 2 teaspoons minced garlic
- 2 teaspoons Worcestershire sauce
- 1 teaspoon freshly grated lemon zest
- ½ teaspoon dried oregano
- ½ teaspoon freshly ground pepper
- ¼ teaspoon salt
- ½ cup shredded part-skim mozzarella cheese, divided
- 2 tablespoons finely chopped fresh basil
- 2 teaspoons extra-virgin olive oil
- 4 4-inch-square slices focaccia bread (about 2 ounces each), toasted

1. **To prepare marinara:** Heat oil in a medium saucepan over medium heat. Add onion and garlic, cover and cook, stirring frequently, until translucent, 5 to 7 minutes. Stir in fresh tomatoes and any juices, sun-dried tomatoes, ½ teaspoon salt and pepper. Bring to a simmer and cook, stirring occasionally, until the tomatoes have broken down, 8 to 10 minutes. Stir in basil and remove from the heat. Transfer to a food processor and pulse to form a coarse-textured sauce. Return to the pan and set aside.

2. To prepare burgers: Place turkey, scallions, garlic, Worcestershire sauce, lemon zest, oregano, pepper and ¼ teaspoon salt in a large bowl. Gently combine, without overmixing, until evenly incorporated. Form into 8 thin patties about 4 inches wide and ⅜ inch thick.

3. Combine ¼ cup cheese and basil and place an equal amount in the center of 4 patties. Cover with the remaining patties and crimp the edges closed.

4. Heat oil in a large nonstick skillet over medium heat (*see Grilling Variation*). Add burgers and cook, turning once, until an instant-read thermometer inserted in the center registers 165°F, 8 to 10 minutes total.

5. Reheat the marinara on the stove. To assemble the burgers, spread 3 tablespoons of marinara on each toasted focaccia, top with a burger, about 3 more tablespoons of marinara and 1 tablespoon of the remaining cheese.

MAKES 4 SERVINGS.

GRILLING VARIATION:

To grill the turkey burgers, preheat a grill to medium-high. Oil the grill rack (*see Note, page 210*). Grill the burgers, turning once, until an instant-read thermometer inserted in the center registers 165°F, 8 to 10 minutes total.

THE 500-CALORIE MENU

SERVE WITH ONE FROM EACH GROUP

Curried Carrot Soup, page 32 (123 cal.)
OR
Baby spinach (1 1/2 cups) with 2 Tbsp. Spicy Mediterranean Vinaigrette, page 75 (125 cal.)

Papaya-Lime Sorbet, page 199 (110 cal.)
OR
Nonfat vanilla frozen yogurt (1/2 cup, 95 cal.)

CHICKEN CURRY WITH RICE

ACTIVE TIME: **40 MINUTES** | TOTAL: **1 HOUR 20 MINUTES**

Fresh ginger and pungent curry powder add big flavor to this one-pot meal, making it extra satisfying to the palate.

1	cup basmati rice
3	teaspoons canola oil, divided
6	skinless, bone-in chicken thighs, trimmed
2	cups finely chopped onions
5	cloves garlic, minced
2	tablespoons minced fresh ginger
2	tablespoons curry powder, preferably Madras
1	tablespoon ground coriander
1/2	teaspoon cayenne pepper, or to taste
2	cups reduced-sodium chicken broth
1	15-ounce can chickpeas, rinsed
1	14-ounce can diced tomatoes, drained
2	cups frozen peas, thawed
1/4	teaspoon salt
	Freshly ground pepper to taste
2	tablespoons chopped fresh cilantro (optional)
	Lime wedges for garnish

1. Preheat oven to 400°F. Soak rice in cold water for 20 minutes. Drain.

2. Meanwhile, heat 1 teaspoon oil in a Dutch oven over medium-high heat. Add chicken and cook until browned on all sides, 6 to 8 minutes. Transfer the chicken to a plate. Reduce the heat to low, add the remaining 2 teaspoons oil and heat until hot. Add onions and cook, stirring, until light golden, 10 to 15 minutes. Stir in garlic, ginger, curry powder, coriander and cayenne; cook, stirring constantly, until fragrant, about 2 minutes.

3. Stir in broth, chickpeas, tomatoes and the rice; bring to a simmer over medium-high heat. Nestle the chicken in the rice. Cover the pot and transfer to the oven. Bake until the rice is tender and most of the liquid has been absorbed, 20 to 25 minutes. Remove the chicken pieces and stir peas into the rice. Season with salt and pepper. Set the chicken back on the rice, and sprinkle with cilantro, if using. Serve with lime wedges, if desired.

MAKES 6 SERVINGS, ABOUT 1 1/3 CUPS EACH.

CHICKEN TETRAZZINI

ACTIVE TIME: **30 MINUTES** | TOTAL: **1 HOUR** | TO MAKE AHEAD:
Prepare through Step 3; cover and refrigerate for up to 2 days.

This classic dish will please kids and *adults. It's also great with leftover turkey.*

6	ounces whole-wheat fettuccine
2	teaspoons canola oil
3	leeks, white parts only, washed and finely chopped (1½ cups)
6	ounces button mushrooms, quartered
1	teaspoon chopped fresh rosemary, divided
3	tablespoons all-purpose flour
3	cups reduced-sodium chicken broth
½	cup low-fat milk
2	cups cubed cooked chicken breast (*see Note, page 209*)
	Grated zest and juice of 1 lemon
¼	teaspoon salt, divided
	Freshly ground pepper to taste
⅓	cup freshly grated Parmesan cheese
¼	cup fine dry breadcrumbs
1	tablespoon finely chopped fresh parsley

1. Preheat oven to 425°F. Coat a 3-quart baking dish with cooking spray.

2. Cook fettuccine in boiling water until just tender, 8 to 10 minutes or according to package directions. Drain and refresh under cold running water. Drain and set aside.

3. Meanwhile, heat oil in a large skillet over medium heat. Add leeks and cook, stirring, until lightly browned, 6 to 8 minutes. Add mushrooms and ½ teaspoon rosemary; cook, stirring, until softened, about 5 minutes. Add flour and cook, stirring, for 1 minute. Add broth and milk; bring to a boil, stirring, until slightly thickened, about 4 minutes more. Remove from heat and stir in chicken. Season with lemon juice, ⅛ teaspoon salt and pepper. Gently mix in the fettuccine. Spoon into the prepared baking dish. Combine lemon zest, Parmesan, breadcrumbs, parsley, the remaining ½ teaspoon rosemary, the remaining ⅛ teaspoon salt and pepper. Sprinkle the mixture over the casserole.

4. Bake the casserole until bubbling, 20 to 30 minutes. Let stand for 5 minutes before serving.

MAKES 6 SERVINGS.

PER SERVING: **290 calories**; 6 g fat (2 g sat, 2 g mono); 45 mg cholesterol; 36 g carbohydrate; 25 g protein; 5 g fiber; 533 mg sodium; 473 mg potassium.
NUTRITION BONUS: Magnesium (19% daily value), Iron (18% dv), Folate & Vitamin A (16% dv).

H✖W   H⬆F   H♥H

THE 500-CALORIE MENU

SERVE WITH ONE FROM EACH GROUP

Mixed greens (1½ cups) with 2 Tbsp. Champagne Vinaigrette, page 74 (120 cal.)
OR
Parmesan Spinach Cakes, page 181 (141 cal.)

Chewy Chocolate Cookies, page 197 (68 cal.)
OR
Chunky Peach Popsicles, page 202 (33 cal.)

PAN-ROASTED CHICKEN & GRAVY

ACTIVE TIME: **25 MINUTES** | TOTAL: **1¼ HOURS**

Most roast chickens are seasoned on top of the skin—making it heartbreaking to remove the skin before eating to save calories. Spreading a flavorful paste under the skin ensures richly flavored meat, so you won't miss the skin.

1	large clove garlic, minced
½	teaspoon kosher salt
¼	teaspoon ground white pepper
1½	teaspoons fresh thyme leaves
1	3½-pound chicken, giblets removed
1	teaspoon peanut oil *or* canola oil
2	teaspoons butter, softened, divided
2	teaspoons all-purpose flour
1½	cups reduced-sodium chicken broth

1. Preheat oven to 400°F.

2. Mash garlic and salt into a paste in a small bowl, using the back of a spoon. Stir in pepper and thyme. With a sharp knife, remove any excess fat from chicken. Dry the inside with a paper towel. With your fingers, loosen the skin over the breasts and thighs to make pockets, being careful not to tear the skin. Rub the garlic mixture over the breast and thigh meat.

3. Heat oil and 1 teaspoon butter in a 12-inch cast-iron skillet over medium heat. Add the chicken and cook, turning often, until nicely browned on all sides, about 10 minutes.

4. Transfer the pan to the oven and roast the chicken until the internal temperature in the thickest part of the thigh reaches 165°F, 50 minutes to 1 hour. Transfer the chicken to a clean cutting board; tent with foil.

5. Meanwhile, mash the remaining 1 teaspoon butter and flour in a small bowl to form a paste. Place the pan over medium-high heat (be careful: the handle will be hot). Add broth and bring to a simmer, stirring to scrape up any browned bits. Gradually whisk in the butter-flour paste a few bits at a time, until the gravy thickens, about 8 minutes. Remove from heat; let stand for 5 minutes. Skim off any fat. Carve the chicken and serve with the gravy.

MAKES 6 SERVINGS.

PER SERVING: **177 calories** (without skin); 6 g fat (2 g sat, 1 g mono); 91 mg cholesterol; 1 g carbohydrate; 28 g protein; 0 g fiber; 333 mg sodium; 375 mg potassium.

H✖W   L↓C   H❤H

THE 500-CALORIE MENU
SERVE WITH ONE FROM EACH GROUP

Salmon & Cucumber Mini Smørrebrød, page 22 (91 cal.)
OR
Sherried Mushrooms, page 25 (49 cal.)

Claire's Mixed Green Salad with Feta Vinaigrette, page 53 (165 cal.)
OR
Parmesan Spinach Cakes, page 181 (141 cal.)

Crushed Red Potatoes with Buttermilk, page 188 (85 cal.)
OR
Polenta (*see Guide, page 190;* ½ cup, 74 cal.)

THE 500-CALORIE MENU

SERVE WITH ONE FROM EACH GROUP

Brown rice (see Guide, page 190; 1/2 cup, 109 cal.)

OR

Whole-wheat egg noodles (1/2 cup, 90 cal.)

Mixed greens (1 1/2 cups) with 2 Tbsp. Cucumber Herb Vinaigrette, page 74 (70 cal.)

OR

Chilled Snap Peas with Creamy Tarragon Dressing, page 179 (61 cal.)

DIET TIP

Remove the skin before cooking poultry in a sauce to trim fat and calories.

BRAISED PAPRIKA CHICKEN

ACTIVE TIME: **1 HOUR** | TOTAL: **1 HOUR 55 MINUTES**
TO MAKE AHEAD: Prepare through Step 2, cool to room temperature and refrigerate for up to 1 day. To serve, finish with Step 3.

Sweet Hungarian paprika gives this creamy braised chicken the best flavor. You may vary the recipe by using well-trimmed, cubed veal shoulder instead of chicken and mushrooms instead of peppers.

2	tablespoons canola oil
1	tablespoon butter
4	cups finely diced onions
	Pinch of sugar
1	cup diced red bell pepper
1/2	cup diced green bell pepper
2	tablespoons tomato paste
2	tablespoons sweet paprika
1	teaspoon crushed red pepper
3-3 1/2	pounds bone-in chicken pieces, skin removed, breasts cut in half crosswise, if using
3/4	teaspoon coarse salt, divided
1/2	teaspoon freshly ground pepper
1	teaspoon dried marjoram
1	cup reduced-sodium chicken broth
1/2	cup reduced-fat sour cream
1	tablespoon all-purpose flour
2	tablespoons finely minced fresh parsley, dill *and/or* chives

1. Heat oil and butter in a Dutch oven over medium heat. Add onions and sprinkle with sugar. Cook, stirring often, until very soft, 10 to 15 minutes.

2. Stir in bell peppers, tomato paste, paprika and crushed red pepper. Season chicken with 1/2 teaspoon salt and pepper; stir gently into the pot. Sprinkle with marjoram and add broth. Cover with a tight-fitting lid; simmer over medium-low heat until the chicken is very tender, about 50 minutes.

3. Whisk sour cream, flour and the remaining 1/4 teaspoon salt in a small bowl until smooth. Transfer the chicken to a plate. Stir the sour cream mixture into the sauce; simmer, stirring, until it coats the spoon. Return the chicken to the pot and reheat on low, about 1 minute. Garnish with herbs.

MAKES 6 SERVINGS.

HAWAIIAN GINGER-CHICKEN STEW

ACTIVE TIME: 35 MINUTES | TOTAL: 35 MINUTES

This chicken stew has a bold ginger-flavored broth and provides a whole serving of dark leafy greens in each bowl.

- 1 tablespoon sesame oil *or* canola oil
- 1 pound chicken tenders, cut into 1-inch pieces
- 1 2-inch piece fresh ginger, peeled and cut into matchsticks or minced
- 4 cloves garlic, thinly sliced
- ½ cup dry sherry (*see Note, page 208*)
- 1 14-ounce can reduced-sodium chicken broth
- 1½ cups water
- 2 tablespoons reduced-sodium soy sauce
- 1 teaspoon Asian red chile sauce, such as sriracha, or to taste
- 1 bunch mustard greens *or* chard, stemmed and chopped (6-7 cups), *or* 2 cups frozen chopped mustard greens

1. Heat oil in a Dutch oven over medium-high heat. Add chicken and cook, stirring occasionally, until just cooked through, about 6 minutes. Transfer to a plate with tongs.

2. Add ginger and garlic to the pot and cook until fragrant, about 10 seconds. Add sherry and cook until mostly evaporated, scraping up any browned bits, 1½ to 3 minutes. Add broth and water, increase heat to high and bring to a boil. Boil for 5 minutes. Add soy sauce, chile sauce and mustard greens (or chard) and cook until the greens are tender, about 3 minutes. Return the chicken and any accumulated juices to the pot and cook until heated through, 1 to 2 minutes.

MAKES 4 SERVINGS, ABOUT 1 CUP EACH.

PER SERVING: **198 calories**; 4 g fat (1 g sat, 1 g mono); 67 mg cholesterol; 7 g carbohydrate; 30 g protein; 3 g fiber; 527 mg sodium; 458 mg potassium.
NUTRITION BONUS: Vitamin A (180% daily value), Vitamin C (100% dv), Folate (40% dv).

H✖W L↓C H♥H

THE 500-CALORIE MENU

SERVE WITH ONE FROM EACH GROUP

Quinoa (*see Guide, page 190*; ½ cup, 111 cal.)
OR
Brown rice (*see Guide, page 190*; ½ cup, 109 cal.)

Chocolate-Dipped Gingersnaps, page 200 (157 cal.)
OR
Pilsner (12-ounce glass, 169 cal.)

DIET TIP

Keep your freezer stocked with frozen chopped greens, such as mustard greens, collards or spinach. They meld into stews and soups in minutes—adding flavor, fiber and lots of healthy nutrients.

PER SERVING: **225 calories**; 6 g fat (1 g sat, 3 g mono); 63 mg cholesterol; 14 g carbohydrate; 27 g protein; 3 g fiber; 448 mg sodium; 796 mg potassium.
NUTRITION BONUS: Vitamin A (110% daily value), Vitamin C (60% dv), Potassium (23% dv), Iron (15% dv).

H✕W L↓C H♥H

THE 500-CALORIE MENU

SERVE WITH ONE FROM EACH GROUP

Brown rice (*see Guide, page 190;* ¾ cup, 164 cal.)
OR
Whole-wheat spaghetti (¾ cup, 131 cal.)

Fast Strawberry Frozen Yogurt, page 201 (100 cal.)
OR
White wine (5-ounce glass, 116 cal.)

DIET TIP

Keep lemons around to zest up almost any dish, without any calories. Stock up when they're on sale and freeze the zest and juice for up to 6 months: pare the rind and freeze in strips, and freeze the juice in ice cube trays.

LEMON CHICKEN STIR-FRY

ACTIVE TIME: **40 MINUTES** | TOTAL: **40 MINUTES**

Spiked with lots of lemon, this delectable chicken stir-fry has a colorful mix of fiber-packed snow peas, carrots and scallions. But feel free to substitute other thinly sliced vegetables, such as bell peppers or zucchini. (Photograph: page 8.)

1	lemon
½	cup reduced-sodium chicken broth
3	tablespoons reduced-sodium soy sauce
2	teaspoons cornstarch
1	tablespoon canola oil
1	pound boneless, skinless chicken breasts, trimmed and cut into 1-inch pieces
10	ounces mushrooms, halved or quartered
1	cup diagonally sliced carrots (¼ inch thick)
2	cups snow peas (6 ounces), stems and strings removed
1	bunch scallions, cut into 1-inch pieces, greens and whites separated
1	tablespoon chopped garlic

1. Grate 1 teaspoon lemon zest and set aside. Juice the lemon and whisk 3 tablespoons of the juice with broth, soy sauce and cornstarch in a small bowl.

2. Heat oil in a large skillet over medium-high heat. Add chicken and cook, stirring occasionally, until just cooked through, 4 to 5 minutes. Transfer to a plate with tongs. Add mushrooms and carrots to the pan and cook until the carrots are just tender, about 5 minutes. Add snow peas, scallion whites, garlic and the reserved lemon zest. Cook, stirring, until fragrant, 30 seconds. Whisk the broth mixture and add to the pan; cook, stirring, until thickened, 2 to 3 minutes. Add scallion greens and the chicken and any accumulated juices; cook, stirring, until heated through, 1 to 2 minutes.

MAKES 4 SERVINGS, ABOUT 1½ CUPS EACH.

JAPANESE CHICKEN-SCALLION RICE BOWL

ACTIVE TIME: 15 MINUTES | TOTAL: 20 MINUTES

Here's the quintessence of Japanese home cooking: an aromatic, protein-rich broth served over rice. While it's traditional to use white rice, upgrading to brown gives the dish an extra punch of slow-digesting, satisfying fiber. Mirin is a low-alcohol rice wine essential to Japanese cooking. Look for it in the Asian section of the supermarket.

- 1 1/2 cups instant brown rice
- 1 cup reduced-sodium chicken broth
- 1 1/2 tablespoons sugar
- 2 tablespoons reduced-sodium soy sauce
- 1 tablespoon mirin *or* 1 tablespoon white wine plus a pinch of sugar
- 2 large egg whites
- 1 large egg
- 8 ounces boneless, skinless chicken breasts, cut into 1/2-inch pieces
- 6 scallions, trimmed and thinly sliced

1. Prepare rice according to package directions.

2. Pour broth into a heavy medium saucepan and add sugar, soy sauce and mirin (or wine plus sugar). Bring to a boil; reduce heat to medium-low.

3. Stir egg whites and whole egg in a small bowl until just mixed. Add chicken to the simmering broth. Gently pour in the egg mixture, without stirring. Sprinkle scallions on top. When the egg starts to firm up, after about 3 minutes, stir it with chopsticks or a knife. (The chicken will be cooked by now.) Divide the rice among 4 deep soup bowls and top with the chicken mixture.

MAKES 4 SERVINGS, 1 1/2 CUPS EACH.

PER SERVING: **258 calories**; 3 g fat (1 g sat, 1 g mono); 86 mg cholesterol; 34 g carbohydrate; 21 g protein; 2 g fiber; 426 mg sodium; 352 mg potassium.
NUTRITION BONUS: Magnesium (17% daily value).

H)(W H♥H

THE 500-CALORIE MENU

SERVE WITH ONE FROM EACH GROUP

Spinach Salad with Japanese Ginger Dressing, page 56 (135 cal.)
OR
Edamame with a drizzle of reduced-sodium soy sauce (1/2 cup, 127 cal.)

Sesame Snap Peas with Carrots & Peppers, page 183 (78 cal.)
OR
Japanese Cucumber Salad, page 57 (46 cal.)

Pineapple chunks (1/2 cup, 41 cal.)
OR
Sliced strawberries (1/2 cup, 27 cal.)

INDIAN WOK-SEARED CHICKEN & VEGETABLES

ACTIVE TIME: 35 MINUTES | TOTAL: 35 MINUTES

Between the sizzles, aromas and flavors, there's a lot to satisfy the palate in this delightful stir-fry. The cooking happens quickly, so it's a good idea to measure out and prepare all the ingredients before you fire up the wok.

- 2 teaspoons coriander seeds
- 1 teaspoon cumin seeds
- 1 teaspoon fennel seeds
- 1 tablespoon cornstarch
- 3/4 teaspoon salt
- 1/2 teaspoon ground turmeric
- 1 pound boneless, skinless chicken breasts, trimmed and cut into 1-inch cubes
- 3 tablespoons canola oil, divided
- 2 large carrots, cut into 1/4-inch-thick slices
- 1 large green bell pepper, cut into 1-inch cubes
- 1 small red onion, cut into 1/2-inch cubes
- 4 large cloves garlic, thinly sliced
- 3 dried red chiles, such as Thai, cayenne *or* chile de arbol, stemmed
- 1 tablespoon lime juice
- 1/2 cup firmly packed fresh mint leaves, finely chopped

1. Grind coriander, cumin and fennel seeds in a spice grinder (such as a clean coffee grinder) or a mortar and pestle until the mixture resembles coarsely ground pepper. Transfer to a medium bowl and add cornstarch, salt and turmeric; stir to combine. Add chicken and stir until coated.

2. Heat a wok or a well-seasoned cast-iron skillet over high heat. Add 2 tablespoons oil. When the oil is shimmering, add carrots, bell pepper, onion, garlic and chiles. Cook, stirring, until the vegetables begin to brown, 4 to 6 minutes. Transfer to a plate.

3. Reduce heat to medium-high and add the remaining 1 tablespoon oil to the pan. Add the chicken and seasonings from the bowl and cook, stirring, until no longer pink in the middle, 5 to 7 minutes. Stir in the vegetables, lime juice and mint and cook until heated through, about 30 seconds.

MAKES 4 SERVINGS, 1 1/4 CUPS EACH.

PER SERVING: **271 calories**; 14 g fat (2 g sat, 7 g mono); 63 mg cholesterol; 13 g carbohydrate; 25 g protein; 4 g fiber; 524 mg sodium; 513 mg potassium.
NUTRITION BONUS: Vitamin A (140% daily value), Vitamin C (70% dv), Iron (20% dv), Potassium (15% dv).

H✖W L↓C H♥H

THE 500-CALORIE MENU

SERVE WITH ONE FROM EACH GROUP

Brown rice with a squeeze of lime (*see Guide, page 190; 3/4* cup, 164 cal.)
OR
Sugar Snap Pea & Barley Salad, page 184 (152 cal.)

Mixed greens (1 1/2 cups) with 2 Tbsp. Buttermilk Dressing, page 76 (34 cal.)
OR
Japanese Cucumber Salad, page 57 (46 cal.)

DIET TIP

In one study, when mice were fed high-fat diets with added curcumin (an active ingredient in the spice turmeric), they gained less weight than a similar group whose diets had no added curcumin. Don't bank on turmeric as a magic bullet for weight loss yet. But go ahead and try it in your cooking—it adds flavor without any calories.

PER SERVING: **286 calories**; 11 g fat (2 g sat, 1 g mono); 65 mg cholesterol; 24 g carbohydrate; 26 g protein; 5 g fiber; 596 mg sodium; 414 mg potassium. NUTRITION BONUS: Vitamin A (150% daily value), Vitamin C (100% dv), Iron (25% dv), Folate (20% dv).

H✳W   L⬇C   H⬆F   H♥H

THE 500-CALORIE MENU

SERVE WITH ONE FROM EACH GROUP

Hot & Sour Slaw, page 60 (64 cal.)
OR
Japanese Cucumber Salad, page 57 (46 cal.)

Hot Fudge Pudding Cake, page 196 (142 cal.)
OR
Red wine (5-ounce glass, 120 cal.)

DIET TIP

The next time you make a sandwich, consider lettuce leaves as a virtually calorie-free alternative to a bread slice or wrap. Just about any filling works beautifully. Try tuna or chicken salad, a stir-fry or even a burger.

FIVE-SPICE TURKEY & LETTUCE WRAPS

ACTIVE TIME: 30 MINUTES | TOTAL: 30 MINUTES
TO MAKE AHEAD: Prepare the filling (through Step 2), cover and refrigerate for up to 1 day. Serve cold or reheat in the microwave.

Based on a popular Chinese dish, these fun wraps make appealing appetizers for entertaining too. They're also a terrific lunch: just pack the lettuce leaves and filling separately.

½ cup instant brown rice
2 teaspoons sesame oil
1 pound 93%-lean ground turkey
1 tablespoon minced fresh ginger
1 large red bell pepper, finely diced
1 8-ounce can water chestnuts, rinsed and chopped
½ cup reduced-sodium chicken broth
2 tablespoons hoisin sauce (*see Note, page 207*)
1 teaspoon five-spice powder (*see Note, page 207*)
½ teaspoon salt
2 heads Boston lettuce, leaves separated
½ cup chopped fresh herbs, such as cilantro, basil, mint *and/or* chives
1 large carrot, shredded

1. Prepare rice according to package directions. Remove from heat.

2. Meanwhile, heat oil in a large nonstick pan over medium-high heat. Add turkey and ginger; cook, crumbling with a wooden spoon, until the turkey is cooked through, about 6 minutes. Stir in the cooked rice, bell pepper, water chestnuts, broth, hoisin sauce, five-spice powder and salt; cook until heated through, about 1 minute.

3. To serve, spoon portions of the turkey mixture into lettuce leaves, top with herbs and carrot and roll into wraps.

MAKES 4 SERVINGS, 1¼ CUPS FILLING EACH.

FISH & SEAFOOD

Work fish into your menu a couple times a week—it's an excellent source of lean protein and it cooks quickly, so you'll have dinner on the table fast (and have less time to be tempted by snacks). Most of the recipes in this chapter take less than 45 minutes start to finish. What to choose? Start with varieties of fish caught or farm-raised in sustainable ways. (All the recipes in this chapter feature sustainable choices but you can check on the status of your favorite fish at *seafoodwatch.org*.)

We love white fish, such as Pacific halibut and tilapia, because they're very low in calories and fat: less than 125 calories and 3 grams of fat for a 3-ounce serving. Don't avoid oily fish like salmon just because it has more calories (184 per 3-ounce serving of wild salmon) and more fat. The fat is in the form of omega-3s, the healthy fats that help keep your heart healthy and may reduce risk for depression and cognitive decline, according to emerging research. And nutrition experts generally consider the ever-versatile shrimp a very heart-healthy choice. It's true that shrimp is high in dietary cholesterol—but it's also very low in saturated fat, which has a much greater impact on blood cholesterol levels. Check out what fish is fresh at your local market. Whatever you choose, you can't go wrong getting more fish into your diet.

A 462-Calorie Dinner (*left*): Linguine with Escarole & Shrimp (*page 127*), 271 calories; Roasted Squash & Fennel with Thyme (*page 180*), 66 calories; Mixed Lettuce Salad with Cucumber Herb Vinaigrette (*page 52*), 83 calories. Serve with ½ cup fresh blueberries, 42 calories, for dessert.

CAJUN CRAB CROQUETTES

ACTIVE TIME: 30 MINUTES | TOTAL: 50 MINUTES

Give crab cakes a Louisiana spin with Cajun spice. Low-calorie onion, bell pepper and corn bulk up the cakes and add great texture and flavor. Although any type of crab works here, we prefer the texture of lump crabmeat.

- **3** teaspoons canola oil, divided
- **1** small onion, finely diced
- **½** cup finely diced green bell pepper
- **½** cup frozen corn kernels, thawed
- **1½** teaspoons Cajun seasoning, divided
- **1** pound pasteurized crabmeat, drained if necessary
- **1** large egg white
- **¾** cup plain dry breadcrumbs, divided
- **¼** cup low-fat mayonnaise
- **½** teaspoon freshly grated lemon zest

1. Preheat oven to 425°F. Coat a baking sheet with cooking spray.

2. Heat 1 teaspoon oil in a large nonstick skillet over medium heat. Add onion, bell pepper, corn and 1 teaspoon Cajun seasoning and cook, stirring, until the vegetables are softened, about 4 minutes. Transfer to a large bowl. Let cool for 5 minutes. Add crab, egg white, ½ cup breadcrumbs, mayonnaise and lemon zest. Mix well.

3. Divide the mixture into 8 equal portions (about ½ cup each). Form each portion into an oblong patty about 4 inches by 2 inches. Place on the prepared baking sheet. Combine the remaining ¼ cup breadcrumbs, ½ teaspoon Cajun seasoning and 2 teaspoons oil in a small bowl. Sprinkle 1 heaping teaspoon of the breadcrumb mixture over the top of each croquette, then gently press it on.

4. Bake the croquettes until heated through and golden brown on top, about 20 minutes.

MAKES 4 SERVINGS, 2 CROQUETTES EACH.

PER SERVING: **246 calories**; 6 g fat (1 g sat, 2 g mono); 132 mg cholesterol; 23 g carbohydrate; 27 g protein; 2 g fiber; 942 mg sodium; 141 mg potassium.
NUTRITION BONUS: Iron (35% daily value), Vitamin C (25% dv), Calcium (15% dv).

H✕W H♥H

THE 500-CALORIE MENU

SERVE WITH ONE FROM EACH GROUP

Baby spinach (1½ cups) with 2 Tbsp. Spicy Mediterranean Vinaigrette, page 75 (125 cal.)
OR
Mississippi Spiced Pecans, page 23 (107 cal.)

Southwestern Calico Corn, page 184 (98 cal.)
OR
Roasted Asparagus with Garlic-Lemon Sauce, page 182 (89 cal.)

Chunky Peach Popsicles, page 202 (33 cal.)
OR
Apple slices with cinnamon (½ cup, 28 cal.)

LINGUINE WITH ESCAROLE & SHRIMP

ACTIVE TIME: 45 MINUTES | TOTAL: 45 MINUTES

Lots of tangy lemon flavors this pasta dish and tames the slightly bitter greens. Don't be put off by 16 cups of escarole; it cooks down to a fraction of that amount and is buttery-tender in this dish. (Photograph: page 124.)

8   ounces whole-wheat linguine
4   teaspoons extra-virgin olive oil, divided
1   pound peeled and deveined raw shrimp (16-20 per pound; *see Note, page 210*)
¾   teaspoon salt, divided
¼   teaspoon freshly ground pepper, plus more to taste
2   tablespoons minced garlic
½   cup white wine
1   pint grape *or* cherry tomatoes, halved
16 cups thinly sliced escarole (2-3 heads) *or* chard leaves
¼   cup clam juice (*see Note, page 208*) *or* water
1   teaspoon cornstarch
1   tablespoon lemon juice
6   lemon wedges for garnish

1. Cook linguine in a large pot of boiling water until just tender, 8 to 10 minutes or according to package directions. Drain and return to the pot.

2. Meanwhile, heat 3 teaspoons oil in a large skillet over medium heat. Add shrimp, ¼ teaspoon salt and ¼ teaspoon pepper and cook until pink and just cooked through, 3 to 4 minutes. Transfer to a plate.

3. Add garlic and the remaining 1 teaspoon oil to the pan; cook, stirring, until fragrant, about 15 seconds. Add wine; cook until reduced by half, 2 to 3 minutes. Stir in tomatoes. Add escarole (or chard) in handfuls, stirring until it wilts before adding more; cook, stirring occasionally, until tender, 5 to 6 minutes. Whisk clam juice (or water) and cornstarch in a small bowl, then add to the pan; simmer until slightly thickened, about 2 minutes. Return the shrimp and any juices to the pan, add lemon juice, the remaining ½ teaspoon salt and pepper and cook until heated through, about 1 minute.

4. Add the sauce to the linguine and toss to coat. Serve with lemon wedges.

MAKES 6 SERVINGS, ABOUT 1⅓ CUPS EACH.

PER SERVING: **271 calories**; 5 g fat (1 g sat, 3 g mono); 112 mg cholesterol; 37 g carbohydrate; 20 g protein; 10 g fiber; 502 mg sodium; 751 mg potassium. NUTRITION BONUS: Vitamin A (70% daily value), Folate (55% dv), Vitamin C (30% dv), Magnesium (25% dv), Potassium (21% dv).

H✖W   H⬆F   H♥H

THE 500-CALORIE MENU

SERVE WITH ONE FROM EACH GROUP

Mixed Lettuce Salad with Cucumber Herb Vinaigrette, page 52 (83 cal.)
OR
Mixed greens (1½ cups) with 2 Tbsp. Champagne Vinaigrette, page 74 (120 cal.)

Roasted Squash & Fennel with Thyme, page 180 (66 cal.)
OR
Simple Sautéed Spinach, page 178 (68 cal.)

Blueberries (½ cup, 42 cal.)
OR
Chunky Peach Popsicles, page 202 (33 cal.)

THE 500-CALORIE MENU

SERVE WITH ONE FROM EACH GROUP

Cauliflower & Couscous Pilaf, page 185 (162 cal.)
OR
Quinoa with chopped fresh herbs (*see Guide, page 190;* ½ cup, 111 cal.)

Papaya-Lime Sorbet, page 199 (110 cal.)
OR
White wine (5-ounce glass, 116 cal.)

LEMON-GARLIC SHRIMP & VEGETABLES

ACTIVE TIME: **35 MINUTES** | TOTAL: **35 MINUTES**

Here's a healthy twist on shrimp scampi: we left out the butter and loaded the dish up with red peppers and asparagus to create an ample and satisfying portion.

4	teaspoons extra-virgin olive oil, divided
2	large red bell peppers, diced
2	pounds asparagus, trimmed and cut into 1-inch lengths
2	teaspoons freshly grated lemon zest
½	teaspoon salt, divided
5	cloves garlic, minced
1	pound raw shrimp (26-30 per pound), peeled and deveined (*see Note, page 210*)
1	cup reduced-sodium chicken broth
1	teaspoon cornstarch
2	tablespoons lemon juice
2	tablespoons chopped fresh parsley

1. Heat 2 teaspoons oil in a large nonstick skillet over medium-high heat. Add bell peppers, asparagus, lemon zest and ¼ teaspoon salt and cook, stirring occasionally, until just beginning to soften, about 6 minutes. Transfer the vegetables to a bowl; cover to keep warm.

2. Add the remaining 2 teaspoons oil and garlic to the pan and cook, stirring, until fragrant, about 30 seconds. Add shrimp and cook, stirring, for 1 minute. Whisk broth and cornstarch in a small bowl until smooth and add to the pan along with the remaining ¼ teaspoon salt. Cook, stirring, until the sauce has thickened slightly and the shrimp are pink and just cooked through, about 2 minutes more. Remove from the heat. Stir in lemon juice and parsley. Serve the shrimp and sauce over the vegetables.

MAKES 4 SERVINGS.

SHRIMP VERACRUZANA

ACTIVE TIME: **30 MINUTES** | TOTAL: **30 MINUTES**

Veracruzana is a dish full of onions, jalapeños and tomatoes from the Mexican state of Veracruz. Here we pair the zesty sauce with shrimp, but it can be served with any type of fish or chicken. The heat of fresh jalapeños varies, so be sure to taste yours as you're adding them to the dish and adjust the amount according to your taste.

2   teaspoons canola oil
1   bay leaf
1   medium onion, halved and thinly sliced
2   jalapeño peppers, seeded and very thinly sliced, or to taste
4   cloves garlic, minced
1   pound peeled and deveined raw shrimp (16-20 per pound; see Note, page 210)
3   medium tomatoes, diced
¼   cup thinly sliced pitted green olives
1   lime, cut into 4 wedges

Heat oil in a large nonstick skillet over medium heat. Add bay leaf and cook for 1 minute. Add onion, jalapeños and garlic and cook, stirring, until softened, about 3 minutes. Stir in shrimp, cover and cook until pink and just cooked through, 3 to 4 minutes. Stir in tomatoes and olives and bring to a simmer, uncovered. Reduce heat to medium-low, cover and cook until the tomatoes are almost broken down, 2 to 3 minutes more. Remove the bay leaf. Serve with lime wedges.

MAKES 4 SERVINGS, ABOUT 1 CUP EACH.

PER SERVING: **192 calories**; 6 g fat (1 g sat, 3 g mono); 172 mg cholesterol; 11 g carbohydrate; 24 g protein; 2 g fiber; 324 mg sodium; 516 mg potassium. NUTRITION BONUS: Vitamin C (40% daily value), Iron & Vitamin A (20% dv).

H�incW   L↓C   H♥H

THE 500-CALORIE MENU

SERVE WITH ONE FROM EACH GROUP

Brown rice (*see Guide, page 190*; ½ cup, 109 cal.)
OR
Warm corn tortilla (6-inch, 70 cal.)

Avocado (one-fourth, 80 cal.)
OR
Basic Sautéed Kale, page 178 (102 cal.)

Nonfat chocolate frozen yogurt (½ cup, 100 cal.)
OR
White wine (5-ounce glass, 116 cal.)

PER SERVING: **326 calories**; 15 g fat (1 g sat, 8 g mono); 19 mg cholesterol; 32 g carbohydrate; 16 g protein; 4 g fiber; 713 mg sodium; 511 mg potassium. NUTRITION BONUS: Vitamin C (35% daily value), Magnesium (31% dv), Folate (25% dv), Iron (15% dv).

THE 500-CALORIE MENU

SERVE WITH

Claire's Mixed Green Salad with Feta Vinaigrette, page 53 (165 cal.)
OR
Spinach Salad with Japanese Ginger Dressing, page 56 (135 cal.)

DIET TIP

Try delicately flavored quinoa instead of rice. It provides high-quality protein (about 8 grams per cup), so it adds some staying power to your meal.

TOASTED QUINOA WITH SCALLOPS & SNOW PEAS

ACTIVE TIME: **50 MINUTES** | TOTAL: **50 MINUTES**

This recipe has great texture in every bite, from crunchy snow peas and red bell pepper to the smooth, creamy scallops.

12	ounces dry sea scallops, cut into ½-inch pieces, *or* dry bay scallops (*see Note, page 210*)
4	teaspoons reduced-sodium tamari *or* soy sauce, divided
4	tablespoons plus 2 teaspoons canola oil, divided
1½	cups quinoa, rinsed well (*see Note, page 208*)
2	teaspoons grated *or* minced garlic
3	cups water
1	teaspoon salt
1	cup trimmed and diagonally sliced snow peas (½ inch thick)
⅓	cup rice vinegar
1	teaspoon toasted sesame oil
1	cup thinly sliced scallions
⅓	cup finely diced red bell pepper
¼	cup finely chopped fresh cilantro for garnish

1. Toss scallops with 2 teaspoons tamari (or soy sauce) in a bowl. Set aside.

2. Place a large, high-sided skillet with a tight-fitting lid over medium heat. Add 1 tablespoon canola oil and quinoa. Cook, stirring, until the quinoa begins to color, 6 to 8 minutes. Add garlic and cook, stirring, for about 1 minute. Add water and salt; bring to a boil. Stir once, cover and cook until the water is absorbed, about 15 minutes. (Do not stir.) Let stand, covered, for 5 minutes. Stir in snow peas, cover and let stand for 5 minutes more.

3. Meanwhile, whisk the remaining 2 teaspoons tamari (or soy sauce), 3 tablespoons canola oil, vinegar and sesame oil in a large bowl. Add the quinoa mixture, scallions and bell pepper; toss to combine.

4. Remove the scallops from the marinade and pat dry. Heat a large skillet over medium-high heat until hot enough to evaporate a drop of water on contact. Add the remaining 2 teaspoons canola oil and cook the scallops, turning once, until golden and just firm, about 2 minutes total. Gently stir the scallops into the quinoa salad. Serve garnished with cilantro, if desired.

MAKES 6 SERVINGS, ABOUT 1 CUP EACH.

GINGER-STEAMED FISH WITH TROY'S HANA-STYLE SAUCE

ACTIVE TIME: 20 MINUTES | TOTAL: 20 MINUTES

This lovely, simple preparation was adapted from Executive Chef David Patterson at the Hotel Hana-Maui, Hawaii. While he uses onaga, a red snapper found in Hawaiian waters, we found that halibut and other white fish are also delicious.

FISH

6   5-ounce portions striped bass *or* Pacific halibut (*see Notes, pages 209 & 210*)
6   ¼-inch-thick slices peeled fresh ginger

SAUCE

¼   cup minced peeled fresh ginger
¼   cup chopped garlic
¼   cup sesame seeds
2   tablespoons grapeseed oil *or* canola oil
2   tablespoons toasted sesame oil
¼   cup reduced-sodium soy sauce
2-3   scallions, thinly sliced, for garnish

1. **To prepare fish:** Bring 1 to 2 inches of water to a boil in a pot large enough to hold a two-tier bamboo steamer. (If you don't have a steamer, improvise by setting mugs upside down in a large pot and resting a large heatproof plate on top.) Put a heatproof plate in each of the steamer baskets. Place 3 portions of fish on each plate with a slice of fresh ginger on top of each portion. Stack the baskets, cover and set over the boiling water. Steam the fish for 7 minutes per inch of thickness.

2. **To prepare sauce:** Meanwhile, combine minced ginger, garlic and sesame seeds in a small bowl. Heat grapeseed (or canola) oil in a medium skillet over medium-high heat. Add the ginger mixture and cook, stirring, until fragrant, 1 minute. Add sesame oil; allow the mixture to get hot. Add soy sauce (be careful, it will splatter a bit) and cook for 1 minute more.

3. Transfer the fish to a deep platter. Discard the ginger slices. Pour the sauce over the fish and garnish with scallions.

MAKES 6 SERVINGS.

PER SERVING: **298 calories**; 15 g fat (1 g sat, 6 g mono); 45 mg cholesterol; 6 g carbohydrate; 32 g protein; 1 g fiber; 350 mg sodium; 727 mg potassium.
NUTRITION BONUS: Magnesium (31% daily value), Potassium (20% dv), source of omega-3s.

H✂W   L⬇C   H❤H

THE 500-CALORIE MENU
SERVE WITH ONE FROM EACH GROUP

Sesame Snap Peas with Carrots & Peppers, page 183 (78 cal.)
OR
Glazed Mini Carrots, page 179 (74 cal.)

Brown rice (*see Guide, page 190*; ½ cup, 109 cal.)
OR
Whole-Grain Rice Pilaf, page 186 (97 cal.)

DIET TIP

Steaming lean fish fillets preserves their delicate texture and mild flavor without adding a single calorie. This simple method works well with any flaky white fish.

THE 500-CALORIE MENU

SERVE WITH ONE FROM EACH GROUP

Roasted Asparagus with Garlic-Lemon
Sauce, page 182 (89 cal.)
OR
Basic Sautéed Kale, page 178 (102 cal.)

Raspberry Applesauce, page 201
(67 cal.)
OR
Chewy Chocolate Cookies, page 197
(68 cal.)

DIET TIP

Slow down when you eat—it can help
make your meal feel more satisfying.
Eating a whole fish is a fun way to slow
down because it gives you plenty of work
to do.

GRILLED WHOLE TROUT WITH LEMON-TARRAGON BEAN SALAD

ACTIVE TIME: **35 MINUTES** | TOTAL: **45 MINUTES** | EQUIPMENT: Fish-grilling basket

This freshwater favorite is a snap on the grill—and provides easy portion control: one whole trout (about 5 ounces after cleaning) makes an ample amount for one person. Grilling with the skin on keeps the fish from falling apart and gives the skin a delightful crispy texture. No fish basket? The trout can be grilled directly on a well-oiled grill.

¼ cup chopped fresh tarragon, plus 4 whole sprigs
3 tablespoons lemon juice
2 tablespoons extra-virgin olive oil
1 tablespoon chopped shallot
1 teaspoon kosher salt, divided
¼ teaspoon sugar
¼ teaspoon freshly ground pepper, divided
1 15-ounce can small white beans, rinsed
⅓ cup chopped roasted red peppers
4 cleaned whole rainbow trout (about 5 ounces each; *see Note, page 210*)
12 thin slices of lemon (1-2 lemons)

1. Whisk chopped tarragon, lemon juice, oil, shallot, ¼ teaspoon salt, sugar and ⅛ teaspoon pepper in a medium bowl until combined. Reserve 2 tablespoons of the dressing; add beans and peppers to the rest and toss to combine.

2. Preheat grill to medium-high. Coat a large fish-grilling basket with cooking spray. Stuff each trout with 3 lemon slices and 1 tarragon sprig. Sprinkle inside and out with the remaining ¾ teaspoon salt and ⅛ teaspoon pepper. Place in the basket.

3. Grill the fish until the skin is golden and crispy, 4 to 5 minutes per side. Carefully remove the lemon and tarragon, drizzle the fish with the reserved dressing and serve with the bean salad.

MAKES 4 SERVINGS.

CASHEW SALMON WITH APRICOT COUSCOUS

ACTIVE TIME: 35 MINUTES | TOTAL: 35 MINUTES

Yogurt sauce flavored with lemon, cumin and cilantro tops this Indian-inspired grilled salmon. (Photograph: front cover.)

- ½ cup nonfat plain yogurt
- 3 scallions, sliced, greens and whites separated
- 2 tablespoons lemon juice
- 2 tablespoons chopped fresh cilantro
- ½ teaspoon ground cumin
- ¾ teaspoon salt, divided
- ½ teaspoon freshly ground pepper, divided
- 1 tablespoon extra-virgin olive oil
- ¼ cup chopped dried apricots
- 1 tablespoon minced fresh ginger
- 1¼ cups water
- 1 cup whole-wheat couscous
- 1 pound salmon fillet, preferably wild Pacific, skinned (*see Note, page 209*) and cut into 4 portions
- 2 tablespoons chopped toasted cashews (*see Note, page 208*)

1. Preheat grill to medium-high or position rack in upper third of oven and preheat broiler.

2. Combine yogurt, scallion greens, lemon juice, cilantro, cumin, ¼ teaspoon salt and ¼ teaspoon pepper in a medium bowl. Set aside.

3. Heat oil in a large saucepan over medium heat. Add apricots, ginger, the scallion whites and ¼ teaspoon salt. Cook, stirring, until softened, about 2 minutes. Add water and bring to a boil over high heat. Stir in couscous. Remove from heat, cover and let stand until the liquid is absorbed, about 5 minutes. Fluff with a fork.

4. Meanwhile, rub salmon with the remaining ¼ teaspoon each salt and pepper. If grilling, oil the grill rack (*see Note, page 210*). If broiling, coat a broiler pan with cooking spray. Grill or broil the salmon until browned and just cooked through, about 3 minutes per side. Serve with the couscous, topped with the yogurt sauce and cashews.

MAKES 4 SERVINGS.

PER SERVING: **487 calories**; 15 g fat (2 g sat, 6 g mono); 73 mg cholesterol; 57 g carbohydrate; 35 g protein; 9 g fiber; 527 mg sodium; 621 mg potassium.
NUTRITION BONUS: Vitamin A (19% daily value), Potassium (18% dv), source of omega-3s.

H⬆F H♥H

THE 500-CALORIE MENU
SERVE WITH

Steamed broccoli with a pinch of cumin and a squeeze of lemon (*see Guide, page 191*; ½ cup, 22 cal.)
OR
Steamed snap peas (*see Guide, page 191*; ½ cup, 35 cal.)

PER SERVING: **187 calories**; 9 g fat (2 g sat, 4 g mono); 55 mg cholesterol; 2 g carbohydrate; 23 g protein; 0 g fiber; 287 mg sodium; 439 mg potassium. NUTRITION BONUS: Source of omega-3s.

H✣W   L↓C   H♥H

THE 500-CALORIE MENU

SERVE WITH ONE FROM EACH GROUP

Sugar Snap Pea & Barley Salad, page 184 (152 cal.)
OR
Spinach Salad with Japanese Ginger Dressing, page 56 (135 cal.)

Quinoa with a squeeze of lime (*see Guide, page 190;* ½ cup, 111 cal.)
OR
Brown rice with chopped fresh scallion greens (*see Guide, page 190;* ½ cup, 109 cal.)

Cubed watermelon (1 cup, 46 cal.)
OR
Chunky Peach Popsicles, page 202 (33 cal.)

SALMON BURGERS WITH GREEN GODDESS SAUCE

ACTIVE TIME: **25 MINUTES** | TOTAL: **45 MINUTES** | TO MAKE AHEAD: Prepare through Step 1, cover and refrigerate for up to 2 hours.

The key to perfect salmon burgers is to handle the fish delicately: don't over-season, overhandle or overcook it. Cutting the salmon into small pieces by hand takes a little while, but it helps ensure tender burgers. Serve over a bed of salad greens with the sauce dolloped on top, and you'll never miss the bun.

1	pound salmon fillet, preferably wild Pacific, skinned (*see Note, page 209*)
2	tablespoons finely chopped red onion *or* scallion
2	tablespoons chopped fresh cilantro
½	teaspoon finely chopped peeled fresh ginger
¼	teaspoon kosher *or* sea salt, plus a pinch, divided
⅛	teaspoon freshly ground pepper, plus more to taste
3	tablespoons low-fat mayonnaise
1	tablespoon reduced-fat sour cream
1	anchovy fillet, rinsed and finely chopped
2	teaspoons finely chopped fresh chives
1	teaspoon finely chopped fresh parsley
1	teaspoon capers, rinsed and finely chopped
½	teaspoon freshly grated lemon zest
½	teaspoon fresh lemon juice
1	tablespoon extra-virgin olive oil *or* canola oil

1. With a large chef's knife, chop salmon using quick, even, straight-up-and-down motions (do not rock the knife or the fish will turn mushy) until you have a mass of roughly ¼-inch pieces. Transfer to a large bowl; gently stir in onion (or scallion), cilantro, ginger, ¼ teaspoon salt and ⅛ teaspoon pepper (do not overmix). Divide the mixture into 4 patties, about 1 inch thick. Chill in the refrigerator for at least 20 minutes (or up to 2 hours).

2. Mix mayonnaise, sour cream, anchovy, chives, parsley, capers, lemon zest, lemon juice, the remaining pinch of salt and pepper in a small bowl.

3. Heat oil in a large nonstick skillet over medium heat. Add the burgers and cook until browned on both sides and just cooked through, 4 to 6 minutes total. Serve with the sauce.

MAKES 4 SERVINGS.

SALMON WITH PEPITA-LIME BUTTER

ACTIVE TIME: 20 MINUTES | TOTAL: 20 MINUTES

Lime juice, chili powder and pepitas combined with just a bit of butter makes a rich Mexican-flavored sauce for this salmon.

2	tablespoons unsalted pepitas (*see Note, page 208*)
1	tablespoon butter
½	teaspoon freshly grated lime zest
2	tablespoons lime juice
¼	teaspoon chili powder
1	pound salmon fillet, preferably wild Pacific, skinned (*see Note, page 209*) and cut into 4 portions
½	teaspoon salt
¼	teaspoon freshly ground pepper

1. Place pepitas in a small dry skillet and cook over medium-low heat, stirring constantly, until fragrant and lightly browned, 2 to 4 minutes. Transfer to a small bowl and add butter, lime zest, lime juice and chili powder.

2. Generously coat a large nonstick skillet with cooking spray and place over medium heat. Sprinkle salmon with salt and pepper, add to the pan and cook until browned and just cooked through in the center, 2 to 4 minutes per side. Remove the pan from the heat. Transfer the salmon to a plate. Add the butter-lime mixture to the hot pan; stir until the butter is melted. Serve the salmon topped with the sauce.

MAKES 4 SERVINGS.

PER SERVING: **185 calories**; 9 g fat (3 g sat, 2 g mono); 61 mg cholesterol; 2 g carbohydrate; 24 g protein; 0 g fiber; 349 mg sodium; 466 mg potassium.
NUTRITION BONUS: Source of omega-3s.

H✖W   L↓C   H♥H

THE 500-CALORIE MENU

SERVE WITH ONE FROM EACH GROUP

Brown rice with lime juice and chopped fresh cilantro (*see Guide, page 190;* ½ cup, 109 cal.)
OR
Maple-Roasted Sweet Potatoes, page 189 (96 cal.)

Southwestern Calico Corn, page 184 (98 cal.)
OR
Simple Sautéed Spinach, page 178 (68 cal.)

Pineapple-Raspberry Parfaits, page 201 (112 cal.)
OR
White wine (5-ounce glass, 116 cal.)

DIET TIP

Choosing wild over farmed salmon can save you calories. Since farmed salmon are often fattened to increase market weight (and don't have as much room to swim), their flesh tends to be fattier than that of their wild counterparts.

PER SERVING: **161 calories**; 5 g fat (1 g sat, 2 g mono); 53 mg cholesterol; 5 g carbohydrate; 23 g protein; 0 g fiber; 252 mg sodium; 457 mg potassium. NUTRITION BONUS: Source of omega-3s.

H✖W   L↓C   H♥H

THE 500-CALORIE MENU

SERVE WITH ONE FROM EACH GROUP

Zucchini and red bell pepper tossed with 1 tsp. extra-virgin olive oil (1 cup, 75 cal.)

OR

Sesame Snap Peas with Carrots & Peppers, page 183 (78 cal.)

Wild Rice with Shiitakes & Toasted Almonds, page 185 (158 cal.)

OR

Whole-wheat pasta with 1 tsp. melted butter (½ cup, 120 cal.)

Apple Cider Granita, page 203 (103 cal.)

OR

Fast Strawberry Frozen Yogurt, page 201 (100 cal.)

HONEY-SOY BROILED SALMON

ACTIVE TIME: 20 MINUTES | TOTAL: 40 MINUTES

A sweet, tangy and salty mixture of soy sauce, rice vinegar and honey does double duty as marinade and sauce, and it keeps the salmon unbelievably flavorful and moist. Tuck the leftovers into a whole-wheat wrap for a tasty, filling lunch.

2 tablespoons reduced-sodium soy sauce
1 tablespoon rice vinegar
1 tablespoon honey
1 scallion, minced
1 teaspoon minced fresh ginger
1 pound center-cut salmon fillet, preferably wild Pacific, skinned (*see Note, page 209*) and cut into 4 portions
1 teaspoon toasted sesame seeds (*see Note, page 208*)

1. Whisk soy sauce, vinegar, honey, scallion and ginger in a medium bowl until the honey is dissolved. Place salmon in a sealable plastic bag, add 3 tablespoons of the sauce and refrigerate; let marinate for 15 minutes. Reserve the remaining sauce.

2. Preheat broiler. Line a small baking pan with foil and coat with cooking spray.

3. Transfer the salmon to the pan, skinned-side down. (Discard the marinade.) Broil the salmon 4 to 6 inches from the heat source until cooked through, 6 to 10 minutes. Drizzle with the reserved sauce and garnish with sesame seeds.

MAKES 4 SERVINGS.

THE 500-CALORIE MENU

SERVE WITH ONE FROM EACH GROUP

Brussels Sprouts with Bacon-Horseradish Cream, page 181 (80 cal.)
OR
Sicilian-Style Broccoli, page 183 (63 cal.)

Pearl barley (*see Guide, page 190;* 1/2 cup, 97 cal.)
OR
Polenta (*see Guide, page 190;* 1/2 cup, 74 cal.)

Baby Tiramisù, page 200 (107 cal.)
OR
White wine (5-ounce glass, 116 cal.)

DIET TIP

Instead of topping cooked fish (or meat or poultry) with a sauce, use vegetables, such as peppers, onions and tomatoes. They'll add plenty of flavor and nutrients—and at the same time, boost portion size without adding a lot of calories.

TUNA STEAKS PROVENÇAL

ACTIVE TIME: **30 MINUTES** | TOTAL: **40 MINUTES**

A colorful mixture of yellow and red bell peppers, red onion, tomatoes and olives is a quick and flavorful topping for simple tuna steaks. (Photograph: page 19.)

2	tomatoes
3	teaspoons extra-virgin olive oil, divided
1	red bell pepper, chopped
1	yellow bell pepper, chopped
1	small red onion, sliced
2	cloves garlic, minced
1/4	cup fish stock *or* water
2	tablespoons dry red wine
2	tablespoons sliced pitted good-quality black olives
1	tablespoon red-wine vinegar
1 1/2	teaspoons chopped fresh rosemary *or* oregano *or* 1/2 teaspoon dried
3/4	teaspoon salt, divided
1/2	teaspoon freshly ground pepper, divided
4	4-ounce tuna steaks (*see Note, page 210*), about 1 inch thick

1. Preheat oven to 400°F.

2. Core and halve tomatoes crosswise. Scoop out the seeds with a hooked finger and discard them. Chop the tomatoes.

3. Heat 2 teaspoons oil in a wide saucepan over medium heat. Add bell peppers, onion and garlic and cook, stirring, until softened, 2 to 3 minutes. Add the tomatoes, fish stock (or water) and wine and bring to a boil. Cook over high heat, stirring frequently, until thickened, about 10 minutes. Stir in olives, vinegar, rosemary (or oregano) and 1/4 teaspoon each salt and pepper. Remove from the heat.

4. Meanwhile, season both sides of tuna steaks with the remaining 1/2 teaspoon salt and 1/4 teaspoon pepper. Heat the remaining 1 teaspoon oil in an ovenproof nonstick skillet over medium-high heat. Sear the tuna until lightly browned on one side, 1 to 2 minutes. Turn the tuna over and transfer the pan to the oven. Bake until the fish is opaque in the center, 9 to 10 minutes. Serve with the tomato mixture on top.

MAKES 4 SERVINGS.

MIDDLE EASTERN TUNA SALAD

ACTIVE TIME: **15 MINUTES** | TOTAL: **15 MINUTES**

Here's a fresh, light spin on the traditional tuna-with-mayo combination. It's packed with fabulous flavor from tahini, lemon, garlic and parsley.

- ⅓ cup nonfat plain yogurt
- 2 tablespoons tahini *or* fruity extra-virgin olive oil
- 1 teaspoon lemon juice
- 2 cloves garlic, very finely chopped
- 1 teaspoon ground cumin
- 1 6-ounce can chunk light tuna in water (*see Note, page 210*), drained and flaked
- 1 8-ounce can chickpeas (¾ cup), rinsed
- ¼ cup chopped flat-leaf parsley
- ¼ teaspoon salt
  Freshly ground pepper to taste

Whisk yogurt, tahini (or oil), lemon juice, garlic and cumin in a bowl. Stir in tuna, chickpeas and parsley and season with salt and pepper.

MAKES 3 SERVINGS.

PER SERVING: **216 calories**; 7 g fat (1 g sat, 2 g mono); 18 mg cholesterol; 19 g carbohydrate; 21 g protein; 4 g fiber; 525 mg sodium; 321 mg potassium. NUTRITION BONUS: Vitamin C (20% daily value), Folate & Iron (15% dv).

H✴W L↓C H♥H

THE 500-CALORIE MENU
SERVE WITH ONE FROM EACH GROUP

Toasted whole-grain baguette (2 inches, 132 cal.)
OR
Small whole-wheat crackers (about 15, 130 cal.)

Baby spinach (1 cup) with a drizzle (1 tsp.) of olive oil (52 cal.)
OR
Mixed greens (1½ cups) with 2 Tbsp. Buttermilk Dressing, page 76 (33 cal.)

Pineapple-Raspberry Parfaits, page 201 (112 cal.)
OR
Apple Cider Granita, page 203 (103 cal.)

DIET TIP

Keep a can or two of chickpeas in the pantry. They have a meaty texture and a nutty flavor along with plenty of satiating fiber and a little protein—perfect when you're watching your weight.

PER SERVING: **360 calories**; 6 g fat (1 g sat, 3 g mono); 9 mg cholesterol; 62 g carbohydrate; 20 g protein; 11 g fiber; 218 mg sodium; 280 mg potassium. NUTRITION BONUS: Magnesium (30% daily value), Iron (17% dv).

THE 500-CALORIE MENU

SERVE WITH ONE FROM EACH GROUP

Lemon-Dill Green Beans, page 180 (74 cal.)

OR

Roasted Asparagus with Garlic-Lemon Sauce, page 182 (89 cal.)

Chunky Peach Popsicles, page 202 (33 cal.)

OR

Cubed honeydew melon (½ cup, 31 cal.)

SPAGHETTI WITH TUNA & TOMATO SAUCE

ACTIVE TIME: 30 MINUTES | TOTAL: 30 MINUTES

Italian tuna packed in olive oil is a must for this pasta dish: the flavorful oil is drained from the tuna and a little is used for cooking the sauce. The result is incredibly unctuous and tasty.

1	6-ounce can tuna in olive oil (*see Note, page 210*), preferably Italian
3	cloves garlic, finely chopped
1	28-ounce can plum tomatoes
½	teaspoon crushed red pepper
1	pound whole-wheat spaghetti
4	tablespoons chopped fresh parsley, divided
¼	teaspoon salt
	Freshly ground pepper to taste

1. Put a large pot of water on to boil. Drain tuna in a sieve set over a small bowl, pressing out as much oil as possible (reserve the oil). Break up the tuna with a fork.

2. Heat 1 tablespoon of the tuna oil in a large nonstick skillet over medium heat. Add garlic and cook, stirring, for 30 seconds. Add tomatoes with their juice and crushed red pepper; break up the tomatoes with a fork. Simmer over low heat until slightly thickened, about 15 minutes. Stir in the tuna.

3. Meanwhile, cook spaghetti in the boiling water until just tender, 8 to 10 minutes or according to package directions. Drain and return it to the pot. Add the sauce, 3 tablespoons parsley, salt and pepper; toss to combine. Transfer to a serving bowl, sprinkle with the remaining 1 tablespoon parsley and serve immediately.

MAKES 6 SERVINGS.

PASTA WITH WHITE CLAM SAUCE

ACTIVE TIME: 30 MINUTES | TOTAL: 1 HOUR (including roasting garlic)

The vibrant combination of garlicky seafood, lemon zest and parsley is a perfect match for whole-wheat pasta's assertive, nutty flavor.

1	tablespoon extra-virgin olive oil
1	large shallot, minced
1½	teaspoons dried marjoram *or* 1 teaspoon fresh
⅛	teaspoon crushed red pepper
1	cup dry white wine
2	heads garlic, roasted (*see Note, page 207*)
3	6-ounce cans chopped clams, drained, juices reserved
¼	cup finely chopped fresh parsley
1	pound whole-wheat linguine *or* spaghetti
2	tablespoons lemon juice
2	teaspoons butter
	Lemon wedges for garnish

GREMOLATA

¼	cup finely chopped fresh parsley
1	teaspoon freshly grated lemon zest
1	clove garlic, finely chopped

1. Heat oil in a saucepan over low heat. Add shallot; cook until softened, 1 to 2 minutes. Add marjoram and crushed red pepper; cook until aromatic, about 30 seconds. Add wine and bring to a boil. Increase heat to medium-high and cook until reduced to ¼ cup, 10 to 14 minutes. (The wine will be nearly evaporated.) Reduce heat to low; squeeze roasted garlic cloves out of the skins into the pan, add the reserved clam juice and whisk until well combined. Stir in clams and parsley; heat gently over low heat. Keep warm.

2. Cook pasta in a large pot of boiling salted water until just tender, 8 to 10 minutes or according to package directions.

3. **To prepare gremolata:** Combine parsley, lemon zest and garlic.

4. Drain the pasta and transfer to a large, warm serving bowl. Stir lemon juice and butter into the sauce and pour over the pasta. Toss gently, then sprinkle the gremolata over the top. Serve immediately, with lemon wedges.

MAKES 8 SERVINGS.

PER SERVING: **286 calories**; 4 g fat (1 g sat, 1 g mono); 14 mg cholesterol; 48 g carbohydrate; 14 g protein; 8 g fiber; 428 mg sodium; 213 mg potassium.
NUTRITION BONUS: Fiber (30% daily value), Magnesium (22% dv), Iron (20% dv), Vitamin C (16% dv).

H⋈W   H↑F   H♥H

THE 500-CALORIE MENU

SERVE WITH ONE FROM EACH GROUP

Simple Sautéed Spinach, page 178 (68 cal.)
OR
Sicilian-Style Broccoli, page 183 (63 cal.)

Mixed greens (1½ cups) with 2 Tbsp. Champagne Vinaigrette, page 74 (119 cal.)
OR
White wine (5-ounce glass, 116 cal.)

DIET TIP

Roast garlic to turn it into a terrific, creamy butter substitute. Here, it adds flavor and texture to the sauce, so nobody will miss the traditional butter.

EATINGWELL FISH STICKS

ACTIVE TIME: **30 MINUTES** | TOTAL: **40 MINUTES**

You can make these homemade fish sticks in about the same amount of time it takes to bake a box of the frozen kind—with a fraction of the fat and calories.

Canola oil cooking spray
1 cup whole-wheat dry breadcrumbs (*see Note, page 207*) or ½ cup plain dry breadcrumbs
1 cup whole-grain cereal flakes
1 teaspoon lemon pepper
½ teaspoon garlic powder
½ teaspoon paprika
¼ teaspoon salt
½ cup all-purpose flour
2 large egg whites, beaten
1 pound tilapia fillets (*see Note, page 210*), cut into ½-by-3-inch strips

1. Preheat oven to 450°F. Set a wire rack on a baking sheet; coat with cooking spray.

2. Place breadcrumbs, cereal flakes, lemon pepper, garlic powder, paprika and salt in a food processor or blender and process until finely ground. Transfer to a shallow dish.

3. Place flour in a second shallow dish and egg whites in a third shallow dish. Dredge each strip of fish in the flour, dip it in the egg and then coat all sides with the breadcrumb mixture. Place on the prepared rack. Coat both sides of the breaded fish with cooking spray.

4. Bake until the fish is cooked through and the breading is golden brown and crisp, about 10 minutes.

MAKES 4 SERVINGS.

PER SERVING: **289 calories**; 3 g fat (1 g sat, 1 g mono); 57 mg cholesterol; 37 g carbohydrate; 31 g protein; 4 g fiber; 373 mg sodium; 436 mg potassium.
NUTRITION BONUS: Folate (19% daily value).

H✱W H♥H

THE 500-CALORIE MENU

SERVE WITH ONE FROM EACH GROUP

Butternut & Barley Pilaf, page 187 (176 cal.)

OR

Cheesy Broccoli-Potato Mash, page 188 (135 cal.)

Shredded cabbage with lemon, salt, pepper and ½ tsp. extra-virgin olive oil (½ cup, 38 cal.)

OR

Steamed asparagus with chopped fresh chives (*see Guide, page 191;* ½ cup, 20 cal.)

DIET TIP

Skip regular tartar sauce, which contains 69 calories per tablespoon. Try a splash of hot red pepper sauce (0 calories) instead. Or make your own low-cal tartar sauce: combine ¼ cup low-fat mayonnaise with 2 tablespoons sweet pickle relish for 17 calories per tablespoon.

MEAT

When you hear "diet," juicy steak probably doesn't come to mind. And you do need to be careful when you choose cuts of meat because some are loaded with fat, which has twice as many calories as protein. There are many lean cuts of steak— filet mignon, sirloin, strip steak, flank steak. If you can't remember the names, use your eyes. Pick steaks that are deep red with a relatively small amount of marbling (fat).

For pork, lean choices include tenderloin, loin, chops and cutlets. If you love lamb, then leg, shoulder, chops and rack are all good choices. Ground meat is easier to decipher than the various cuts. Just check the label for the "percentage lean." Beef labeled 93%-lean means the other 7% is fat. We usually stick with ground meats that are 90%-lean or leaner.

And as with all things diet, you have to watch your portions. Even the "petite filet," which weighs in at 8 ounces at your local restaurant, is too much. A healthy serving of meat, whether you're watching your weight or not, is 3 ounces, cooked. If you start with 4 ounces of raw meat, it will cook down to 3 ounces. So if you're cooking for four people, start with a pound. That 32-ounce Porterhouse on the menu at the steakhouse? That's enough for eight people.

Bottom line is, if you love meat then keep on eating it. This chapter is proof that anything from steaks and chops to meatloaf and meatballs should come to mind when you think "diet."

A 471-Calorie Dinner (left): Seared Steaks with Caramelized Onions & Gorgonzola (*page 150*), 306 calories; Crushed Red Potatoes with Buttermilk (*page 188*), 85 calories; 1 cup of asparagus drizzled with 1 teaspoon olive oil, 80 calories.

THE 500-CALORIE MENU

SERVE WITH ONE FROM EACH GROUP

Polenta (*see Guide, page 190;* ½ cup, 74 cal.)

OR

Crushed Red Potatoes with Buttermilk, page 188 (85 cal.)

Asparagus drizzled with 1 tsp. olive oil (1 cup, 80 cal.)

OR

Sautéed chard with 1 tsp. olive oil and a squeeze of lemon (1 cup, 76 cal.)

SEARED STEAKS WITH CARAMELIZED ONIONS & GORGONZOLA

ACTIVE TIME: **30 MINUTES** | TOTAL: **30 MINUTES**

Beef tenderloin is naturally lean and mild-flavored, so it's great paired with the intense flavors of sweet caramelized onions and salty Gorgonzola cheese. (Photograph: page 148.)

2	tablespoons canola oil, divided
2	large onions, sliced (about 4 cups)
1	tablespoon brown sugar
½	cup reduced-sodium beef broth
1	tablespoon balsamic vinegar
½	teaspoon salt, divided
¼	teaspoon freshly ground pepper
1	pound beef tenderloin (filet mignon) *or* sirloin steak, 1-1¼ inches thick, trimmed and cut into 4 steaks
¼	cup crumbled Gorgonzola *or* blue cheese

1. Heat 1 tablespoon oil in a large skillet over medium heat. Add onions and brown sugar and cook, stirring often, until the onions are very tender and golden brown, about 15 minutes. Add broth, vinegar and ¼ teaspoon salt and cook, stirring, until the liquid has almost evaporated, 3 to 4 minutes more. Transfer the onions to a bowl; cover to keep warm. Clean and dry the pan.

2. Sprinkle the remaining ¼ teaspoon salt and pepper on both sides of each steak. Heat the remaining 1 tablespoon oil in the pan over medium-high heat. Add the steaks and cook until browned, 3 to 5 minutes. Turn them over and top with cheese. Reduce heat to medium-low, cover and cook until the cheese is melted and the steaks are cooked to desired doneness, 3 to 5 minutes for medium-rare. Serve with the caramelized onions.

MAKES 4 SERVINGS.

FLEMISH BEEF STEW

ACTIVE TIME: 45 MINUTES | TOTAL: 8¾ HOURS | TO MAKE AHEAD: Prepare through Step 2; cover and refrigerate for up to 1 day before cooking. | EQUIPMENT: 6-quart slow cooker (*or see Stovetop Variation*)

Here's an easy, slow-cooker interpretation of Carbonnades Flamandes, *a hearty Flemish stew made with beer. If you can't find a brown ale, use a strong, dark beer (but not a stout).*

- 4 teaspoons canola oil, divided
- 2 pounds bottom round, trimmed and cut into 1-inch cubes
- 12 ounces cremini *or* white button mushrooms, sliced
- 3 tablespoons all-purpose flour
- 2 cups brown ale *or* dark beer
- 4 large carrots, cut into 1-inch pieces
- 1 large onion, chopped
- 1 clove garlic, minced
- 1½ tablespoons Dijon mustard
- 1 teaspoon caraway seeds
- ¾ teaspoon salt
- ½ teaspoon freshly ground pepper
- 1 bay leaf

1. Heat 2 teaspoons oil in a Dutch oven over medium heat. Add half the beef and brown on all sides, turning frequently, about 5 minutes. Transfer to a 6-quart slow cooker. Drain any fat from the pan. Add the remaining 2 teaspoons oil and brown the remaining beef. Transfer to the slow cooker.

2. Return the pot to medium heat, add mushrooms and cook, stirring often, until they give off their liquid and it evaporates into a glaze, 5 to 7 minutes. Sprinkle flour over the mushrooms; cook undisturbed for 10 seconds, then stir and cook for 30 seconds more. Pour in ale (or beer); bring to a boil, whisking constantly to reduce foaming, until thickened and bubbling, about 3 minutes. Transfer the mushroom mixture to the slow cooker. Add carrots, onion, garlic, mustard, caraway seeds, salt, pepper and bay leaf to the slow cooker. Stir to combine.

3. Put the lid on and cook on low until the beef is very tender, about 8 hours. Discard the bay leaf before serving.

MAKES 8 SERVINGS, ABOUT 1 CUP EACH.

PER SERVING: **303 calories**; 10 g fat (3 g sat, 5 g mono); 84 mg cholesterol; 17 g carbohydrate; 31 g protein; 2 g fiber; 361 mg sodium; 645 mg potassium.
NUTRITION BONUS: Vitamin A (160% daily value), Zinc (33% dv), Potassium (17% dv), Iron (15% dv).

H♥W L↓C H♥H

THE 500-CALORIE MENU

SERVE WITH ONE FROM EACH GROUP

Brown rice (*see Guide, page 190;* ½ cup, 109 cal.)
OR
Whole-wheat orzo (½ cup, 87 cal.)

Brussels Sprouts with Bacon-Horseradish Cream, page 181 (80 cal.)
OR
Roasted Squash & Fennel with Thyme, page 180 (66 cal.)

STOVETOP VARIATION:

Step 1: Transfer the browned beef to a plate.

Step 2: Add 3 cups ale (or beer). Add the remaining vegetables and the browned beef to the mushrooms in the pot.

Step 3: Cover and cook on the stovetop over low heat, stirring occasionally, for 3 hours.

PER SANDWICH: **294 calories**; 10 g fat
(3 g sat, 5 g mono); 35 mg cholesterol;
27 g carbohydrate; 22 g protein; 2 g fiber;
598 mg sodium; 439 mg potassium.
NUTRITION BONUS: Vitamin C (210% daily
value), Vitamin A (30% dv), Zinc (23% dv).

H ✖ W   H ♥ H

THE 500-CALORIE MENU

SERVE WITH ONE FROM EACH GROUP

Cheesy Broccoli-Potato Mash, page 188
(135 cal.)

OR

Roasted red potatoes (see Guide, page
193; ½ cup, 97 cal.)

Roasted asparagus (see Guide, page 193;
½ cup, 77 cal.)

OR

Mixed greens (1½ cups) with 2 Tbsp.
Cucumber Herb Vinaigrette, page 74
(69 cal.)

DIET TIP

For a lighter meal, skip the bread and
serve the sliced steak and peppers on a
larger amount (say, 4 cups) of the salad
greens instead. Toss with the aïoli and
a squeeze of lemon. You'll save about
100 calories.

BISTRO FLANK STEAK SANDWICH

ACTIVE TIME: **45 MINUTES** | TOTAL: **45 MINUTES**

*Make this bistro-style sandwich, sauce and all, completely on the grill. If
you're in a hurry, just grill the steak and garlic and substitute jarred
roasted peppers for the grilled ones.*

6	cloves garlic, unpeeled
1	tablespoon extra-virgin olive oil
12	ounces flank steak, trimmed
½	teaspoon salt, divided
¼	teaspoon freshly ground pepper
1	medium red bell pepper
1	medium yellow bell pepper
4	large slices whole-wheat country bread, cut in half
2	tablespoons low-fat mayonnaise
1	cup mixed salad greens

1. Preheat grill to medium-high.

2. Place garlic on a piece of foil, drizzle with oil and seal to form a packet.
Sprinkle both sides of steak with ¼ teaspoon salt and pepper. Place the
garlic packet over indirect heat or the coolest part of the grill. Place the
steak and bell peppers over direct heat or the hottest part of the grill. Cook
the garlic until soft and golden brown, 8 to 10 minutes. Cook the peppers,
turning occasionally, until the skin is blistered on all sides, about 10 minutes total. Cook the steak, turning once, until desired doneness, about
6 minutes per side for medium. Transfer the garlic packet, peppers and
steak to a clean platter. Tent the steak with foil to keep warm. Grill bread,
turning once, until toasted, about 1 minute per side.

3. Peel the peppers; discard the stems, seeds and ribs. Slice into wide strips
and toss with the remaining ¼ teaspoon salt in a small bowl. Peel the garlic
and place it and the oil from the packet in another small bowl. Add mayonnaise and mash with a fork until combined. Slice the steak very thinly.

4. To assemble sandwiches, spread 1 scant teaspoon of the roasted garlic
aïoli on each piece of bread. Divide greens, the sliced steak and grilled
peppers among 4 slices of bread; top with the remaining bread.

MAKES 4 SANDWICHES.

PER SERVING: **209 calories**; 12 g fat (4 g sat, 5 g mono); 94 mg cholesterol; 5 g carbohydrate; 20 g protein; 0 g fiber; 391 mg sodium; 338 mg potassium.
NUTRITION BONUS: Zinc (20% dv).

H ✳ W   L ↓ C

THE 500-CALORIE MENU

SERVE WITH ONE FROM EACH GROUP

Cheesy Broccoli-Potato Mash, page 188 (135 cal.)
OR
Zesty Dill Potato Salad, page 189 (123 cal.)

Glazed Mini Carrots, page 179 (74 cal.)
OR
Lemon-Dill Green Beans, page 180 (74 cal.)

Apple Cider Granita, page 203 (103 cal.)
OR
Nonfat vanilla frozen yogurt (½ cup, 95 cal.)

DIET TIP

Baking meatloaves or casseroles like shepherd's pie in muffin tins or ramekins creates perfect portion-controlled servings. The other benefit is that it cuts down on baking time.

MINI MEATLOAVES

ACTIVE TIME: **10 MINUTES** | TOTAL: **40 MINUTES**

Traditional meatloaf is made with ground beef, pork and veal; here we replace the veal with ground turkey for a tender, flavorful and leaner version of the classic. If you can't find lean ground pork in your supermarket, it's easy enough to make yourself if you have a food processor: just trim the leanest pork you can find (loin is ideal) and cut into chunks, then pulse in the processor.

8	ounces lean (90% or leaner) ground beef
8	ounces lean ground pork
8	ounces ground turkey breast
1	large egg, lightly beaten
¼	cup quick-cooking oats
¼	cup chopped fresh parsley
¼	cup ketchup, divided
3	tablespoons low-fat milk
1	small onion, chopped
¾	teaspoon salt
⅛	teaspoon freshly ground pepper
1½	teaspoons Worcestershire sauce

1. Preheat oven to 375°F. Coat 8 muffin cups with cooking spray.

2. Mix beef, pork, turkey, egg, oats, parsley, 2 tablespoons ketchup, milk, onion, salt and pepper in a large bowl.

3. Form the mixture into 8 balls and place in the prepared muffin cups. Combine the remaining 2 tablespoons ketchup and Worcestershire sauce and spread about ½ teaspoon over each mini meatloaf.

4. Place the muffin pan on a baking sheet. Bake the meatloaves until their internal temperature reaches 160°F, 25 to 30 minutes. Pour off fat before serving.

MAKES 8 SERVINGS.

INDISPENSABLE MEAT SAUCE FOR PASTA

ACTIVE TIME: 20 MINUTES | TOTAL: 2 HOURS 10 MINUTES
TO MAKE AHEAD: Refrigerate for up to 5 days or freeze for up to 6 months.

Prosciutto, wine and mushrooms dress up this all-purpose spaghetti sauce; keep some handy in your freezer for a quick dinner. We add bulgur to reduce the amount of ground beef (and boost the amount of satisfying fiber).

8 ounces lean (90% or leaner) ground beef
1 teaspoon canola oil
1 ounce prosciutto, finely chopped (generous ¼ cup)
1 large onion, finely chopped
1 green bell pepper, seeded and finely chopped
2 carrots, finely chopped
2 stalks celery, finely chopped
8 ounces mushrooms, trimmed and thinly sliced
3 cloves garlic, minced
½ cup dry red wine
2 28-ounce cans plum tomatoes (with juices), chopped
1 tablespoon chopped fresh thyme *or* 1½ teaspoons dried
½ teaspoon dried oregano
½ teaspoon freshly ground pepper
¼ teaspoon crushed red pepper
¼ teaspoon salt
2 cups water
¼ cup bulgur (*see Note, page 208*)

1. Heat a large Dutch oven over medium heat. Add ground beef and cook, breaking up the meat with a wooden spoon, until browned, 3 to 5 minutes. Set aside in a colander to drain fat. Add oil to the pot and heat over medium-low heat. Add prosciutto, onion, bell pepper, carrots and celery and cook, stirring, until softened, about 10 minutes. Add mushrooms and garlic and cook, stirring frequently, for 10 minutes more. Add wine, increase heat to medium-high and cook until the wine has evaporated, about 3 minutes. Stir in tomatoes, thyme, oregano, pepper, crushed red pepper, salt and the reserved beef. Simmer, uncovered, stirring often, for 1 hour.

2. Add water and bulgur; bring to a boil. Reduce heat to a simmer and cook until the bulgur is tender, about 15 minutes.

MAKES ABOUT 8 CUPS.

PER ½-CUP SERVING: **76 calories**; 2 g fat (1 g sat, 1 g mono); 11 mg cholesterol; 9 g carbohydrate; 5 g protein; 2 g fiber; 247 mg sodium; 365 mg potassium.
NUTRITION BONUS: Vitamin A & Vitamin C (29% daily value).

THE 500-CALORIE MENU

SERVE WITH ONE FROM EACH GROUP

Whole-wheat pasta (1 cup, 174 cal.)

Roasted Asparagus with Garlic-Lemon Sauce, page 182 (89 cal.)
OR
Basic Sautéed Kale, page 178 (102 cal.)

Chocolate-Dipped Gingersnaps, page 200 (157 cal.)
OR
Red wine (5-ounce glass, 120 cal.)

THE 500-CALORIE MENU

SERVE WITH ONE FROM EACH GROUP

Brown rice (*see Guide, page 190;* 1/2 cup, 109 cal.)

OR

Whole-wheat fettuccine (1/2 cup, 87 cal.)

Sesame Snap Peas with Carrots & Peppers, page 183 (78 cal.)

OR

Raspberry Applesauce, page 201 (67 cal.)

SZECHUAN BRAISED MEATBALLS

ACTIVE TIME: **35 MINUTES** | TOTAL: **35 MINUTES**

Szechuan cuisine, from western China, is full of fiery-hot peppercorns and braised dishes. This recipe gets its heat from prepared Szechuan sauce and crushed red pepper.

- 1 pound 93%-lean ground beef
- 1 5- to 6-ounce can water chestnuts, rinsed and finely chopped
- 2 teaspoons plus 1 tablespoon cornstarch, divided
- 1/2 teaspoon five-spice powder (*see Note, page 207*)
- 1/4 teaspoon salt
- 1 cup reduced-sodium beef broth
- 4 teaspoons canola oil, divided
- 2 cloves garlic, minced
- 1/2 teaspoon crushed red pepper, or to taste
- 1/4 cup Szechuan sauce (*see Note, page 207*)
- 4 cups shredded napa cabbage
- 1 15-ounce can straw mushrooms, rinsed
- 2 scallions, sliced (optional)

1. Gently mix beef, water chestnuts, 2 teaspoons cornstarch, five-spice powder and salt in a medium bowl until combined. Shape the mixture into 12 balls (use about 2 tablespoons each to make 1 1/2-inch meatballs). Whisk broth and the remaining 1 tablespoon cornstarch in a small bowl until smooth; set aside.

2. Heat 2 teaspoons oil in a large nonstick skillet or nonstick wok over medium-high heat. Add the meatballs and cook, turning once, until brown, about 3 minutes total. Transfer to a plate.

3. Add the remaining 2 teaspoons oil to the pan. Add garlic and crushed red pepper and cook, stirring, until fragrant, 15 to 30 seconds. Add the reserved broth mixture, Szechuan sauce, cabbage and mushrooms; cook, stirring, until the cabbage is just wilted, about 2 minutes. Reduce heat to a simmer, return the meatballs to the pan, cover and cook until the sauce is thickened and the meatballs are cooked through, 8 to 10 minutes. Serve sprinkled with scallions (if using).

MAKES 4 SERVINGS, 3 MEATBALLS EACH.

BEEF & BEAN CHILE VERDE

ACTIVE TIME: **20 MINUTES** | TOTAL: **30 MINUTES**

TO MAKE AHEAD: Cover and refrigerate for up to 3 days. Reheat just before serving.

Chile Verde, usually a slow-cooked stew of pork, jalapeños and tomatillos, becomes an easy weeknight meal with quick-cooking lean ground beef and store-bought green salsa. It's even more delicious a day later and freezes well; make a double batch and store in single-serving portions for easy lunches to go.

1	pound 93%-lean ground beef
1	large red bell pepper, chopped
1	large onion, chopped
6	cloves garlic, chopped
1	tablespoon chili powder
2	teaspoons ground cumin
¼	teaspoon cayenne pepper, or to taste
1	16-ounce jar green salsa, green enchilada sauce *or* green taco sauce
¼	cup water
1	15-ounce can pinto *or* kidney beans, rinsed

Cook beef, bell pepper and onion in a large saucepan over medium heat, crumbling the meat with a wooden spoon, until the meat is browned, 8 to 10 minutes. Add garlic, chili powder, cumin and cayenne; cook until fragrant, about 15 seconds. Stir in salsa (or sauce) and water; bring to a simmer. Reduce heat to medium-low, cover and cook, stirring occasionally, until the vegetables are tender, 10 to 15 minutes. Stir in beans and cook until heated through, about 1 minute.

MAKES 4 SERVINGS, ABOUT 1½ CUPS EACH.

PER SERVING: **309 calories**; 8 g fat (3 g sat, 3 g mono); 64 mg cholesterol; 29 g carbohydrate; 27 g protein; 6 g fiber; 516 mg sodium; 641 mg potassium.
NUTRITION BONUS: Vitamin C (100% daily value), Vitamin A & Zinc (40% dv), Folate (20% dv), Potassium (18% dv).

H✳W H⬆F H♥H

THE 500-CALORIE MENU

SERVE WITH ONE FROM EACH GROUP

Quinoa with a squeeze of lime (*see Guide, page 190;* ½ cup, 111 cal.)
OR
Avocado (one-fourth) with 1 Tbsp. reduced-fat sour cream (100 cal.)

Banana Pudding Pops, page 202 (82 cal.)
OR
Chewy Chocolate Cookies, page 197 (68 cal.)

DIET TIP

We like 93%-lean ground beef because it's not as dry as ultra-lean (95% or leaner) beef. It's not always available, so stock up when you find it and freeze it in 1-pound portions. Or mix your own with a combination of 90%- and 95%-lean beef.

THE 500-CALORIE MENU

SERVE WITH ONE FROM EACH GROUP

Mixed greens (1 1/2 cups) with 2 Tbsp. Parmesan-Pepper Dressing, page 77 (37 cal.)
OR
Simple Sautéed Spinach, page 178 (68 cal.)

Orange Crisps with Citrus Fruit Salad, page 198 (128 cal.)
OR
Red wine (5-ounce glass, 120 cal.)

DIET TIP

Try prosciutto instead of bacon or pepperoni. It's exceptionally lean and flavorful—and the paper-thin slices fool the eye into thinking "abundance." In truth, the prosciutto only contributes a mere 20 or so calories to each serving.

ARUGULA & PROSCIUTTO PIZZA

ACTIVE TIME: **35 MINUTES** | TOTAL: **35 MINUTES**

Topping the hot-out-of-the-oven crust with fresh greens and diced tomatoes gives this white pizza a summery twist, while the little bit of prosciutto and fontina cheese make it taste like a splurge.

- 1 pound prepared pizza dough, preferably whole-wheat
- 2 tablespoons extra-virgin olive oil
- 1 medium onion, halved and thinly sliced
- 2 ounces very thinly sliced prosciutto, cut into thin strips (about 1/2 cup)
- 1/4 teaspoon crushed red pepper
- 1 cup shredded fontina *or* part-skim mozzarella cheese
- 2 cups packed coarsely chopped arugula
- 1 cup chopped tomato

1. Position oven rack in the lowest position; preheat to 450°F. Coat a large baking sheet with cooking spray.

2. Roll out dough on a lightly floured surface to about the size of the baking sheet. Transfer to the baking sheet. Bake until puffed and lightly crisped on the bottom, 8 to 10 minutes.

3. Meanwhile, heat oil in a large nonstick skillet over medium heat. Add onion, prosciutto and crushed red pepper and cook, stirring, until the onion is beginning to brown, about 3 minutes.

4. Spread the onion mixture evenly over the hot crust and top with cheese. Bake until crispy and golden and the cheese is melted, 8 to 10 minutes. Remove from the oven and top with arugula and tomato.

MAKES 6 SERVINGS.

THE 500-CALORIE MENU

SERVE WITH ONE FROM EACH GROUP

Roasted asparagus (see Guide, page 193; 77 cal.)

OR

Chilled Snap Peas with Creamy Tarragon Dressing, page 179 (61 cal.)

Toasted whole-wheat English muffin (134 cal.)

OR

Whole-Grain Rice Pilaf, page 186 (97 cal.)

DIET TIP

Watch out for traditional Hollandaise sauce, which is made from butter, lemon and egg yolks—a mere ¼ cup of it has 340 calories. Try this lighter creamy sauce made with low-fat mayo, nonfat plain yogurt and lemon juice instead.

ARTICHOKE-SCRAMBLED EGGS BENEDICT

ACTIVE TIME: **30 MINUTES** | TOTAL: **30 MINUTES**

Roasted artichoke bottoms stand in for English muffins in this quick yet elegant supper, saving calories while adding filling fiber. Look for them near other canned vegetables; if unavailable, use two 14-ounce cans artichoke hearts. For a vegetarian option, substitute roasted mushrooms for the pancetta.

8 canned artichoke bottoms (1 ½ cans), rinsed
4 teaspoons extra-virgin olive oil, divided
3 teaspoons chopped fresh oregano, divided
⅓ cup chopped pancetta
2 tablespoons low-fat mayonnaise
2 tablespoons nonfat plain yogurt
2 teaspoons lemon juice
1 teaspoon water
6 large eggs
4 large egg whites
2 tablespoons reduced-fat cream cheese (Neufchâtel)
¼ teaspoon salt

1. Preheat oven to 425°F.

2. Toss artichoke bottoms with 2 teaspoons oil and 2 teaspoons chopped oregano. Place them top-side down on half of a large baking sheet. Spread pancetta in an even layer on the other half. Roast until the artichokes are just beginning to brown and the pancetta is crispy, 12 to 14 minutes.

3. Meanwhile, whisk mayonnaise, yogurt, lemon juice and water in a small bowl until smooth; set aside. Beat eggs and egg whites in a large bowl. Heat the remaining 2 teaspoons oil in a large nonstick skillet over medium-high heat. Add the eggs; cook, folding and stirring frequently with a heatproof rubber spatula, until almost set, about 2 minutes. Remove from the heat; fold in cream cheese, salt and the remaining 1 teaspoon oregano.

4. To serve, divide the artichoke bottoms among 4 plates. Top each artichoke with equal portions scrambled egg, crispy pancetta and creamy lemon sauce.

MAKES 4 SERVINGS.

BLACK-EYED PEAS WITH PORK & GREENS

ACTIVE TIME: 30 MINUTES | TOTAL: 45 MINUTES

This boldly flavored spin on Hoppin' John replaces fatty salt pork or bacon with lean pork chops. Greens are a traditional accompaniment with the dish; we like the earthiness of kale, but collards or turnip greens would be wonderful too.

1	pound boneless pork chops, trimmed, cut into 1/2-inch pieces
1/2	teaspoon salt, divided
1/4	teaspoon freshly ground pepper
1	tablespoon canola oil
1	medium onion, chopped
2	tablespoons tomato paste
1	cup instant brown rice
8	cups coarsely chopped kale leaves (about 1 small bunch), tough stems removed
4	cloves garlic, minced
1	14-ounce can reduced-sodium chicken broth
2	tablespoons cider vinegar *or* sherry vinegar
1/2	teaspoon smoked paprika (*see Note, page 207*), preferably hot
1	15-ounce can black-eyed peas, rinsed

1. Toss pork with 1/4 teaspoon salt and pepper. Heat oil in a large nonstick skillet over medium heat. Add the pork and cook, stirring, until just cooked through, 4 to 6 minutes. Transfer to a bowl with a slotted spoon.

2. Add onion, tomato paste and rice to the pan and cook until the onion softens, about 4 minutes. Add kale and garlic and cook until the kale begins to wilt, 1 to 2 minutes. Stir in broth, vinegar, paprika and the remaining 1/4 teaspoon salt. Bring to a boil. Cover, reduce heat and simmer until the rice is done, 15 to 20 minutes. Stir in black-eyed peas and the reserved pork and heat through, about 1 minute.

MAKES 6 SERVINGS, ABOUT 1 1/3 CUPS EACH.

PER SERVING: **279 calories**; 8 g fat (1 g sat, 3 g mono); 44 mg cholesterol; 32 g carbohydrate; 22 g protein; 5 g fiber; 526 mg sodium; 796 mg potassium. NUTRITION BONUS: Vitamin A (280% daily value), Vitamin C (190% dv), Potassium (21% dv), Magnesium (20% dv), Calcium & Iron (15% dv).

THE 500-CALORIE MENU

SERVE WITH ONE FROM EACH GROUP

Golden Summer Squash & Corn Soup, page 33 (111 cal.)
OR
Red wine (5-ounce glass, 120 cal.)

Apple Cider Granita, page 203 (103 cal.)
OR
Baby Tiramisù, page 200 (107 cal.)

DIET TIP

When a dish calls for smoked pork or bacon, try reducing or omitting the meat and adding smoked paprika. Made from smoke-dried red peppers, its complex flavor restores some welcome smokiness without the calories and fat. Look for it in large supermarkets and at *tienda.com*.

PER SERVING: **257 calories**; 10 g fat (2 g sat, 5 g mono); 66 mg cholesterol; 20 g carbohydrate; 24 g protein; 5 g fiber; 378 mg sodium; 818 mg potassium. NUTRITION BONUS: Vitamin C (140% daily value), Vitamin A (25% dv), Potassium (23% dv).

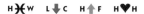

THE 500-CALORIE MENU

SERVE WITH ONE FROM EACH GROUP

Cauliflower & Couscous Pilaf, page 185 (162 cal.)

OR

Quinoa with chopped fresh tarragon (*see Guide, page 190;* ½ cup, 111 cal.)

Banana Pudding Pops, page 202 (82 cal.)

OR

Fast Strawberry Frozen Yogurt, page 201 (100 cal.)

PORK CHOPS WITH ORANGE & FENNEL SALAD

ACTIVE TIME: **35 MINUTES** | TOTAL: **35 MINUTES**

Fennel seed–crusted pork chops with a warm citrus-and-fresh-fennel salad is a terrific antidote to a dreary winter day. To keep calories down (and satisfying protein up) select the leanest chops you can find, preferably from the loin.

- 3 navel oranges
- 1 teaspoon lemon juice
- ½ teaspoon sugar
- ½ teaspoon cornstarch
- ½ teaspoon salt, divided
- 4 4-ounce boneless pork chops, ½ inch thick, trimmed
- 2 teaspoons fennel seeds, coarsely chopped *or* coarsely ground
- ¼ teaspoon freshly ground pepper
- 1 tablespoon extra-virgin olive oil
- 1 large fennel bulb, cored and thinly sliced
- 1 shallot, chopped
- 3 cups watercress *or* arugula, tough stems removed

1. Remove skin and white pith from oranges with a sharp knife. Working over a bowl, cut segments from surrounding membranes. (*See photos, page 208.*) Squeeze juice into the bowl before discarding membranes. Transfer the segments with a slotted spoon to another bowl; set aside. Whisk lemon juice, sugar, cornstarch and ¼ teaspoon salt into the orange juice; set aside.

2. Season pork chops on both sides with fennel seeds, the remaining ¼ teaspoon salt and pepper. Heat oil in a large nonstick skillet over medium heat. Add the chops and cook until browned and just cooked through, 2 to 3 minutes per side. Transfer to a plate and tent with foil to keep warm.

3. Add sliced fennel and shallot to the pan and cook, stirring, for 1 minute. Add watercress (or arugula) and cook, stirring, until it begins to wilt, 1 to 2 minutes more. Stir in the reserved orange segments, then transfer everything to a platter.

4. Add the reserved orange juice mixture and any juices from the pork chops to the pan. Cook, stirring constantly, until slightly thickened, about 1 minute. Serve the chops on the fennel salad, drizzled with the pan sauce.

MAKES 4 SERVINGS.

PORK TENDERLOIN WITH ROASTED GRAPE SAUCE

ACTIVE TIME: 45 MINUTES | TOTAL: 45 MINUTES

Here, we roast grapes to bring out their succulent sweetness, then combine them with thyme, mustard and Madeira in an easy, savory sauce for pork tenderloin.

4	cups red *and/or* green grapes
1-1¼	pounds pork tenderloin, trimmed
½	teaspoon salt
½	teaspoon freshly ground pepper
1	tablespoon extra-virgin olive oil
¼	cup finely chopped shallots
½	cup Madeira (*see Note, page 208*) *or* white wine
½	cup reduced-sodium chicken broth
1	tablespoon chopped fresh thyme *or* 1 teaspoon dried
2	teaspoons Dijon mustard
2	teaspoons water
1½	teaspoons cornstarch

1. Position racks in the middle and lower third of oven; preheat to 425°F.

2. Place grapes on a rimmed baking sheet. Roast on the lower rack, shaking the pan occasionally to turn the grapes, until shriveled, 25 to 30 minutes.

3. Meanwhile, rub pork with salt and pepper. Heat oil in a large ovenproof skillet over medium-high heat. Add the pork and brown on one side, about 2 minutes. Turn the pork over and transfer the pan to the top oven rack. Roast the pork until just barely pink in the center and an instant-read thermometer registers 145°F, 12 to 14 minutes. Transfer the pork to a clean cutting board to rest before slicing.

4. Place the pan over medium heat (be careful: the handle will still be hot), add shallots and cook, stirring, until softened, 1 to 2 minutes. Add Madeira (or wine) and cook until reduced by half, 2 to 4 minutes. Stir in broth, thyme and mustard; bring to a simmer. Combine water and cornstarch in a small bowl and stir into the pan sauce. Cook until thickened, 30 seconds to 1 minute. Stir in the grapes. Serve the sliced pork with the grape sauce.

MAKES 4 SERVINGS.

PER SERVING: **298 calories**; 6 g fat (1 g sat, 4 g mono); 74 mg cholesterol; 31 g carbohydrate; 26 g protein; 2 g fiber; 459 mg sodium; 824 mg potassium. NUTRITION BONUS: Vitamin C (30% daily value), Potassium (23% dv), Zinc (16% dv).

H✄W   H♥H

THE 500-CALORIE MENU

SERVE WITH ONE FROM EACH GROUP

Pearl barley (*see Guide, page 190*; ½ cup, 97 cal.)
OR
Crushed Red Potatoes with Buttermilk, page 188 (85 cal.)

Mixed greens (1½ cups) with 2 Tbsp. Champagne Vinaigrette, page 74 (120 cal.)
OR
Simple Sautéed Spinach, page 178 (68 cal.)

DIET TIP

If you've got extra grapes, toss them in the freezer for an easy snack. Because they're sweet and you savor them individually and slowly, you'll get a lot of satisfaction for just a handful of calories.

THE 500-CALORIE MENU

SERVE WITH ONE FROM EACH GROUP

Japanese Cucumber Salad, page 57 (46 cal.)

OR

Steamed snow peas with a splash of reduced-sodium soy sauce (½ cup, 35 cal.)

Wild Rice with Shiitakes & Toasted Almonds, page 185 (158 cal.)

OR

Brown rice with a drizzle (1 tsp.) of sesame oil (*see Guide, page 190;* ½ cup, 149 cal.)

Orange Crisps with Citrus Fruit Salad, page 198 (128 cal.)

OR

Papaya-Lime Sorbet, page 199 (110 cal.)

DIET TIP

At just 5 grams of fat in a 3-ounce portion, pork tenderloin is about as lean as skinless chicken breast and every bit as versatile. When you shop, avoid salty "enhanced" tenderloins that have been plumped up with a sodium solution to boost juiciness.

GRILLED PORK TENDERLOIN MARINATED IN SPICY SOY SAUCE

ACTIVE TIME: **20 MINUTES** | TOTAL: **2 HOURS 20 MINUTES** (including 2 hours marinating time)

These sweet and spicy soy sauce–marinated pork tenderloin medallions make for a delicious, healthful and elegant entree. Try this marinade with chicken also. We love the flavor and heat of Thai red chiles—small red or green chiles, about 1½ inches long. Look for them in well-stocked supermarkets and Asian markets.

¼   cup reduced-sodium soy sauce
2   tablespoons sugar
1   large clove garlic, peeled and finely grated or minced
1   tablespoon finely grated fresh ginger
1   fresh red Thai chile *or* cayenne chile pepper, stemmed, seeded and minced
1   tablespoon toasted sesame oil
1½   pounds pork tenderloin, trimmed and cut into 1-inch-thick medallions

1. Whisk soy sauce and sugar in a medium bowl until the sugar is completely dissolved. Stir in garlic, ginger, chile and oil.

2. Place pork in a sealable plastic bag. Add the marinade and seal the bag, squeezing air out. Turn the bag to coat the medallions. Refrigerate for 2 hours, turning the bag once to redistribute the marinade.

3. Preheat grill to medium. Remove the pork from the marinade. (Discard the marinade.) Grill the medallions until just cooked through, 3 to 5 minutes per side.

MAKES 6 SERVINGS.

LAMB CHOPS WITH LEBANESE GREEN BEANS

ACTIVE TIME: **45 MINUTES** | TOTAL: **45 MINUTES**

Simple pan-roasted lamb chops are served alongside spiced stewed green beans and tomatoes in a riff on a Lebanese favorite, lubiyeh.

- 1 tablespoon plus **1** teaspoon extra-virgin olive oil, divided
- 1 medium yellow onion, chopped
- 2 tablespoons chopped fresh mint *or* 2 teaspoons dried, divided
- ½ teaspoon ground cinnamon
- 1 teaspoon salt, divided
- ¼ teaspoon freshly ground pepper, plus more to taste
- 3 cups diced tomatoes (4-5 medium)
- ⅓ cup water
- 12 ounces green beans, trimmed
- 8 lamb loin chops, trimmed (1½-1¾ pounds total)

1. Preheat oven to 400°F.

2. Heat 1 tablespoon oil in a large saucepan over medium heat. Add onion and cook, stirring occasionally, until tender and light brown, about 5 minutes. Add 1 tablespoon fresh mint (or 1 teaspoon dried), cinnamon, ½ teaspoon salt and pepper to taste; cook, stirring, until fragrant, about 30 seconds. Add tomatoes and water and increase heat to high. Cook, stirring occasionally, until the tomatoes begin to break down, 2 to 3 minutes. Stir in green beans. Reduce heat to medium, cover and cook, stirring occasionally, until the green beans are tender, about 12 minutes.

3. Meanwhile, sprinkle both sides of lamb chops with the remaining ½ teaspoon salt and ¼ teaspoon pepper. Heat the remaining 1 teaspoon oil in a large ovenproof skillet over medium-high heat. Add the lamb chops and cook until browned on one side, about 2 minutes. Turn them over and transfer the pan to the oven. Roast until an instant-read thermometer inserted horizontally into a chop registers 140°F for medium-rare, 6 to 10 minutes, depending on thickness.

4. Stir the remaining mint into the green bean mixture. Serve the lamb chops with the green beans.

MAKES 4 SERVINGS, 2 CHOPS & 1 CUP VEGETABLES EACH.

PER SERVING: **327 calories**; 15 g fat (4 g sat, 8 g mono); 96 mg cholesterol; 15 g carbohydrate; 33 g protein; 5 g fiber; 676 mg sodium; 876 mg potassium.
NUTRITION BONUS: Vitamin C (45% daily value), Vitamin A (35% dv), Potassium (25% dv), Folate & Iron (20% dv).

H⫲W   L⬇C   H⬆F

THE 500-CALORIE MENU

SERVE WITH ONE FROM EACH GROUP

Whole-Grain Rice Pilaf, page 186 (97 cal.)
OR
Bulgur tossed with chopped fresh mint (*see Guide, page 190*; ½ cup, 96 cal.)

Raspberry Applesauce, page 201 (67 cal.)
OR
Chewy Chocolate Cookies, page 197 (68 cal.)

THE 500-CALORIE MENU

SERVE WITH ONE FROM EACH GROUP

Roasted Asparagus with Garlic-Lemon Sauce, page 182 (89 cal.)
OR
Basic Sautéed Kale, page 178 (102 cal.)

Nonfat chocolate frozen yogurt (100 cal.)
OR
Red wine (5 ounce glass, 120 cal.)

RACK OF LAMB WITH WARM APPLE & LENTIL SALAD

ACTIVE TIME: **40 MINUTES** | TOTAL: **40 MINUTES**

Mustard and rosemary complement rich lamb in this elegant meal. Don't let rack of lamb intimidate you—it's actually simple to prepare.

2 tablespoons coarse dry breadcrumbs, preferably whole-wheat
1½ teaspoons extra-virgin olive oil, divided
1 teaspoon chopped fresh rosemary, divided
¾ teaspoon kosher salt, divided
¼ teaspoon freshly ground pepper, divided
1 1½-pound rack of lamb, Frenched (*see Note, page 209*) and trimmed
3 teaspoons Dijon mustard, divided
2 shallots, finely chopped
1 15-ounce can lentils, rinsed, *or* 1⅓ cups cooked lentils
1 Granny Smith apple, finely chopped
2 stalks celery with leaves, finely chopped
¾ cup reduced-sodium chicken broth *or* water
2 teaspoons sherry vinegar *or* cider vinegar

1. Preheat oven to 450°F.

2. Mix breadcrumbs, ½ teaspoon oil, ½ teaspoon rosemary, ½ teaspoon salt and ⅛ teaspoon pepper in a small bowl. Heat the remaining 1 teaspoon oil in a large ovenproof skillet over medium-high heat. Add lamb, meat-side down, and sear until browned, about 1½ minutes. Turn it over and spread 2 teaspoons mustard over the meat. Sprinkle the breadcrumb mixture over the mustard. Transfer the pan to the oven and roast until an instant-read thermometer inserted in the center registers 140°F for medium-rare, 15 to 20 minutes. Transfer the lamb to a plate and tent with foil to keep warm.

3. Return the pan to medium-high heat (be careful: the handle will still be hot). Add shallots, the remaining ½ teaspoon rosemary, ¼ teaspoon salt and ⅛ teaspoon pepper; cook, stirring constantly, until starting to soften, about 1 minute. Stir in lentils, apple, celery, broth (or water), vinegar and the remaining 1 teaspoon mustard. Cook at a lively simmer, stirring occasionally, until slightly reduced and the celery and apple begin to soften, about 4 minutes. Cut the lamb into 8 chops and serve over the lentils.

MAKES 4 SERVINGS.

SIDES

Just as shoes can make an outfit, sides really do make a meal. After all, who hasn't picked an entree at a restaurant primarily because it includes a side of cheesy mashed potatoes? (And is your favorite Thanksgiving food *really* the turkey?)

The best side dishes don't just enhance the flavor of your meal: they elevate the nutrition too. Roasted root vegetables offer vitamin C and loads of beta carotene, a powerful antioxidant that can protect your eyesight. Green vegetables, such as spinach, peas, broccoli and kale, contain both of those nutrients plus folate, an important B vitamin that promotes the growth of healthy cells. (They're also really low in calories.) Even white potatoes deliver vitamin C—but we boost the nutrition of our cheesy mash by adding some broccoli (*see page 188*). Barley, brown rice, quinoa and other whole grains will help you get your fill of fiber and provide antioxidants that may help to prevent conditions like heart disease and cancer.

And, really, the healthiest plate is one that's half filled with veggies, a quarter with whole grains and a quarter with a source of lean protein, such as chicken, fish or pork. So let the sides shine.

A 501-Calorie Dinner (*left*): Sugar Snap Pea & Barley Salad (*page 184*), 152 calories; grilled bone-in pork chop (6 ounces cooked), 177 calories; 2 cups mixed green salad with 2 tablespoons Roasted Garlic Dressing (*page 75*), 172 calories.

PER SERVING: **106 calories**; 6 g fat (1 g sat, 3 g mono); 35 mg cholesterol; 12 g carbohydrate; 3 g protein; 3 g fiber; 180 mg sodium; 294 mg potassium. NUTRITION BONUS: Vitamin A (60% daily value), Folate (17% dv), Vitamin C (15% dv).

H✖W L↓C H↑F H♥H

SHREDDED ROOT VEGETABLE PANCAKES

ACTIVE TIME: 30 MINUTES | TOTAL: 45 MINUTES

Red beets and golden carrots look especially festive in these zesty horseradish- and bacon-flecked cakes. Avoid parsnips, which need to be cored, in this recipe, as trying to shred the smaller cored pieces might result in nicked knuckles. Try the pancakes with seared steaks or make them bite-size for a beautiful appetizer.

1	large egg, lightly beaten
¼	cup whole-wheat flour
3	tablespoons chopped scallions
1	tablespoon chopped fresh dill *or* 1 teaspoon dried
1	tablespoon prepared horseradish
¼	teaspoon salt
¼	teaspoon freshly ground pepper
4	cups peeled and shredded root vegetables, such as beets, carrots, rutabaga *and/or* turnips (about 1 ½ pounds)
2	slices cooked bacon, crumbled (optional)
6	teaspoons canola oil, divided
	Reduced-fat sour cream for garnish
	Dill sprigs for garnish

1. Preheat oven to 400°F. Coat a baking sheet with cooking spray.

2. Whisk egg, flour, scallions, dill, horseradish, salt and pepper in a large bowl. Stir in vegetables and bacon (if using).

3. Heat 2 teaspoons oil in a large nonstick skillet over medium heat. Cook 4 pancakes per batch: place about ¼ cup vegetable mixture in a little of the oil and press with the back of a spatula to flatten into a 2- to 3-inch pancake. Cook until crispy and golden, 1½ to 3 minutes per side. Transfer the pancakes to the prepared baking sheet. Continue with 2 more batches, using the remaining 4 teaspoons oil and vegetable mixture. Transfer the baking sheet to the oven and bake for 15 minutes. Serve garnished with sour cream and dill sprigs, if desired.

MAKES 6 SERVINGS, 2 PANCAKES EACH.

BASIC SAUTÉED KALE

ACTIVE TIME: **10 MINUTES** | TOTAL: **25 MINUTES**

1	tablespoon plus 1 teaspoon extra-virgin olive oil, divided
1-1 ½	pounds kale, ribs removed, coarsely chopped
½	cup water
2	cloves garlic, minced
¼	teaspoon crushed red pepper
2-3	teaspoons sherry vinegar *or* red-wine vinegar
¼	teaspoon salt

Heat 1 tablespoon oil in a Dutch oven over medium heat. Add kale and cook, tossing with two large spoons, until bright green, about 1 minute. Add water, reduce heat to medium-low, cover and cook, stirring occasionally, until the kale is tender, 12 to 15 minutes. Push kale to one side,

BASIC SAUTÉED KALE

add the remaining 1 teaspoon oil to the empty side and cook garlic and crushed red pepper in it until fragrant, 30 seconds to 1 minute. Remove from the heat and toss together. Stir in vinegar to taste and salt.

MAKES 4 SERVINGS, ABOUT ½ CUP EACH.
PER SERVING: **102 calories**; 5 g fat (1 g sat, 4 g mono); 0 mg cholesterol; 12 g carbohydrate; 4 g protein; 2 g fiber; 195 mg sodium; 516 mg potassium.
NUTRITION BONUS: Vitamin A (350% daily value), Vitamin C (230% dv), Calcium (15% dv).

SIMPLE SAUTÉED SPINACH

ACTIVE TIME: **20 MINUTES** | TOTAL: **20 MINUTES**

2	tablespoons extra-virgin olive oil
4	cloves garlic, thinly sliced
20	ounces fresh spinach, trimmed (about 20 cups)
1	tablespoon lemon juice
¼	teaspoon salt
¼	teaspoon crushed red pepper

Heat oil in a Dutch oven over medium heat. Add garlic and cook until beginning to brown, 1 to 2 minutes. Add spinach and toss to coat. Cover and cook until wilted, 3 to 5 minutes. Remove from the heat and add lemon juice, salt and crushed red pepper. Toss to coat and serve immediately.

MAKES 6 SERVINGS, ABOUT ½ CUP EACH.
PER SERVING: **68 calories**; 5 g fat (1 g sat, 4 g mono); 0 mg cholesterol; 4 g carbohydrate; 3 g protein; 2 g fiber; 172 mg sodium; 540 mg potassium.
NUTRITION BONUS: Vitamin A (180% daily value), Folate (46% dv), Vitamin C (45% dv), Iron & Potassium (15% dv).

GLAZED MINI CARROTS

H✖W L⬇C H⬆F H♥H

⏱ ACTIVE TIME: **5 MINUTES** | TOTAL: **10 MINUTES**

3 cups mini carrots (about 1 pound)
⅓ cup water
1 tablespoon honey
2 teaspoons butter
¼ teaspoon salt, or to taste
1 tablespoon lemon juice
   Freshly ground pepper to taste
2 tablespoons chopped fresh parsley

Combine carrots, water, honey, butter and salt in a large skillet. Bring to a simmer over medium-high heat. Cover and cook until tender, 5 to 7 minutes. Uncover and cook, stirring often, until the liquid is a syrupy glaze, 1 to 2 minutes. Stir in lemon juice and pepper. Sprinkle with parsley.

MAKES 4 SERVINGS, ½ CUP EACH.

PER SERVING: **74 calories**; 2 g fat (1 g sat, 1 g mono); 5 mg cholesterol; 14 g carbohydrate; 1 g protein; 2 g fiber; 236 mg sodium; 287 mg potassium.
NUTRITION BONUS: Vitamin A (320% daily value).

CHILLED SNAP PEAS WITH CREAMY TARRAGON DRESSING

H✖W L⬇C H⬆F H♥H

⏱ ACTIVE TIME: **15 MINUTES** | TOTAL: **35 MINUTES**
TO MAKE AHEAD: Refrigerate peas and dressing separately for up to 1 day. Toss together just before serving.

1 pound sugar snap peas, trimmed (about 4 cups)

CHILLED SNAP PEAS WITH CREAMY TARRAGON DRESSING

2 tablespoons low-fat mayonnaise
2 tablespoons low-fat plain yogurt *or* nonfat buttermilk
1 tablespoon chopped fresh tarragon *or* 1 teaspoon dried
¼ teaspoon salt
   Freshly ground pepper to taste

1. Bring an inch of water to a boil in a large saucepan fitted with a steamer basket. Add peas, cover and steam, stirring once, until crisp-tender, 5 to 7 minutes. Transfer to a baking sheet lined with paper towels. Refrigerate until chilled, about 20 minutes.
2. Whisk mayonnaise, yogurt (or buttermilk), tarragon, salt and pepper in a medium bowl. Add peas; toss well to coat. Serve chilled.

MAKES 4 SERVINGS, ¾ CUP EACH.

PER SERVING: **61 calories**; 1 g fat (0 g sat, 0 g mono); 0 mg cholesterol; 10 g carbohydrate; 4 g protein; 3 g fiber; 220 mg sodium; 251 mg potassium.
NUTRITION BONUS: Vitamin C (110% daily value), Vitamin A (25% dv).

LEMON-DILL GREEN BEANS

MAKES 4 SERVINGS, ABOUT 1 CUP EACH.
PER SERVING: **74 calories**; 4 g fat (1 g sat, 3 g mono);
0 mg cholesterol; 10 g carbohydrate; 2 g protein; 4 g fiber;
163 mg sodium; 177 mg potassium.
NUTRITION BONUS: Vitamin C (20% daily value), Vitamin A
(15% dv).

ROASTED SQUASH & FENNEL WITH THYME

ACTIVE TIME: 30 MINUTES | TOTAL: 30 MINUTES

- 2 small summer squash (about 12 ounces total)
- 1 ½ cups sliced fennel bulb (about 1 small bulb), plus 1 tablespoon chopped fennel fronds, divided
- 1 tablespoon extra-virgin olive oil
- 1 tablespoon chopped fresh thyme
- ¼ teaspoon salt
- ¼ teaspoon freshly ground pepper
- ¼ cup thinly sliced garlic

1. Preheat oven to 450°F.
2. Quarter squash lengthwise, then cut crosswise into 1-inch pieces. Combine the squash with sliced fennel, oil, thyme, salt and pepper in a large bowl. Spread the mixture evenly on a large, rimmed baking sheet. Roast for 10 minutes. Stir in garlic and roast until the vegetables are tender and the fennel is beginning to brown, about 5 minutes more. Stir in fennel fronds and serve.

MAKES 4 SERVINGS, ABOUT ⅔ CUP EACH.
PER SERVING: **66 calories**; 4 g fat (1 g sat, 3 g mono);
0 mg cholesterol; 8 g carbohydrate; 2 g protein; 2 g fiber;
167 mg sodium; 388 mg potassium.
NUTRITION BONUS: Vitamin C (35% daily value).

LEMON-DILL GREEN BEANS

ACTIVE TIME: 15 MINUTES | TOTAL: 25 MINUTES

- 1 pound green beans, trimmed
- 4 teaspoons chopped fresh dill
- 1 tablespoon minced shallot
- 1 tablespoon extra-virgin olive oil
- 1 tablespoon lemon juice
- 1 teaspoon whole-grain mustard
- ¼ teaspoon salt
- ¼ teaspoon freshly ground pepper

1. Bring an inch of water to a boil in a large saucepan fitted with a steamer basket. Add green beans, cover and steam until tender-crisp, 5 to 7 minutes.
2. Meanwhile, whisk dill, shallot, oil, lemon juice, mustard, salt and pepper in a large bowl. Add the green beans and toss to coat. Let stand for about 10 minutes before serving to blend flavors.

BRUSSELS SPROUTS WITH BACON-HORSERADISH CREAM

H✖W L⬇C H⬆F H♥H

⏱ ACTIVE TIME: 20 MINUTES | TOTAL: 20 MINUTES

- 1½ pounds Brussels sprouts, trimmed and halved
- 4 strips crisp-cooked bacon, finely chopped
- ¼ cup reduced-fat sour cream
- 2 teaspoons prepared horseradish
- ¼ teaspoon salt
- ⅛ teaspoon freshly ground pepper

1. Bring an inch of water to a boil in a large saucepan fitted with a steamer basket. Add Brussels sprouts, cover and steam until tender, 6 to 8 minutes.

2. Mix bacon, sour cream, horseradish, salt and pepper in a medium bowl. Add the Brussels sprouts and toss to coat.

MAKES 6 SERVINGS, 1 CUP EACH.

PER SERVING: **80 calories**; 3 g fat (1 g sat, 1 g mono); 8 mg cholesterol; 9 g carbohydrate; 5 g protein; 3 g fiber; 222 mg sodium; 431 mg potassium.

NUTRITION BONUS: Vitamin C (130% daily value), Vitamin A (20% dv), Folate (19% dv).

PARMESAN SPINACH CAKES

L⬇C

⏱ ACTIVE TIME: 15 MINUTES | TOTAL: 40 MINUTES
EQUIPMENT: Muffin pan with 12 (½-cup) muffin cups

- 12 ounces fresh spinach, trimmed (about 12 cups)
- 2 large eggs, beaten
- ½ cup part-skim ricotta cheese *or* low-fat cottage cheese
- ½ cup finely shredded Parmesan cheese, plus more for garnish
- 1 clove garlic, minced
- ¼ teaspoon salt
- ¼ teaspoon freshly ground pepper

1. Preheat oven to 400°F.

2. Pulse spinach in three batches in a food processor until finely chopped. Transfer to a medium bowl. Add eggs, ricotta (or cottage cheese), ½ cup Parmesan, garlic, salt and pepper; stir to combine.

3. Coat 8 cups of the muffin pan with cooking spray. Divide the spinach mixture among the 8 cups (they will be very full).

4. Bake the spinach cakes until set, about 20 minutes. Let stand in the pan for 5 minutes. Loosen the edges with a knife and turn out onto a clean cutting board or large plate. Serve warm, sprinkled with more Parmesan, if desired.

MAKES 4 SERVINGS, 2 SPINACH CAKES EACH.

PER SERVING: **141 calories**; 8 g fat (4 g sat, 3 g mono); 123 mg cholesterol; 6 g carbohydrate; 13 g protein; 2 g fiber; 456 mg sodium; 560 mg potassium.

NUTRITION BONUS: Vitamin A (170% daily value), Folate (46% dv), Vitamin C (40% dv), Calcium (30% dv), Potassium (16% dv).

PARMESAN SPINACH CAKES

ROASTED ASPARAGUS WITH GARLIC-LEMON SAUCE

ACTIVE TIME: **15 MINUTES** | TOTAL: **25 MINUTES**

- 2 bunches asparagus (about 2 pounds), trimmed
- 2 teaspoons extra-virgin olive oil, divided
- 1/8 teaspoon salt
- 2 tablespoons low-fat mayonnaise
- 2 tablespoons shredded Parmesan cheese
- 2 tablespoons water
- 1 tablespoon lemon juice
- 2 anchovy fillets, minced
- 1 small clove garlic, minced
- 2 chopped hard-boiled eggs (optional; *see Note, page 209*)

1. Preheat oven to 425°F.
2. Toss asparagus with oil and salt in a large bowl. Spread on a baking sheet and roast, stirring once halfway through, until tender, 15 to 20 minutes.
3. Combine mayonnaise, Parmesan, water, lemon juice, anchovies and garlic in a small bowl. Drizzle the asparagus with the sauce and top with hard-boiled egg (if using).

MAKES 4 SERVINGS.

PER SERVING: **89 calories**; 4 g fat (1 g sat, 2 g mono); 4 mg cholesterol; 10 g carbohydrate; 6 g protein; 4 g fiber; 282 mg sodium; 464 mg potassium.
NUTRITION BONUS: Folate (74% daily value), Vitamin A (40% dv), Vitamin C (30% dv).

QUICK PICKLED BEETS

ACTIVE TIME: **10 MINUTES** | TOTAL: **40 MINUTES**
TO MAKE AHEAD: Cover and refrigerate for up to 1 week.

- 1 small red onion, halved and sliced
- 1/2 cup red-wine vinegar

ROASTED ASPARAGUS WITH GARLIC-LEMON SAUCE

QUICK PICKLED BEETS

2 tablespoons sugar
1 cinnamon stick
4 whole peppercorns
2 whole cloves
3 cups steamed sliced beets, 1/2-1 inch thick
  (*see Guide, page 191, and Note, page 209*)

Combine onion, vinegar, sugar, cinnamon stick, peppercorns and cloves in a large saucepan. Bring to a boil over medium-high heat. Cover, reduce heat to medium-low and simmer until the onion is tender-crisp, 4 to 6 minutes. Stir in beets. Transfer to a large bowl and let marinate, stirring occasionally, for 30 minutes.

MAKES 6 SERVINGS, ABOUT 1/2 CUP EACH.
PER SERVING: **44 calories**; 0 g fat (0 g sat, 0 g mono);
0 mg cholesterol; 10 g carbohydrate; 2 g protein; 2 g fiber;
66 mg sodium; 276 mg potassium.
NUTRITION BONUS: Folate (18% daily value).

SICILIAN-STYLE BROCCOLI

H✖W L⬇C H⬆F H♥H

ACTIVE TIME: **20 MINUTES** | TOTAL: **20 MINUTES**
(Photograph: page 19.)

1 bunch broccoli (about 1 1/4 pounds)
2 teaspoons extra-virgin olive oil
2 tablespoons capers, rinsed
1 clove garlic, finely chopped
1/2 cup water
1/4 teaspoon salt
  Freshly ground pepper to taste

1. Cut off and separate broccoli florets. Trim the tough ends of the stalks; peel the stalks, if desired, and cut crosswise into 3/8-inch-thick slices.
2. Heat oil in a large skillet over medium heat. Add capers and garlic and cook, stirring, until the garlic is golden, about 1 minute. Add the broccoli florets and stalks and

water; bring to a simmer. Reduce the heat to medium-low, cover and cook until the broccoli is tender, about 5 minutes. Uncover, increase the heat to high and cook, stirring, until any remaining water evaporates, about 1 minute. Season with salt and pepper.

MAKES 4 SERVINGS.
PER SERVING: **63 calories**; 3 g fat (0 g sat, 2 g mono);
0 mg cholesterol; 8 g carbohydrate; 4 g protein; 4 g fiber;
156 mg sodium; 465 mg potassium.
NUTRITION BONUS: Vitamin C (220% dv), Vitamin A (90% daily value), Folate (25% dv).

SESAME SNAP PEAS WITH CARROTS & PEPPERS

H✖W L⬇C H⬆F H♥H

ACTIVE TIME: **20 MINUTES** | TOTAL: **20 MINUTES**

8 ounces sugar snap peas, trimmed (about 2 cups)
1 small red bell pepper, cut into strips
1 large carrot, peeled and thinly sliced
1 tablespoon reduced-sodium soy sauce
1 tablespoon toasted sesame oil
1 teaspoon sesame seeds
  Freshly ground pepper to taste

Bring an inch of water to a boil in a large saucepan fitted with a steamer basket. Add peas, bell pepper and carrot, cover and steam, stirring once, until crisp-tender, 5 to 7 minutes. Toss with soy sauce, oil, sesame seeds and pepper.

MAKES 4 SERVINGS, 3/4 CUP EACH.
PER SERVING: **78 calories**; 4 g fat (1 g sat, 2 g mono);
0 mg cholesterol; 9 g carbohydrate; 2 g protein; 3 g fiber;
118 mg sodium; 245 mg potassium.
NUTRITION BONUS: Vitamin A (130% daily value), Vitamin C (110% dv).

SOUTHWESTERN CALICO CORN

SOUTHWESTERN CALICO CORN

H W L C H F H H

ACTIVE TIME: 25 MINUTES | TOTAL: 25 MINUTES

- 1 tablespoon canola oil
- 1 poblano pepper, diced
- 1 small red bell pepper, diced
- 2 cups fresh corn kernels (*see Note, page 209*)
- 1 teaspoon chili powder
- 1/2 teaspoon ground cumin
- 1/4 teaspoon salt
- 1 14-ounce can hominy (*see Note, page 208*), rinsed

Heat oil in a large nonstick skillet over medium-high heat. Add poblano, bell pepper and corn; cook, stirring occasionally, until just tender, 3 to 5 minutes. Stir in chili powder, cumin and salt; cook for 30 seconds more. Add hominy and cook, stirring, until heated through, about 2 minutes more.

MAKES 6 SERVINGS, 2/3 CUP EACH.

PER SERVING: **98 calories**; 3 g fat (0 g sat, 2 g mono); 0 mg cholesterol; 16 g carbohydrate; 2 g protein; 3 g fiber; 186 mg sodium; 185 mg potassium.

NUTRITION BONUS: Vitamin C (40% daily value).

SUGAR SNAP PEA & BARLEY SALAD

H W H F H H

ACTIVE TIME: 30 MINUTES | TOTAL: 30 MINUTES
(Photograph: page 174.)

- 2 cups water
- 1 cup quick-cooking barley
- 8 ounces sugar snap peas, trimmed and sliced into matchsticks
- 1/2 cup chopped flat-leaf parsley
- 1/4 cup finely chopped red onion
- 2 tablespoons extra-virgin olive oil
- 2 tablespoons lemon juice
- 3/4 teaspoon salt
- 1/4 teaspoon freshly ground pepper

1. Bring water to a boil in a medium saucepan. Add barley, reduce heat to low and simmer, covered, for 10 to 12 minutes, or according to package directions. Remove from the heat and let stand, covered, for 5 minutes.
2. Rinse the barley under cool water, drain and transfer to a large bowl. Add snap peas, parsley, onion, oil, lemon juice, salt and pepper and toss to combine.

MAKES 6 SERVINGS, ABOUT 2/3 CUP EACH.

PER SERVING: **152 calories**; 5 g fat (1 g sat, 4 g mono);
0 mg cholesterol; 23 g carbohydrate; 4 g protein; 4 g fiber;
301 mg sodium; 108 mg potassium.

NUTRITION BONUS: Vitamin C (25% daily value), Vitamin A
(15% dv).

CAULIFLOWER & COUSCOUS PILAF

ACTIVE TIME: 25 MINUTES | TOTAL: 25 MINUTES

1 tablespoon extra-virgin olive oil
4 cups finely chopped cauliflower florets
  (about 1 medium head)
1/2 teaspoon salt
3/4 cup reduced-sodium chicken broth
1 teaspoon freshly grated orange zest
1/4 cup orange juice
1/4 cup currants
2/3 cup whole-wheat couscous
1/2 cup sliced scallion greens

Heat oil in a large saucepan over medium heat. Add cauliflower and salt; cook, stirring, until softened, about 3 minutes. Add broth, orange zest, juice and currants; bring to a boil over high heat. Stir in couscous and scallions. Remove from the heat and let stand, covered, until the liquid is absorbed, about 5 minutes. Fluff with a fork.

MAKES 6 SERVINGS, GENEROUS 3/4 CUP EACH.

PER SERVING: **162 calories**; 3 g fat (0 g sat, 2 g mono);
0 mg cholesterol; 31 g carbohydrate; 6 g protein; 6 g fiber;
291 mg sodium; 381 mg potassium.

NUTRITION BONUS: Vitamin C (80% daily value), Folate
(15% dv).

WILD RICE WITH SHIITAKES & TOASTED ALMONDS

H✳W   H↑F   H♥H

ACTIVE TIME: 20 MINUTES | TOTAL: 1 HOUR 5 MINUTES

Toasted almonds enhance the nutty flavor of wild rice in this simple yet luxurious side dish. You could give it an Asian twist by substituting sesame oil for the butter and adding a drizzle of soy sauce.

2 1/4 cups reduced-sodium chicken broth *or*
      vegetable broth
2 cups sliced shiitake mushroom caps *or*
      button mushrooms (3 ounces)
1 cup wild rice
6 tablespoons sliced almonds
1 teaspoon butter
1 bunch scallions, trimmed and thinly sliced
      (about 2 cups)
      Freshly ground pepper to taste

1. Bring broth to a boil in a medium saucepan over high heat. Stir in mushrooms and wild rice. Return to a boil. Reduce heat to very low, cover, and simmer until the rice has "blossomed" and is just tender, 45 to 55 minutes. Drain any remaining liquid and transfer the rice to a serving bowl.
2. Meanwhile, toast almonds in a small dry skillet over medium-low heat, stirring constantly, until golden brown and fragrant, 2 to 3 minutes. Transfer to a plate to cool.
3. About 5 minutes before the rice is done, melt butter in a medium nonstick skillet over medium heat. Add scallions and cook, stirring often, until softened and still bright green, 2 to 3 minutes. Stir the scallions and almonds into the rice; season with pepper. Serve warm.

MAKES 6 SERVINGS, 3/4 CUP EACH.

PER SERVING: **158 calories**; 4 g fat (1 g sat, 2 g mono);
2 mg cholesterol; 26 g carbohydrate; 7 g protein; 4 g fiber;
216 mg sodium; 339 mg potassium.

NUTRITION BONUS: Magnesium (18% daily value).

WHOLE-GRAIN RICE PILAF

H✕W L⬇C H♥H

⏱ ACTIVE TIME: 15 MINUTES | TOTAL: 30 MINUTES

2 teaspoons extra-virgin olive oil *or* canola oil
½ cup broken whole-wheat spaghetti pieces
⅓ cup finely diced onion
1 14-ounce can reduced-sodium chicken broth
1 cup instant brown rice
¼ teaspoon salt
1 bay leaf
1 tablespoon chopped fresh parsley

Heat oil in a saucepan over medium-high heat. Add pasta and onion; cook, stirring, until starting to brown, about 3 minutes. Add broth, rice, salt and bay leaf; bring to a boil. Reduce heat to low, cover and cook until the liquid is absorbed and the rice is tender, 10 to 12 minutes. Let stand for 5 minutes. Discard the bay leaf. Fluff with a fork and stir in parsley.

MAKES 6 SERVINGS, ABOUT ⅔ CUP EACH.
PER SERVING: **97 calories**; 2 g fat (0 g sat, 1 g mono); 0 mg cholesterol; 17 g carbohydrate; 3 g protein; 2 g fiber; 253 mg sodium; 88 mg potassium.

GARLIC & HERB PITA CHIPS

H✕W L⬇C H♥H

ACTIVE TIME: 20 minutes | TOTAL: 20 minutes | TO MAKE AHEAD: Store in an airtight container for up to 4 days.

⏱ *You can make your own tasty pita chips in a matter of minutes. Just cut pita bread into wedges (stale pitas work very well), brush them with a little olive oil and bake. You'll save money—and cut calories by 16 percent.*

4 6-inch whole-wheat pitas
2 tablespoons extra-virgin olive oil

1 teaspoon Italian seasoning
½ teaspoon garlic powder
¼ teaspoon salt

1. Position racks in middle and lower third of oven; preheat to 350°F. Coat 2 large baking sheets with nonstick cooking spray.
2. Cut pitas into 8 wedges each and separate each wedge at the fold. Place the pita wedges, rough-side up, in an even layer on the prepared baking sheets. Brush with oil and sprinkle with Italian seasoning, garlic powder and salt.
3. Bake the pita wedges, switching the baking sheets halfway through, until golden and crispy, 6 to 10 minutes (depending on the thickness).

MAKES 8 SERVINGS, 8 CHIPS EACH.
PER SERVING: **117 calories**; 4 g fat (1 g sat, 3 g mono); 0 mg cholesterol; 18 g carbohydrate; 3 g protein; 2 g fiber; 243 mg sodium; 61 mg potassium.

QUINOA WITH LATIN FLAVORS

H✕W H⬆F H♥H

⏱ ACTIVE TIME: 30 MINUTES | TOTAL: 45 MINUTES

1 cup quinoa, rinsed well (*see Note, page 208*)
2 teaspoons canola oil
1 medium onion, chopped
1 4-ounce can chopped green chiles
2 cloves garlic, minced
1 14-ounce can reduced-sodium chicken broth *or* vegetable broth
¼ cup pepitas, toasted (*see Note, page 208*)
¾ cup coarsely chopped fresh cilantro
½ cup chopped scallions
2 tablespoons lime juice
¼ teaspoon salt

QUINOA WITH LATIN FLAVORS

BUTTERNUT & BARLEY PILAF

1. Toast quinoa in a large dry skillet over medium heat, stirring often, until it crackles and becomes aromatic, 3 to 5 minutes. Transfer to a fine sieve and rinse thoroughly.
2. Heat oil in a large saucepan over medium heat. Add onion and cook, stirring often, until softened, 2 to 3 minutes. Add chiles and garlic; cook, stirring, for 30 seconds. Add the quinoa and broth; bring to a simmer. Reduce heat to maintain a gentle simmer, cover and cook until the quinoa is tender and most of the liquid has been absorbed, 20 to 25 minutes.
3. Add pepitas, cilantro, scallions, lime juice and salt to the quinoa; mix gently and fluff with a fork.

MAKES 6 SERVINGS, 2/3 CUP EACH.
PER SERVING: **171 calories**; 6 g fat (1 g sat, 2 g mono); 0 mg cholesterol; 24 g carbohydrate; 7 g protein; 3 g fiber; 331 mg sodium; 363 mg potassium.
NUTRITION BONUS: Magnesium (23% daily value), Vitamin C (20% dv), Folate (15%), Iron (15% dv).

BUTTERNUT & BARLEY PILAF

H✱W H↑F H♥H

ACTIVE TIME: 20 MINUTES | TOTAL: 1 HOUR

- 2 teaspoons extra-virgin olive oil
- 1 medium onion, chopped
- 1 14-ounce can reduced-sodium chicken broth *or* vegetable broth
- 1 3/4 cups water
- 2 cups cubed peeled butternut squash (3/4-inch cubes) (*see Note, page 209*)
- 1 cup pearl barley
- 1/3 cup chopped flat-leaf parsley
- 1 teaspoon freshly grated lemon zest
- 1 tablespoon lemon juice
- 1 clove garlic, minced
- 1/4 teaspoon salt, or to taste
- Freshly ground pepper to taste

Heat oil in a large saucepan over medium heat. Add onion and cook, stirring often, until softened, 2 to 3 minutes. Add broth, water, squash and barley; bring to a simmer, reduce heat to medium-low and simmer until the squash and barley are tender and most of the liquid has been absorbed, about 45 minutes. Add parsley, lemon zest, lemon juice, garlic, salt and pepper; mix gently.

MAKES 6 SERVINGS, ⅔ CUP EACH.
PER SERVING: **176 calories**; 2 g fat (0 g sat, 1 g mono); 0 mg cholesterol; 36 g carbohydrate; 5 g protein; 7 g fiber; 269 mg sodium; 400 mg potassium.
NUTRITION BONUS: Vitamin A (110% daily value), Vitamin C (30% dv).

CHEESY BROCCOLI-POTATO MASH

H✕W L↓C H♥H

⏱ ACTIVE TIME: **30 MINUTES** | TOTAL: **30 MINUTES**

CHEESY BROCCOLI-POTATO MASH

1 pound Yukon Gold potatoes, scrubbed and cut into wedges
¾ pound broccoli crowns, chopped (4 cups)
¾ cup shredded fontina cheese
½ cup nonfat milk, heated
½ teaspoon salt
    Freshly ground pepper to taste

Bring an inch of water to a boil in a large saucepan fitted with a steamer basket. Add potatoes, cover and steam for 10 minutes. Place broccoli on top, cover and steam until the potatoes and broccoli are tender, 6 to 8 minutes more. Transfer the broccoli to a large bowl and coarsely mash with a potato masher. Add the potatoes, cheese, milk, salt and pepper and continue mashing to desired consistency. Serve immediately.

MAKES 6 SERVINGS, ⅔ CUP EACH.
PER SERVING: **135 calories**; 4 g fat (3 g sat, 1 g mono); 16 mg cholesterol; 17 g carbohydrate; 7 g protein; 2 g fiber; 330 mg sodium; 196 mg potassium.
NUTRITION BONUS: Vitamin C (100% daily value), Vitamin A (30% dv).

CRUSHED RED POTATOES WITH BUTTERMILK

H✕W L↓C H♥H

⏱ ACTIVE TIME: **10 MINUTES** | TOTAL: **25 MINUTES**
(Photograph: page 148.)

2 pounds red potatoes (about 6), scrubbed
1 teaspoon salt, plus more to taste
½ cup nonfat buttermilk
2 tablespoons chopped fresh chives
    Freshly ground pepper to taste

Place potatoes in a large saucepan and cover with cold water. Add 1 teaspoon salt and bring to a simmer over medium heat. Cook until tender, 12 to 15 minutes. Drain and transfer to a medium bowl. Coarsely crush the potatoes with a potato masher or the back of a large spoon. Gently stir in buttermilk and chives. Season with salt and pepper.

MAKES 6 SERVINGS.
PER SERVING: **85 calories**; 0 g fat (0 g sat, 0 g mono); 0 mg cholesterol; 19 g carbohydrate; 3 g protein; 2 g fiber; 311 mg sodium; 522 mg potassium.
NUTRITION BONUS: Potassium & Vitamin C (15% daily value).

ZESTY DILL POTATO SALAD

ACTIVE TIME: 15 MINUTES | TOTAL: 35 MINUTES

1   pound medium red potatoes, scrubbed
2   tablespoons balsamic vinegar
1   tablespoon white-wine vinegar
1   tablespoon extra-virgin olive oil
¼   cup diced red bell pepper
¼   cup diced green bell pepper
¼   cup chopped scallions
1   tablespoon chopped fresh dill
½   teaspoon salt
    Freshly ground white *or* black pepper
    to taste

1. Place potatoes in a saucepan and cover with cold water. Bring to a boil and cook until tender, about 20 minutes. Drain. When cool enough to handle, cut in half lengthwise, then into ½-inch slices. Place in a serving bowl.
2. Sprinkle the potatoes with balsamic vinegar, white-wine vinegar and oil, tossing gently to coat. Add red and green bell peppers, scallions, dill, salt and pepper; toss gently to mix. Serve at room temperature.

MAKES 4 SERVINGS.

PER SERVING: **123 calories**; 4 g fat (1 g sat, 3 g mono); 0 mg cholesterol; 21 g carbohydrate; 2 g protein; 2 g fiber; 302 mg sodium; 576 mg potassium.
NUTRITION BONUS: Vitamin C (50% daily value), Potassium (16% dv).

MAPLE-ROASTED SWEET POTATOES

ACTIVE TIME: 10 MINUTES | TOTAL: 1 HOUR 10 MINUTES | TO MAKE AHEAD: Cover and refrigerate for up to 1 day. Just before serving, reheat at 350°F until hot, about 15 minutes.

2½   pounds sweet potatoes, peeled and cut into
     1½-inch pieces (about 8 cups)
⅓   cup pure maple syrup
2   tablespoons butter, melted
1   tablespoon lemon juice
½   teaspoon salt
     Freshly ground pepper to taste

1. Preheat oven to 400°F.
2. Arrange sweet potatoes in an even layer in a 9-by-13-inch glass baking dish. Combine maple syrup, butter, lemon juice, salt and pepper in small bowl. Pour the mixture over the sweet potatoes; toss to coat. Cover with foil.
3. Bake the sweet potatoes for 15 minutes. Remove the foil. Stir and continue baking, stirring every 15 minutes, until tender and starting to brown, 45 to 50 minutes more.

MAKES 12 SERVINGS, ABOUT ½ CUP EACH.
PER SERVING: **96 calories**; 2 g fat (1 g sat, 0 g mono); 5 mg cholesterol; 19 g carbohydrate; 1 g protein; 2 g fiber; 118 mg sodium; 189 mg potassium.
NUTRITION BONUS: Vitamin A (89% daily value), Vitamin C (23% dv).

GRAIN-COOKING GUIDE

Start with **1 cup uncooked grain**; serving size is ½ cup cooked. See the chart below for prep instructions and timing.

	LIQUID (WATER/BROTH)	YIELD	DIRECTIONS	ANALYSIS PER SERVING
BARLEY Quick-cooking	2 cups	2 cups	Bring liquid to a boil; add barley. Reduce heat to low and simmer, covered, 10-12 minutes.	129 calories; 28 g carbohydrate; 4 g fiber
Pearl	2½ cups	3-3½ cups	Bring barley and liquid to a boil. Reduce heat to low and simmer, covered, 35-50 minutes.	97 calories; 22 g carbohydrate; 3 g fiber
BULGUR (see Note, page 208)	1½ cups	2½-3 cups	Bring bulgur and liquid to a boil. Reduce heat to low; simmer, covered, until tender and most of the liquid has been absorbed, 10-15 minutes.	76 calories; 17 g carbohydrate; 4 g fiber
COUSCOUS Whole-wheat	1¾ cups	3-3½ cups	Bring liquid to a boil; stir in couscous. Remove from heat and let stand, covered, 5 minutes. Fluff with a fork.	70 calories; 15 g carbohydrate; 2 g fiber
POLENTA (cornmeal)	4⅓ cups	4-4⅓ cups	Bring cold water and 1 teaspoon salt to a boil. Slowly whisk in cornmeal until smooth. Reduce heat to low, cover and cook, stirring occasionally, until very thick and creamy, 10 to 15 minutes.	55 calories; 12 g carbohydrate; 1 g fiber
QUINOA (see Note, page 208)	2 cups	3 cups	Rinse in several changes of cold water. Bring quinoa and liquid to a boil. Reduce heat to low and simmer, covered, until tender and most of the liquid has been absorbed, 15-20 minutes. Fluff with a fork.	111 calories; 20 g carbohydrate; 3 g fiber
RICE Brown	2½ cups	3 cups	Bring rice and liquid to a boil. Reduce heat to low and simmer, covered, until tender and most of the liquid has been absorbed, 40-50 minutes. Let stand 5 minutes, then fluff with a fork.	109 calories; 23 g carbohydrate; 2 g fiber
Wild	At least 4 cups	2-2½ cups	Cook rice in a large saucepan of lightly salted boiling water until tender, 45-55 minutes. Drain.	83 calories; 18 g carbohydrate; 1 g fiber

IN A HURRY? Make instant brown rice or quick-cooking wild rice, ready in under 10 minutes (follow package directions).

VEGETABLE-STEAMING GUIDE

TO STEAM VEGETABLES:

Bring an inch of water to a steady boil in a large saucepan over high heat. Prepare the vegetable of your choice and place in a steamer basket in the saucepan. Cover and steam until just tender. See the chart below for prep instructions and timing.

	AMOUNT FOR 4 SERVINGS	STEAMING TIME	ANALYSIS PER SERVING
ASPARAGUS	1½ pounds (1-2 bunches), trimmed	4 minutes	37 calories; 7 g carbohydrate; 3 g fiber
BEETS	1½ pounds, greens removed, ends trimmed, peeled, cut into 1-inch pieces or wedges	10 to 15 minutes	75 calories; 17 g carbohydrate; 3 g fiber
BROCCOLI	1 pound (about 1 head), cut into 1-inch florets	5 to 6 minutes	32 calories; 6 g carbohydrate; 3 g fiber
BRUSSELS SPROUTS	1 pound, stems trimmed	6 to 8 minutes	41 calories; 8 g carbohydrate; 3 g fiber
CARROTS	1½ pounds, cut into ⅛-inch-thick rounds	4 minutes	60 calories; 14 g carbohydrate; 5 g fiber
CAULIFLOWER	1½-2 pounds (1 head), cut into 1-inch florets	5 minutes	39 calories; 7 g carbohydrate; 4 g fiber
GREEN BEANS	1 pound, trimmed	5 minutes	40 calories; 9 g carbohydrate; 4 g fiber
RED POTATOES, BABY	1½ pounds, scrubbed	10 to 15 minutes	140 calories; 30 g carbohydrate; 2 g fiber
SNAP PEAS	1 pound, trimmed	4 to 5 minutes	53 calories; 9 g carbohydrate; 3 g fiber
SUMMER SQUASH	1½ pounds, cut into ¼-inch-thick rounds	4 to 5 minutes	27 calories; 6 g carbohydrate; 2 g fiber

VEGETABLE-ROASTING GUIDE

TO ROAST VEGETABLES:
Preheat oven to 450°F. Prepare the vegetable of your choice (see the chart below for prep instructions). Toss with 4 teaspoons extra-virgin olive oil (or canola oil), ½ teaspoon salt and ¼ teaspoon pepper. Follow roasting times below.

	AMOUNT FOR 4 SERVINGS	ROASTING TIME	ANALYSIS PER SERVING
ASPARAGUS	1½ pounds (1-2 bunches), trimmed	10 to 15 minutes	77 calories; 7 g carbohydrate; 3 g fiber
BEETS	1½ pounds, greens removed, ends trimmed, peeled, cut into 1-inch pieces or wedges	20 to 25 minutes	116 calories; 16 g carbohydrate; 5 g fiber
BROCCOLI	1 pound (about 1 head), florets cut into 1-inch pieces	15 to 20 minutes	74 calories; 6 g carbohydrate; 3 g fiber
BRUSSELS SPROUTS	1 pound, stems trimmed, large quartered, small halved	15 to 20 minutes	91 calories; 10 g carbohydrate; 4 g fiber
BUTTERNUT SQUASH	2 pounds, peeled, seeded, cut into 1-inch pieces	25 to 35 minutes	120 calories; 20 g carbohydrate; 6 g fiber
CARROTS	1½ pounds, peeled, cut into ¼-inch slices	20 to 25 minutes	105 calories; 15 g carbohydrate; 4 g fiber
CAULIFLOWER	1½ -2 pounds (1 head), cut into 1-inch florets	5 to 20 minutes	71 calories; 6 g carbohydrate; 3 g fiber
GREEN BEANS	1 pound, trimmed	15 to 20 minutes	78 calories; 8 g carbohydrate; 4 g fiber
RED POTATOES	1½ pounds, scrubbed, cut into 1-inch pieces or wedges	25 to 35 minutes	194 calories; 33 g carbohydrate; 3 g fiber
SWEET POTATOES	1½ pounds, scrubbed, cut into 1-inch pieces or wedges	20 to 25 minutes	196 calories; 35 g carbohydrate; 6 g fiber

DESSERTS

You see it trumpeted on bumper stickers and on T-shirts: "Life is uncertain, so eat dessert first." People love this saying because, well, who doesn't love dessert? We don't really recommend eating dessert *first*, but we're all for having dessert—especially when you're dieting. Treating yourself to something sweet keeps you from feeling deprived, which is essential for sticking with your healthy-eating habits long-term.

Of course, if you're trying to lose weight, you'll have to "budget" in calories for dessert and that takes planning. First you should decide what you really want—and be honest. If chocolate is your thing, you're not going to feel satisfied with a baked apple. Go for the chocolate—we have plenty of recipes in this chapter for you! Now, the very important point: budget the calories into your day. If you're trying to lose weight you can have a rich dessert but not on top of a big decadent meal. Lucky for you, our 500-calorie menus eliminate the need for calculations. And you'll find plenty of options for 100 calories or less—from fruit pops to a quick tiramisù—so you don't have to stick with just a salad to enjoy dessert with dinner.

There's room for something sweet in a 500-calorie menu. Try this Hot Fudge Pudding Cake (*page 196*), 142 calories.

PER SERVING: **142 calories**; 4 g fat (2 g sat, 1 g mono); 23 mg cholesterol; 25 g carbohydrate; 3 g protein; 2 g fiber; 204 mg sodium; 85 mg potassium.

H✖W   H♥H

HOT FUDGE PUDDING CAKE

ACTIVE TIME: **20 MINUTES** | TOTAL: **1 HOUR**

Serve this dense, fudgy pudding cake with vanilla frozen yogurt. Use coffee instead of hot water if you want a richer-tasting cake with a hint of coffee flavor. (Photograph: page 194.)

1	cup whole-wheat pastry flour (*see Note, page 208*)
⅓	cup sugar
¼	cup plus 2 tablespoons unsweetened cocoa powder, divided
2	teaspoons baking powder
½	teaspoon salt
½	cup nonfat milk
1	large egg, lightly beaten
2	tablespoons butter, melted
1	teaspoon vanilla extract
¼	cup pecan halves, toasted (*see Note, page 208*)
¾	cup brown sugar
1 ½	cups hot water *or* brewed coffee

1. Preheat oven to 375°F. Lightly coat an 8-inch-square baking dish with cooking spray.

2. Whisk flour, sugar, ¼ cup cocoa, baking powder and salt in a large bowl. Combine milk, egg, butter and vanilla in a glass measuring cup or bowl. Make a well in the center of the dry ingredients and gradually pour in the milk mixture, stirring until combined. Stir in pecans. Spread evenly in the prepared pan.

3. Combine brown sugar with the remaining 2 tablespoons cocoa in a small bowl; sprinkle evenly over the batter. Pour hot water (or coffee) over the top.

4. Bake until a toothpick inserted in the center comes out clean, about 25 minutes. Let stand for 10 minutes; serve hot or warm.

MAKES 12 SERVINGS.

CHEWY CHOCOLATE COOKIES

ACTIVE TIME: **20 MINUTES** | TOTAL: **1 ½ HOURS**

PER COOKIE: **68 calories**; 1 g fat (1 g sat, 0 g mono); 0 mg cholesterol; 14 g carbohydrate; 1 g protein; 1 g fiber; 51 mg sodium; 54 mg potassium.

We can't resist big, soft, fudgy cookies, like those found in glass jars on bake-shop counters. These freeze exceptionally well—layer them in a freezer-safe container between sheets of wax paper; thaw for 15 minutes at room temperature before serving.

- ¾ cup all-purpose flour
- ¾ cup whole-wheat pastry flour
- 3 tablespoons unsweetened cocoa powder
- ½ teaspoon baking soda
- ½ teaspoon salt
- 6 large egg whites
- ¾ cup granulated sugar
- 1 ½ cups packed dark brown sugar
- 1 tablespoon vanilla extract
- 3 ounces unsweetened chocolate, chopped and melted (*see Note, page 208*)

1. Position rack in center of oven; preheat to 350°F. Line a large baking sheet with parchment paper or a silicone baking mat.

2. Whisk all-purpose flour, whole-wheat flour, cocoa, baking soda and salt in a medium bowl. Beat egg whites in a large bowl with an electric mixer until foamy, about 1 minute. Beat in granulated sugar in a slow, steady stream. Scrape down the sides, then beat in brown sugar 1 tablespoon at a time. Beat until smooth, about 3 minutes. Beat in vanilla and melted chocolate. Stir in the dry ingredients with a wooden spoon until just incorporated.

3. Drop the batter by tablespoonfuls onto the prepared baking sheet, 1½ inches apart.

4. Bake the cookies until flat yet springy, with slightly cracked tops, 10 to 12 minutes. Cool on the pan for 5 minutes, then transfer to a wire rack to cool completely. Let the pan cool for a few minutes before baking another batch; replace parchment paper if torn or scorched.

MAKES ABOUT 45 COOKIES.

DIET TIP

Try not to drink your fruits too often—their calories will go down with you hardly noticing. Enjoy the whole fruit instead—it's more satisfying.

ORANGE CRISPS WITH CITRUS FRUIT SALAD

ACTIVE TIME: **20 MINUTES** | TOTAL: **1 HOUR** | TO MAKE AHEAD: Store cookies in an airtight container, with parchment or wax paper between layers, for up to 2 days.

These ultra-thin, crisp cookies are a snap to make and have a fortune cookie-inspired flavor. Serve alongside purchased fruit salad to increase your fruit servings for the day while still satisfying your sweet tooth. Look for already-prepared citrus fruit salad in jars in the refrigerated produce section in the supermarket. Or make your own with a mixture of orange and grapefruit segments (see Note, page 208).

½ cup white whole-wheat flour *or* whole-wheat pastry flour (*see Notes, page 208*)

⅓ cup sugar

¼ cup unsalted butter, melted

½ teaspoon freshly grated orange zest

2 tablespoons orange juice

2 teaspoons vanilla extract

4 cups prepared citrus fruit salad

1. Position racks in upper and lower thirds of oven; preheat to 300°F. Coat 2 large baking sheets with cooking spray.

2. Mix flour, sugar, butter, orange zest, orange juice and vanilla in a medium bowl until smooth. Spread 1 tablespoon of batter into a 2½-inch circle on the prepared baking sheet. Repeat with the remaining batter, making 6 cookies per baking sheet, spacing them about 4 inches apart.

3. Bake the cookies until lightly browned around the edges, switching the pans back to front and top to bottom once halfway through, 16 to 18 minutes. Immediately and carefully transfer the cookies from the pan to a wire rack using a thin metal spatula. Let cool completely.

4. For dessert for 4, serve 1 cup citrus fruit salad with 1 cookie each.

MAKES 1 DOZEN COOKIES.

PAPAYA-LIME SORBET

ACTIVE TIME: 30 MINUTES | TOTAL: 40 MINUTES (plus overnight freezing time) | TO MAKE AHEAD: The sorbet will keep in the freezer, without freezing solid, for up to 3 hours. (*Alternatively, prepare through Step 3, transfer to a shallow pan, cover and freeze for up to 1 month. Before serving, let defrost for 30 minutes, break into small chunks and process in small batches in a food processor until smooth and scoopable.*)

In Mexico, papayas are served with a wedge of lime and a pinch of salt. This sorbet honors the sweet-tart combination and transforms it into an elegant dessert. It's like a tropical vacation in your mouth. (Photograph: page 79.)

- 8 cups peeled, seeded and diced ripe papaya (about 1 very large *or* 8 small; *see Note, page 208*)
- ½ cup water
- ½ cup sugar
- ¼ cup "lite" coconut milk, divided
- 2 tablespoons lime juice, divided
- 1 teaspoon lime zest, divided
- 2 pinches of salt

1. Line a large baking sheet with parchment or wax paper. Arrange diced papaya in a single layer and freeze overnight.

2. Combine water and sugar in a small saucepan. Bring to a boil over high heat, stirring constantly, until the sugar is completely dissolved and syrupy, 3 to 5 minutes. Pour the syrup into a glass measuring cup and let cool for 15 minutes. Remove the papaya from the freezer to thaw slightly while the syrup is cooling.

3. Transfer half the frozen papaya to a food processor. Add half the syrup, 2 tablespoons coconut milk, 1 tablespoon lime juice, ½ teaspoon lime zest and a pinch of salt. Pulse two or three times, then process until smooth, stopping to scrape down the sides and stir as necessary. Transfer the sorbet to a large serving bowl. Repeat with the remaining ingredients; add to the serving bowl. Serve immediately or freeze until ready to use.

MAKES 8 SERVINGS, ¾ CUP EACH.

PER SERVING: **110 calories**; 1 g fat (0 g sat, 0 g mono); 0 mg cholesterol; 27 g carbohydrate; 1 g protein; 3 g fiber; 43 mg sodium; 365 mg potassium.
NUTRITION BONUS: Vitamin C (150% daily value), Vitamin A (30% dv).

H✼W H♥H

CHOCOLATE-DIPPED GINGERSNAPS

H♥H

ACTIVE TIME: 15 MINUTES | TOTAL: 45 MINUTES
TO MAKE AHEAD: Refrigerate in an airtight container for up to 5 days.

A sprinkling of crystallized ginger and dried cranberries makes these easy, chocolate-dipped gingersnaps festive. (Photograph: page 17.)

- 8 small gingersnaps
- 1/3 cup bittersweet chocolate chips, melted (*see Note, page 208*)
- 1 tablespoon finely chopped crystallized ginger
- 1 tablespoon finely chopped dried cranberries

Dip gingersnaps into melted chocolate. Let the excess drip off. Place on a wax paper-lined plate. Sprinkle with crystallized ginger and cranberries. Refrigerate until the chocolate is set, about 30 minutes.

MAKES 4 SERVINGS, 2 COOKIES EACH.
PER SERVING: **157 calories**; 6 g fat (3 g sat, 1 g mono); 0 mg cholesterol; 28 g carbohydrate; 2 g protein; 1 g fiber; 97 mg sodium; 96 mg potassium.

BABY TIRAMISÙ

H✂W L↓C H♥H

ACTIVE TIME: 15 MINUTES | TOTAL: 45 MINUTES
TO MAKE AHEAD: Cover and refrigerate for up to 1 day.

If you're a fan of the classic Italian dessert Tiramisù, try this quick, lower-calorie variation the next time you need a dessert in a hurry. Both types of ladyfingers—spongy and crunchy—work well.

- 1/2 cup nonfat ricotta cheese (4 ounces)
- 2 tablespoons confectioners' sugar
- 1/2 teaspoon vanilla extract
- 1/8 teaspoon ground cinnamon
- 12 ladyfingers (about 1 3/4 ounces)
- 4 tablespoons brewed espresso *or* strong coffee, divided
- 2 tablespoons bittersweet chocolate chips, melted (*see Note, page 208*)

1. Combine ricotta, sugar, vanilla and cinnamon in a medium bowl.
2. Place 6 ladyfingers in a 9-by-5-inch (or similar size) loaf pan. Drizzle with 2 tablespoons espresso (or coffee). Spread the ricotta mixture over the ladyfingers. Place another layer of ladyfingers over the ricotta and drizzle with the remaining 2 tablespoons espresso (or coffee). Drizzle with melted chocolate. Refrigerate until the chocolate is set, about 30 minutes.

MAKES 6 SERVINGS.
PER SERVING: **107 calories**; 2 g fat (1 g sat, 0 g mono); 3 mg cholesterol; 18 g carbohydrate; 3 g protein; 0 g fiber; 125 mg sodium; 29 mg potassium.

BABY TIRAMISÙ

PINEAPPLE-RASPBERRY PARFAITS

PINEAPPLE-RASPBERRY PARFAITS

H♓W H♥H

ACTIVE TIME: 5 MINUTES | TOTAL: 5 MINUTES

You won't mind serving dessert on a busy weeknight after assembling these quick parfaits.

- **2** 8-ounce containers (2 cups) nonfat peach yogurt
- **1/2** pint fresh raspberries (about 1 1/4 cups)
- **1 1/2** cups fresh, frozen *or* canned pineapple chunks

Layer yogurt, raspberries and pineapple into 4 glasses.

MAKES 4 PARFAITS.

PER SERVING: **112 calories**; 0 g fat (0 g sat, 0 g mono); 3 mg cholesterol; 24 g carbohydrate; 5 g protein; 3 g fiber; 58 mg sodium; 114 mg potassium.

NUTRITION BONUS: Vitamin C (73% daily value).

RASPBERRY APPLESAUCE

H♓W L↓C H♥H

ACTIVE TIME: 10 MINUTES | TOTAL: 10 MINUTES

Simplicity itself, applesauce from a jar becomes quite special when warmed and laced with raspberries.

- **1** cup prepared "chunky" applesauce
- **2/3** cup frozen unsweetened raspberries (*not* thawed)

Stir applesauce and raspberries in a small microwaveable bowl. Cover with plastic wrap and microwave on High until heated through, about 1½ minutes. Stir gently to avoid breaking down the raspberries. (*Alternatively, warm applesauce in a small saucepan over medium heat. Remove from the heat and stir in raspberries; let stand until they are thawed.*)

MAKES 2 SERVINGS, 3/4 CUP EACH.

PER SERVING: **67 calories**; 0 g fat (0 g sat, 0 g mono); 0 mg cholesterol; 18 g carbohydrate; 0 g protein; 3 g fiber; 2 mg sodium; 133 mg potassium.

NUTRITION BONUS: Vitamin C (50% daily value).

FAST STRAWBERRY FROZEN YOGURT

H♓W H♥H

ACTIVE TIME: 10 MINUTES | TOTAL: 10 MINUTES

Even without an ice cream maker, you can still enjoy homemade frozen yogurt. (Photograph: page 99.)

- **1** 16-ounce package frozen strawberries (about 3 1/2 cups)
- **1/2** cup sugar, preferably superfine
- **1/2** cup nonfat plain yogurt *or* buttermilk

1 tablespoon lemon juice
1 cup diced frozen *or* fresh strawberries for garnish

Combine strawberries and sugar in a food processor and pulse until coarsely chopped. Combine yogurt (or buttermilk) and lemon juice in a measuring cup; with the machine on, gradually pour the mixture through the feed tube. Process until smooth and creamy, scraping down the sides once or twice. Serve garnished with diced strawberries, if desired.

MAKES 6 SERVINGS, ABOUT ½ CUP EACH.
PER SERVING: **100 calories**; 0 g fat (0 g sat, 0 g mono); 0 mg cholesterol; 26 g carbohydrate; 1 g protein; 2 g fiber; 13 mg sodium; 115 mg potassium.
NUTRITION BONUS: Vitamin C (56% daily value).

CHUNKY PEACH POPSICLES

H✕W L↓C H♥H

ACTIVE TIME: **15 MINUTES** | TOTAL. 2¼ HOURS (including freezing time) TO MAKE AHEAD: Store in the freezer for up to 3 weeks. | EQUIPMENT: Twelve 2-ounce freezer-pop molds or small paper cups and frozen-treat sticks

Make sure to reserve a portion of the peaches as you puree the mixture so the pops will be packed with icy cold, chunky bits of fruit. For a grown-up twist, try adding 1 to 2 teaspoons finely chopped fresh mint, lemon verbena or basil.

1¼ pounds ripe peaches (3-4 medium), halved and pitted
     Juice of 1 lemon
¼ cup freshly squeezed orange juice
¼ cup sugar, or to taste
¼ teaspoon vanilla extract

1. Coarsely chop peaches in a food processor. Transfer 1 cup of the chunky peaches to a medium bowl. Add lemon juice,

orange juice and sugar to taste (depending on the sweetness of the peaches) to the food processor. Puree until smooth. Add to the bowl with the chunky peaches and stir in vanilla.
2. Divide the mixture among freezer-pop molds (or small paper cups). Freeze until beginning to set, about 1 hour. Insert frozen-treat sticks and freeze until completely firm, about 1 hour more.

MAKES 12 POPSICLES, 2 OUNCES EACH.
PER SERVING: **33 calories**; 0 g fat (0 g sat, 0 g mono); 0 mg cholesterol; 9 g carbohydrate; 0 g protein; 1 g fiber; 0 mg sodium; 90 mg potassium.

BANANA PUDDING POPS

H✕W L↓C H♥H

ACTIVE TIME: **20 MINUTES** | TOTAL: 6 HOURS 20 MINUTES (including freezing time) | TO MAKE AHEAD: Store in the freezer for up to 3 weeks. | EQUIPMENT: Ten 3-ounce (or similar-size) freezer-pop molds

These banana popsicles taste rich and decadent but are low-fat and really easy to make. We especially like them with some chocolate chips added. Cool the mixture to room temperature and divide ⅔ cup mini chips among the molds before freezing.

⅓-½ cup light brown sugar
2 tablespoons cornstarch
     Pinch of salt
2 cups low-fat milk
2 teaspoons vanilla extract
2 cups diced bananas (about 2 large)

1. Whisk sugar to taste, cornstarch and salt in a large saucepan. Add milk and whisk until combined. Bring to a boil over medium heat, whisking occasionally. Boil, whisking constantly, for 1 minute. Remove from the heat and stir in vanilla.
2. Put about half the pudding in a food processor or blender and add bananas. Process until smooth (use caution

INDOOR S'MORES

¼ cup sugar
¼ cup Calvados *or* other apple brandy
2 tablespoons lemon juice

Put a shallow metal pan in the freezer to chill. Combine cider, sugar, apple brandy and lemon juice in a bowl. Stir until the sugar dissolves. Pour the mixture into the chilled pan and place in the freezer. Every 30 minutes, stir with a fork, crushing any lumps, until the granita is firm but not frozen solid, about 3 hours.

MAKES 8 SERVINGS, 1 CUP EACH.
PER SERVING: **103 calories**; 0 g fat (0 g sat, 0 g mono); 0 mg cholesterol; 22 g carbohydrate; 0 g protein; 0 g fiber; 0 mg sodium; 5 mg potassium.

when pureeing hot liquids). Stir the mixture back into the remaining pudding.
3. Divide the mixture among freezer-pop molds. Insert the sticks and freeze until completely firm, about 6 hours. Dip the molds briefly in hot water before unmolding.

MAKES ABOUT 10 (3-OUNCE) FREEZER POPS.
PER SERVING: **82 calories**; 1 g fat (0 g sat, 0 g mono); 3 mg cholesterol; 18 g carbohydrate; 2 g protein; 1 g fiber; 41 mg sodium; 112 mg potassium.

APPLE CIDER GRANITA

H✖W H♥H

ACTIVE TIME: 30 MINUTES | TOTAL: 3 HOURS
TO MAKE AHEAD: Transfer to a covered container and store in the freezer for up to 2 days. Stir before serving.

Fresh apple cider and apple brandy make a simple granita that's the perfect ending to a fall meal.

4 cups fresh apple cider

INDOOR S'MORES

H✖W L⬇C H♥H

ACTIVE TIME: 5 MINUTES | TOTAL: 5 MINUTES

You don't have to sit around a fire to enjoy S'mores. Just be sure to watch them carefully under the broiler.

2 whole graham crackers, broken in half
4 marshmallows
2 tablespoons bittersweet chocolate chips, melted (*see Note, page 208*)

1. Position rack in upper third of oven; preheat broiler.
2. Place graham cracker halves on a baking sheet; top each with 1 marshmallow. Broil, with the oven door ajar and watching carefully, until the marshmallows are golden brown, 45 to 75 seconds. Drizzle each S'more with a little melted chocolate.

MAKES 4 SERVINGS.
PER SERVING: **98 calories**; 3 g fat (1 g sat, 0 g mono); 0 mg cholesterol; 18 g carbohydrate; 1 g protein; 0 g fiber; 70 mg sodium; 33 mg potassium.

RESOURCES

When it comes to sticking with any healthy eating plan half the battle is making sure it's easy. Running around to three different stores for random ingredients an hour before dinner: *not easy*. So if you're going to cook at home, be prepared. Keep a well-stocked pantry so that you have most of the ingredients for a healthy dinner ready to go when you are. On the following pages you'll find a list of our favorite ingredients to keep on hand and where to look for them. You'll also find instructions for helpful techniques, such as how to skin a salmon fillet and how to make fresh breadcrumbs. Another way to save yourself time and effort is to make sure you have the tools you need—pans, knives, cutting boards, etc.—to get the job done. It's a whole lot speedier to dice up an onion (and not spend a half hour crying) when you have a sharp knife and good cutting board.

Here's what else you'll find in this section of the book: a handy calorie counter (*page 212*), information on how we prepare the nutritional analyses for our recipes (*page 211*) and of course the indexes to all the information and recipes in this book (*page 214*). Get cooking!

Cooking healthy dinners at home is easier when you have a well-stocked pantry. Canned beans, canned tuna, brown rice, whole-grain pasta, olive oil, lemons, nonfat milk and frozen vegetables (*left*) are just a few of the items that belong in the healthy pantry. For more, see page 206.

THE HEALTHY PANTRY

While a good shopping list is the key to a quick and painless trip to the supermarket, a well-stocked pantry is the best way to ensure you'll have everything you need to cook once you get home. Our Healthy Pantry includes many of the items you need to prepare the recipes in this book plus a few other ingredients that will make impromptu meals easier.

OILS, VINEGARS & CONDIMENTS

Oils: extra-virgin olive, canola

Vinegars: balsamic, red-wine, white-wine, rice, cider

Asian condiments: reduced-sodium soy sauce, fish sauce, hoisin sauce, oyster sauce, chile-garlic sauce, toasted sesame oil

Barbecue sauce

Hot sauce

Worcestershire sauce

Mustard: Dijon, whole-grain

Ketchup

Mayonnaise, low-fat

FLAVORINGS

Salt: kosher, iodized table

Black peppercorns

Herbs and spices, assorted dried

Onions

Garlic, fresh

Ginger, fresh

Olives: Kalamata, green

Capers

Anchovies or anchovy paste

Lemons, limes, oranges

DRY GOODS

Pasta, whole-wheat (assorted shapes)

Barley: pearl, quick-cooking

Bulgur

Couscous, whole-wheat

Quinoa

Rice: brown, instant brown, wild

Dried lentils

Flour: whole-wheat, whole-wheat pastry (store opened packages in the refrigerator or freezer), all-purpose

Rolled oats

Cornmeal

Breadcrumbs: plain dry, coarse whole-wheat

Crackers, whole-grain

Buttermilk powder

Unsweetened cocoa powder

Bittersweet chocolate

Sweeteners: granulated sugar, brown sugar, honey, pure maple syrup

CANNED & BOTTLED GOODS

Broth: reduced-sodium beef, chicken and/or vegetable (or go to *eatingwell.com* for broth recipes)

Clam juice

"Lite" coconut milk

Tomatoes, tomato paste

Beans: black, cannellini, kidney, pinto, great northern, chickpeas, lentils

Chunk light tuna

Wild Pacific salmon

Wine: red, white or nonalcoholic

Madeira

Sherry: cream, dry

NUTS, SEEDS & FRUITS

(Store opened packages of nuts and seeds in the refrigerator or freezer.)

Nuts: walnuts, pecans, almonds, hazelnuts, peanuts, pine nuts

Natural peanut butter

Seeds: pepitas, sesame seeds

Tahini (sesame paste)

Dried fruits: apricots, prunes, cherries, cranberries, dates, figs, raisins

REFRIGERATOR ITEMS

Milk, low-fat or nonfat

Yogurt, plain and/or vanilla, low-fat or nonfat

Sour cream, reduced-fat or nonfat

Parmesan cheese, good-quality

Cheddar cheese, sharp

Eggs (large) or egg substitute, such as Egg Beaters

Orange juice

Tofu, water-packed

Tortillas: corn, whole-wheat

FREEZER BASICS

Fruit: berries, other fruit

Vegetables: peas, spinach, broccoli, corn

Ice cream or frozen yogurt, low-fat or nonfat

CONDIMENTS & FLAVORINGS

Black bean-garlic sauce, a savory, salty sauce used in Chinese cooking, is made from fermented black soybeans, garlic and rice wine. Look for it in the Asian-food section of your supermarket and in Asian markets. It will keep in the refrigerator for up to 1 year. Use it in stir-fries and marinades for beef, chicken or tofu.

Chile-garlic sauce (also labeled chili-garlic sauce, or paste) is a blend of ground chiles, garlic and vinegar. Look for it in the Asian-food section of your supermarket and in Asian markets. It will keep in the refrigerator for up to 1 year.

Chipotle chile peppers in adobo sauce are smoked jalapeños packed in a spicy sauce. Look for the small cans with the Mexican foods in large supermarkets. Once opened, they'll keep for at least 2 weeks in the refrigerator or 6 months in the freezer. **Ground chipotle pepper**, made from dried smoked jalapeños, can be found in the specialty-spice section of most supermarkets or online at *penzeys.com*.

Often a blend of cinnamon, cloves, fennel seed, star anise and Szechuan peppercorns, **five-spice powder** was originally considered a cure-all miracle blend encompassing the five elements (sour, bitter, sweet, pungent, salty). Look for it in the supermarket spice section.

To roast garlic, rub off the excess papery skin without separating the cloves. Slice the tips off the head (or heads), exposing the ends of the cloves. Place the garlic on a piece of foil, drizzle with 1 tablespoon oil and wrap into a package. Put in a baking dish and bake at 350°F until the garlic is very soft, 40 minutes to 1 hour. Unwrap and let cool slightly.

Herbes de Provence can be found in the specialty spice section. Or mix your own with equal amounts of dried thyme, sage, rosemary, marjoram, savory and fennel seed.

Hoisin sauce is a dark brown, thick, spicy-sweet sauce made from soybeans, chiles, garlic and spices. Look for it in the Asian-food section of your supermarket and in Asian markets. It will keep in the refrigerator for up to 1 year.

Miso is fermented bean paste made from barley, rice or soybeans and is used in Japanese cooking to add flavor to dishes, such as soups, sauces and salad dressings. A little goes a long way because of its concentrated, salty taste. Miso is available in different colors, depending on the type of grain or bean and how long it's been fermented. In general, the lighter the color, the more mild the flavor. Find it near tofu at your supermarket. It will keep in the refrigerator for at least 1 year.

Smoked paprika is a spice made from grinding smoke-dried red peppers. It's available in sweet, bittersweet and hot. Find it in the spice section of large supermarkets or at *tienda.com*.

Piment d'Espelette is a sweet, mildly spicy chile pepper from the Basque region of France, ground into a powder. Find it with other specialty spices or online at *spanishtable.com*.

The dried stigma from *Crocus sativus*, **saffron** adds flavor and golden color to a variety of Middle Eastern, African and European foods. Find it in the spice section of supermarkets, gourmet shops and at *tienda.com*. It will keep in an airtight container for several years.

Szechuan sauce is a hot and spicy Chinese sauce made from a blend of tamari, ginger, plum, sesame and chiles. Look for it in the Asian-food section of your supermarket and in Asian markets. It will keep in the refrigerator for up to 1 year.

DRY GOODS
See also Grain-Cooking Guide, page 190.

To **make fresh breadcrumbs,** trim crusts from whole-wheat bread. Tear bread into pieces and process in a food processor until coarse crumbs form. One slice of bread makes about 1/2 cup fresh crumbs. For **dry breadcrumbs**, spread the fresh crumbs on a baking sheet and bake at 250°F until crispy, about 15 minutes. One slice of fresh bread makes about 1/3 cup dry crumbs. Or use prepared coarse dry breadcrumbs. We like Ian's brand labeled "Panko breadcrumbs." Find them in the natural-foods section of large supermarkets.

Bulgur is made by parboiling, drying and coarsely grinding or cracking wheat berries. Don't confuse bulgur with cracked wheat, which is simply that—cracked wheat. Since the parboiling step is skipped, cracked wheat must be cooked for up to an hour whereas bulgur simply needs a quick soak in hot water for most uses. Look for it in the natural-foods section of large supermarkets, near other grains.

Quinoa is a delicately flavored, protein-rich grain. Toasting the grain before cooking enhances the flavor, and rinsing removes any residue of saponin, quinoa's natural, bitter protective coating. Find it in natural-foods stores and the natural-foods sections of many supermarkets.

CANNED & BOTTLED GOODS

Some **bottled clam juices** are high in sodium, so salt the recipe accordingly. We like the Bar Harbor brand (120 mg sodium per 2-ounce serving). Find it with the canned fish or in the seafood department of your supermarket.

Hominy is white or yellow corn that has been treated with lime to remove the tough hull and germ. Dried, ground hominy is the main ingredient in grits. Canned, cooked hominy can be found in the Mexican or canned-vegetable section of large supermarkets—near the beans.

Madeira, a fortified wine from the Portuguese island of Madeira, has a sweet, mellow flavor somewhat like sherry. Find it at liquor stores or in the supermarket.

Cooking sherry can be high in sodium. Instead, look for **dry sherry** with other fortified wines in a supermarket or liquor store. **Cream sherry** is a fortified wine used to flavor sauces. Find it near other fortified wines in a wine or liquor store. Opened bottles will keep in a cool, dry place for months.

BAKING SUPPLIES

To **melt chocolate**: Place in a bowl and microwave on Medium for 1 minute. Stir, then continue microwaving on Medium in 20-second intervals until most of the chocolate has melted, stirring well after each heating. Remove the bowl and continue stirring until all the chocolate has completely melted. Or place in the top of a double boiler over hot, but not boiling, water. Stir until melted.

White whole-wheat flour, made from a special variety of white wheat, is light in color and flavor but has the same nutri-tional properties as regular whole-wheat. **Whole-wheat pastry flour** is milled from soft wheat. It contains less gluten-forming potential than regular whole-wheat flour and helps ensure a tender result in delicate baked goods while providing the nutritional benefits of whole grains. Store opened bags in the freezer. Sources: King Arthur Flour, *kingarthur flour.com*; Bob's Red Mill, *bobsredmill.com*.

NUTS & SEEDS

Find **pepitas** (hulled pumpkin seeds) in the bulk-foods section of natural-foods stores or Mexican markets. To toast them, place pepitas in a small dry skillet and cook over medium-low heat, stirring constantly, until fragrant and lightly browned, 2 to 4 minutes.

To **toast chopped nuts**, cook in a small dry skillet over medium-low heat, stirring constantly, until fragrant and lightly browned, 2 to 4 minutes.

To **toast sesame seeds**, heat a small dry skillet over low heat. Add sesame seeds and stir constantly until golden and fragrant, about 2 minutes. Transfer to a bowl to cool.

FRUIT

To **segment citrus fruit**, remove the skin and white pith from the fruit with a sharp knife. Working over a bowl, cut the segments from their surrounding membranes. Squeeze juice into the bowl before discarding the membranes.

Very large **papayas**, 3 to 4 pounds each, are available in many large supermarkets. You may also find smaller papayas (about the size of a mango and yielding about 1 cup of diced fruit each). To select a ripe papaya, look for skin that is about half golden yellow and half green and yields to gentle pressure, like a ripe peach or nectarine. It's common to find very green papayas in the store, but once home, they'll ripen—out of the refrigerator—in 2 to 3 days.

VEGETABLES

See also Vegetable-Steaming Guide, page 191 and Vegetable-Roasting Guide, page 193.

To **prep & steam beets**: Trim greens (if any) and root end; peel the skin with a vegetable peeler. Cut beets into ½- to 1-inch-thick cubes, wedges or slices. Place in a steamer basket over 1 inch of boiling water in a large pot. Cover and steam over high heat until tender, 10 to 15 minutes.

No time to prep beets? Look for Melissa's brand Peeled Baby Red Beets in the produce section of many supermarkets. They're peeled, steamed and ready to eat and contain less sodium than their canned counterparts.

Look for already peeled, seeded and quartered **butternut squash** in the prepared-vegetable section of the produce department.

To **remove corn from the cob**, stand an uncooked ear of corn on its stem end in a shallow bowl and cut the kernels off with a sharp, thin-bladed knife. If making a soup, after cutting off the kernels, you can reverse the knife and use the dull side to press down the length of the ear to push out the rest of the corn and its milk.

DAIRY & EGGS

To **hard-boil eggs:** Place eggs in a single layer in a saucepan; cover with water. Bring to a simmer over medium-high heat. Reduce heat to low and cook at the barest simmer for 10 minutes. Remove from heat, pour out hot water and cover the eggs with ice-cold water. Let stand until cool enough to handle before peeling.

Ghee is a type of clarified butter that has had any water and milk solids removed. It has a higher smoke point than butter, a nutty flavor and is traditionally used in Indian cooking. Look for it in large supermarkets, gourmet or Indian specialty markets.

Greek-style yogurt is made by removing the whey from cultured milk, which gives the yogurt a thick, creamy texture. Look for it with other yogurt in large supermarkets.

MEAT & POULTRY

If you don't have **cooked chicken**, you can cook some quickly by poaching it. Start with 1 pound boneless, skinless chicken breasts to yield about 2 cups cooked cubed or shredded; 1 ½ pounds for 3 cups. Place chicken breasts in a skillet or saucepan. Add lightly salted water (or chicken broth) to cover and bring to a boil. Cover, reduce heat to low

and simmer gently until the chicken is cooked through and no longer pink in the middle, 10 to 15 minutes.

It can be difficult to find an individual **chicken breast** small enough for one portion. Removing the thin strip of meat from the underside of a 5-ounce breast—the "tender"—removes about 1 ounce of meat and yields a perfect 4-ounce portion. Wrap and freeze the trimmed tenders and when you have gathered enough, use them in a stir-fry, for oven-baked chicken fingers or in Hawaiian Ginger-Chicken Stew (*page 117*). **Chicken tenders** can also be purchased separately. Four 1-ounce tenders will yield a 3-ounce cooked portion.

To serve 4 people, look for a rack of **lamb** that has 8 chops. If you can find one that's been "Frenched" (meat cut away at the tips, exposing the bone) and trimmed, you will only need a 1-pound rack. Otherwise, look for a 1 ½-pound rack and ask your butcher to prepare it for you.

FISH & SEAFOOD

For more information about sustainable seafood choices, visit Monterey Bay Aquarium Seafood Watch (seafoodwatch.org).

Wild-caught **halibut** from the U.S. or Canadian Pacific is more sustainably fished and has a more stable population.

Wild-caught **salmon** from the Pacific (Alaska and Washington) are more sustainably fished and have a larger, more stable population. To **skin a salmon fillet**, place the fillet on a clean cutting board, skin side down. Starting at the tail end, slip the blade of a long, sharp knife between the fish flesh and the skin, holding the skin down firmly with your other hand. Gently push the blade along at a 30° angle, separating the fillet from the skin without cutting through either.

Be sure to buy "dry" **scallops**, which are scallops that have not been treated with sodium tripolyphosphate, or STP. Scallops that have been treated with STP ("wet" scallops) have been subjected to a chemical bath and are mushy, less flavorful and won't brown properly. Look for the small, tough muscle on the side of most scallops and pull it off with your fingers before cooking them.

Both wild-caught and farm-raised **shrimp** can damage the surrounding ecosystems when not managed properly. To buy shrimp that have been raised or caught with sound environmental practices, look for fresh or frozen shrimp certified by an independent agency, such as Wild American Shrimp or Marine Stewardship Council. If you can't find certified shrimp, choose wild-caught shrimp from North America—it's more likely to be sustainably caught.

Shrimp is usually sold by the number needed to make one pound. For example, "21-25 count" means there will be 21 to 25 shrimp in a pound. Size names, such as "large" or "extra large," are not standardized, so to be sure you're getting the size you want, order by the count (or number) per pound.

To **peel & devein shrimp**, grasp the legs and hold onto the tail while you twist off the shell. (Save the shells to make a tasty stock: Simmer, in enough water to cover, for 10 minutes, then strain. Try substituting it for clam juice in Linguine with Escarole & Shrimp, page 127.) The "vein" running along a shrimp's back (technically the dorsal surface, opposite the legs) under a thin layer of flesh is really its digestive tract. To devein, use a paring knife to make a slit along the length of the shrimp. Under running water, remove the tract with the knife tip.

Both farmed and wild-caught **striped bass** from the U.S. are sustainably managed and considered best choices for the environment.

Look for U.S. farm-raised **tilapia**, which is usually grown in closed farming systems that limit pollution and prevent escapes. Some Central and South American tilapia is farmed in this manner as well, but avoid tilapia from China and Taiwan, mostly farmed in open systems that can damage the surrounding environment.

U.S. farmed rainbow **trout** is sustainably managed and considered a best choice for the environment. Buy whole trout with the bones and heads removed (easier than cleaning them yourself) or ask your fishmonger to clean them for you. After cleaning, one trout weighs about 5 ounces.

Fresh **albacore tuna** from the U.S. Pacific and British Columbia and most **skipjack tuna** are sustainably managed and considered best choices for the environment. Chunk light canned tuna, which comes from the smaller skipjack or yellowfin, has less mercury than canned white albacore tuna. Due to concerns about mercury harming developing nervous systems, the FDA/EPA advice recommends that pregnant women and young children consume no more than 6 ounces of albacore a week; up to 12 ounces canned light tuna is considered safe.

GRILLING TIP

To **oil a grill rack**: Oil a folded paper towel, hold it with tongs and rub it over the rack. (Do not use cooking spray on a hot grill.)

RECIPE GUIDELINES & NUTRIENT ANALYSES

NUTRITION ICONS

Using our healthy-diet icons, our nutritionists have highlighted recipes likely to be of interest to people following various dietary plans. Recipes with small serving sizes (e.g., salad dressings) don't qualify for icons.

H W To qualify for the **Healthy Weight** icon, an entree has reduced calories and saturated fat, as follows:
calories ≤ 350 sat fat ≤ 5g

For side dishes, muffins, breads, the limits are:
calories ≤ 250 sat fat ≤ 3g

For desserts, the limits are:
calories ≤ 250 sat fat ≤ 5g

For dips (1/4- to 1/2-cup serving), the limits are:
calories ≤ 100 sat fat ≤ 2g

For Combination Meals,* the limits are:
calories ≤ 420 sat fat ≤ 7g

L C The **Lower Carbs** icon means a recipe has 20 grams or less of carbohydrate per serving.

H F The **High Fiber** icon means an entree provides 5 grams or more of fiber per serving (3 grams or more for all other recipes).

H H For the **Healthy Heart** icon, entrees have 3 grams or less of saturated fat (5 grams or less for fish entrees). Side dishes, muffins, breads, desserts have 2 grams or less of saturated fat; dips have 1 gram or less. Combination Meals* have 5 grams or less of saturated fat (7 grams or less for fish entrees).

*Combination Meal: A serving of protein plus a starch **or** vegetable serving.

NUTRITION BONUSES

Nutrition bonuses are indicated for recipes that provide 15% or more of the Daily Value (dv) of specific nutrients. The daily values are the average daily recommended nutrient intakes for most adults. In addition to the nutrients listed on food labels (vitamins A and C, calcium, iron and fiber), we have included information for other nutrients (folate, magnesium, potassium, zinc) when appropriate.

We have chosen to highlight these nutrients because of their importance to good health and the fact that many Americans may have inadequate intakes of them.

ANALYSIS NOTES

Each recipe is analyzed for calories, total fat, saturated (sat) and monounsaturated (mono) fat, cholesterol, carbohydrate, protein, fiber, sodium and potassium. (Numbers less than 0.5 are rounded down to 0; 0.5 to 0.9 are rounded up to 1.) We use The Food Processor SQL© Nutrition Analysis Software from ESHA Research, Salem, Oregon.

Recipes are tested with iodized table salt unless otherwise indicated. Kosher or sea salt is called for when the recipe will benefit from the unique texture or flavor. We assume that rinsing with water reduces the sodium in canned foods by 35%. (Readers on sodium-restricted diets can reduce or eliminate the salt in a recipe.)

When a recipe gives a measurement range of an ingredient, we analyze the first amount. When alternative ingredients are listed, we analyze the first one suggested. Optional ingredients and garnishes are not analyzed. We do not include trimmings or marinade that is not absorbed in analyses. Portion sizes are consistent with healthy-eating guidelines.

OTHER DEFINITIONS

Testers in the EatingWell Test Kitchen keep track of the time needed for each recipe:

Active Time includes prep time (the time it takes to chop, dice, puree, mix, combine, etc. before cooking begins), but it also includes the time spent tending something on the stovetop, in the oven or on the grill—and getting it to the table. If you can't walk away from it for more than 10 minutes, we consider it active time.

Total includes both active and inactive time and indicates the entire amount of time required for each recipe, start to finish.

To Make Ahead gives storage instructions for dishes that taste good made in advance. If special **Equipment** is needed to prepare a recipe, we tell you that too.

Recipes ready to eat in **45 minutes or less** are marked with this icon.

CALORIE COUNTS

CEREAL & GRAIN-BASED FOODS

Bagel, whole-wheat	½ ea.	130
Barley, pearl, cooked	½ cup	97
Bread		
baguette, whole-grain, 2"	2 oz.	131
multigrain	1 piece	80
oatmeal	1 piece	73
pita, whole-wheat, 4"	1 piece	74
rye	1 piece	83
whole-wheat	1 piece	69
Bulgur, whole-wheat	½ cup	76
Buns, hamburger, whole-wheat	1 ea.	114
Couscous, whole-wheat	½ cup	139
Crackers		
graham	1 rectangle	65
matzo, whole-wheat	1 ea.	98
Saltine	6 ea.	76
Croutons, seasoned	½ cup	93
English muffin, whole-wheat	½ ea.	67
Grits, corn, cooked in water	½ cup	71
Oatmeal, cooked in water, plain	½ cup	83
instant, flavored	½ cup	128
Pasta, whole-wheat, cooked	½ cup	87
Popcorn, air-popped	2 cups	62
popped in oil, salted	2 cups	110
Polenta, prepared tube	4 oz.	79
Pretzels, tiny twists, fat-free	1 oz.	101
Quinoa, cooked	½ cup	111
Rice		
brown, cooked	½ cup	109
white, cooked	½ cup	121
wild, cooked	½ cup	83
Tortilla, corn, 6"	1 ea.	70
whole-wheat, 8"	1 ea.	140

CONDIMENTS, FLAVORINGS & BROTHS

Broth, canned		
beef, low-sodium	1 cup	15
chicken, low-sodium	1 cup	15
vegetable, low-sodium	1 cup	30
Honey	1 tsp.	21
Ketchup	1 Tbsp.	15
Mayonnaise		
low-fat	1 Tbsp.	15
regular	1 Tbsp.	100
Mustard, any kind	1 tsp.	2
Oil, any kind	1 tsp.	42
Olives		
green, stuffed	3 ea.	12
Kalamata	3 ea.	35
Peanut butter, natural, chunky or creamy	1 Tbsp.	94
Pesto	1 Tbsp.	78

Pickles, kosher dill, spears	1 ea.	5
Salad dressing		
Caesar	2 Tbsp.	159
Caesar, low-calorie	2 Tbsp.	33
French	2 Tbsp.	146
honey-mustard	2 Tbsp.	102
Italian	2 Tbsp.	86
Italian, low-calorie	2 Tbsp.	53
Ranch	2 Tbsp.	145
Ranch, reduced-fat	2 Tbsp.	59
Soy sauce, low-sodium	1 tsp.	3
Sugar	1 tsp.	16
Vinegar, distilled	1 tsp.	0

DAIRY & EGGS

Butter	1 tsp.	33
whipped	1 tsp.	22
Cheese		
blue, crumbled	¼ cup	119
Brie	1 oz.	95
Cheddar, low-fat, shredded	¼ cup	49
Cheddar, regular, shredded	¼ cup	121
feta, crumbled	¼ cup	99
fontina	1 oz.	110
goat, semisoft	1 oz.	103
Monterey Jack, shredded	¼ cup	105
mozzarella, part-skim, shredded	¼ cup	85
Parmesan, grated	2 Tbsp.	43
ricotta, part-skim	½ cup	171
Swiss, shredded	¼ cup	103
Cottage cheese		
low-fat	½ cup	81
nonfat	½ cup	70
Cream cheese		
reduced-fat	1 Tbsp.	30
whipped, reduced-fat	1 Tbsp.	50
Egg		
large	1 ea.	72
substitute, liquid	¼ cup	53
Frozen yogurt, nonfat		
chocolate	½ cup	100
vanilla or strawberry	½ cup	95
Ice cream, low-fat		
chocolate	½ cup	153
vanilla	½ cup	125
Milk		
low-fat (1%)	1 cup	110
nonfat/skim	1 cup	86
reduced-fat (2%)	1 cup	122
whole	1 cup	146
Sour cream		
reduced-fat	1 Tbsp.	20
regular	1 Tbsp.	23
Soymilk, plain, low-fat	8 oz.	83
Yogurt		
plain, low-fat	½ cup	77
plain, nonfat	½ cup	69
vanilla, low-fat	½ cup	104
vanilla, nonfat	½ cup	111

FISH & SEAFOOD

(See fish and seafood notes, page 209, for best environmental choices.)

Catfish, cooked	3 oz.	129
Cod, cooked	3 oz.	89
Crab		
canned, pasteurized	3 oz.	84
Dungeness, cooked	3 oz.	80
king, leg, cooked	3 oz.	117
Salmon		
wild Pacific, cooked	3 oz.	184
smoked (lox)	1 oz.	33
Sardines, in oil, drained	1 oz.	59
Scallops, cooked	3 oz.	114
Shrimp, cooked	3 oz.	84
Tilapia, cooked	3 oz.	109
Trout, cooked	3 oz.	162
Tuna		
chunk light, canned with water, drained	3 oz.	99
cooked	3 oz.	156

FRUIT & JUICE

Apples, medium, fresh	1 ea.	95
Applesauce, unsweetened	½ cup	51
Apricots, fresh or dried	1 ea.	18
Banana, medium	1 ea.	105
Blackberries, fresh	½ cup	31
Blueberries, fresh	½ cup	42
Cherries		
dried	¼ cup	79
fresh	½ cup	49
Coconut, dried, unsweetened	1 Tbsp.	33
Cranberries, dried	¼ cup	98
Dates, dried	1 oz.	80
Grapefruit, medium	½ ea.	16
Grapes, fresh	1 cup	104
Juice		
apple, unsweetened	½ cup	57
cranberry, unsweetened	½ cup	58
lemon, fresh	1 Tbsp.	4
orange, fresh	½ cup	56
tomato, low-sodium	½ cup	25
vegetable, low-sodium	½ cup	26
Kiwi, fresh, medium	1 ea.	46
Mango, fresh	½ ea.	67
Melon		
cantaloupe, cubed	1 cup	54
honeydew, cubed	1 cup	61
watermelon, cubed	1 cup	46
Nectarines, fresh, medium	1 ea.	62
Oranges, fresh, medium	1 ea.	62
Papaya, fresh, cubed	½ cup	27
Peaches, fresh, medium	1 ea.	60
Pears, fresh, medium	1 ea.	103

	Quantity	Calories
Pineapple, fresh, diced	1/2 cup	41
Plums, fresh	1 ea.	30
Prunes, dried, pitted	1 oz.	78
Raisins, seedless	1/4 cup	108
Raspberries, fresh	1/2 cup	32
Strawberries, fresh	1/2 cup	27
Tangerines, fresh, medium	1 ea.	47

MEATS & POULTRY

	Quantity	Calories
Bacon		
Canadian, cooked	1 oz.	45
regular, cooked	1 piece	43
turkey, cooked	1 piece	31
Beef, ground, cooked		
7% fat (93%-lean)	3 oz.	170
10% fat (90%-lean)	3 oz.	182
Beef		
filet mignon, cooked	3 oz.	175
strip steak, lean, cooked	3 oz.	161
top sirloin or round steak, cooked	3 oz.	151
Chicken		
breast, deli, sliced	1 oz.	27
breast, no skin, cooked	3 oz.	140
dark meat, no skin, cooked	3 oz.	178
tenders, cooked	3 oz.	105
Ham, deli, lean, sliced	1 oz.	30
Pork		
tenderloin, cooked	3 oz.	122
loin chop, bone-in, cooked	6 oz.	177
Prosciutto, sliced	1 oz.	61
Salami, sliced	1 oz.	74
Turkey		
breast, deli, sliced	1 oz.	29
ground, 93%-lean, cooked	3 oz.	150
ground, 99%-lean, cooked	3 oz.	120
dark meat, no skin, cooked	3 oz.	159
light meat, no skin, cooked	3 oz.	134

NUTS, SEEDS & BEANS

	Quantity	Calories
Almonds, dry-roasted	2 Tbsp.	103
Cashews, dry-roasted	2 Tbsp.	98
Peanuts, dry-roasted	2 Tbsp.	107
Pecans, dry-roasted	2 Tbsp.	89
Pine nuts, dried	2 Tbsp.	114
Pistachios, shelled	2 Tbsp.	88
Walnuts, dried, halves	2 Tbsp.	82
Seeds		
pumpkin (pepitas)	2 Tbsp.	36
sesame	1 Tbsp.	52
sunflower, toasted	2 Tbsp.	93
Beans		
baked	1/2 cup	150
black, cooked	1/2 cup	114
butter, cooked	1/2 cup	100
chickpeas, cooked	1/2 cup	143
kidney, cooked	1/2 cup	105
lentils, cooked	1/2 cup	115
pinto, cooked	1/2 cup	122
white, cooked	1/2 cup	153
Soy		
edamame, cooked	1/2 cup	100
tofu, extra-firm, cubed	1/2 cup	128
tofu, seasoned, baked, cubed	1/2 cup	267

VEGETABLES

	Quantity	Calories
Artichoke hearts, water-canned	1/2 cup	38
Arugula, fresh	1 cup	5
Asparagus, cooked	1/2 cup	20
Avocado, fresh	1/4 ea.	80
Beets, slices, cooked	1/2 cup	37
Bok choy, cooked	1/2 cup	10
Broccoli, florets, cooked	1/2 cup	22
Brussels sprouts, cooked	1/2 cup	28
Cabbage, green or red, fresh	1/2 cup	9
Carrots, fresh, chopped	1/2 cup	26
Cauliflower, florets, cooked	1/2 cup	14
Celery, fresh, diced	1/2 cup	8
Corn, kernels, cooked	1/2 cup	66
Cucumber, slices, fresh	1/2 cup	8
Eggplant, diced, cooked	1/2 cup	17
Endive, Belgian, fresh	1 cup	15
Fennel, bulb, fresh, diced	1/2 cup	36
Green beans, cooked	1/2 cup	37
Kale, cooked	1/2 cup	18
Lettuce, fresh, any type	1 cup	8
Mushrooms, fresh	1/2 cup	8
Okra, cooked	1/2 cup	18
Peas		
green, cooked	1/2 cup	67
snow or sugar snap, cooked	1/2 cup	35
Peppers, bell, fresh	1/2 cup	19
Potatoes, cooked		
red	1/2 cup	70
russet	1/2 cup	73
Yukon Gold	1/2 cup	70
Radishes, fresh, sliced	1/2 cup	9
Spinach		
baby, fresh	1 cup	10
steamed	1/2 cup	21
Squash		
butternut, diced, cooked	1/2 cup	41
summer, diced, cooked	1/2 cup	14
Sweet potatoes, diced, cooked	1/2 cup	90
Tomatoes		
fresh	1/2 cup	16
stewed	1/2 cup	33
Turnips, diced, cooked	1/2 cup	17
Watercress, fresh	1 cup	4

EAT BY THE USDA'S MYPYRAMID

Here's how: **1.** Find your daily calorie goal (*see page 12 if you don't know it*). **2.** Follow down the column to see how many servings you need. **3.** MyPyramid defines calorie goals in 200-calorie increments. If your calorie goal falls between levels in the below chart, follow the recommendations for the calorie level closest to your target.

Calorie level	1,200	1,400	1,600	1,800	2,000	2,200	2,400	2,600
Grains*	4 oz.-eq.	5 oz.-eq.	5 oz.-eq.	6 oz.-eq.	6 oz.-eq.	7 oz.-eq.	8 oz.-eq.	9 oz.-eq.
Vegetables**	1.5 cups	1.5 cups	2 cups	2.5 cups	2.5 cups	3 cups	3 cups	3.5 cups
Fruits***	1 cup	1.5 cups	1.5 cups	1.5 cups	2 cups	2 cups	2 cups	2 cups
Milk (or dairy)	2 cups	2 cups	3 cups	3 cups	3 cups	3 cups	3 cups	3 cups
Meat, Beans†	3 oz.-eq.	4 oz.-eq.	5 oz.-eq.	5 oz.-eq.	5.5 oz.-eq.	6 oz.-eq.	6.5 oz.-eq.	6.5 oz.-eq.
Oils	4 tsp.	4 tsp.	5 tsp.	5 tsp.	6 tsp.	6 tsp.	7 tsp.	8 tsp.
Discretionary calories††	171	171	132	195	267	290	362	410

Notes: *1 oz.-equivalent for grain = 1/2 cup pasta, rice or oatmeal, 1 cup whole-grain cold cereal, 1 slice bread, 1/2 an English muffin. **A 1/2 cup of vegetables or 1 cup of raw leafy greens = 1 vegetable serving. ***1 cup cut fruit or 1 medium whole fruit = 1 fruit serving. † 1 oz.-equivalent = 1 oz. lean meat, poultry or fish, 1/4 cup cooked beans or tofu. †† "Discretionary calories" are those remaining after all the food-group portions are consumed. "Spend" them on whatever you want.

SPECIAL INDEXES

RECIPE INDEX

(Page numbers in italics indicate photographs.)

CONTRIBUTORS

Our thanks to these fine food writers whose work was previously published in
EatingWell *Magazine.*

BRUCE AIDELLS | Mozzarella-Stuffed Turkey Burgers, 108

JOHN ASH | Salmon Burgers with Green Goddess Sauce, 138

KATHY FARRELL-KINGSLEY | Roasted Apple & Cheddar Salad, 64; Asian-Style Grilled Tofu with Greens, 73; Maple-Roasted Sweet Potatoes, 189

CHEF JESÚS GONZÁLEZ, RANCHO LA PUERTA | Baja Butternut Squash Soup, 34

JOYCE HENDLEY | Salmon & Cucumber Mini Smørrebrød, 22

SUSAN HERR | Southwestern Rice & Pinto Bean Salad, 89; Chicken, Charred Tomato & Broccoli Salad, 103

RAGHAVAN IYER | Ginger, Split Pea & Vegetable Curry, 94; Indian Wok-Seared Chicken & Vegetables, 121

PATSY JAMIESON | Quinoa with Latin Flavors, 186; Butternut & Barley Pilaf, 187

CHERYL & BILL JAMISON | Grilled Tomato Gazpacho, 40

BARBARA KAFKA | Curried Carrot Soup, 32

WENDY KALEN | Mini Meatloaves, 154

PEGGY KNICKERBOCKER | Mississippi Spiced Pecans, 23

DIANE KOCHILAS | Roasted Eggplant & Feta Dip, 29

PERLA MEYERS | Pan-Roasted Chicken & Gravy, 113; Braised Paprika Chicken, 114

KITTY MORSE | Moroccan Vegetable Soup, 48

ELLEN ECKER OGDEN | Fragrant Fish Soup, 47; Mixed Lettuce Salad with Cucumber Herb Vinaigrette, 52, 74; Baby Greens with Spicy Mediterranean Vinaigrette, 54, 75; Roasted Garlic Dressing, 75; Goat Cheese & Tomato Dressing, 76

DAVID PATTERSON | Ginger-Steamed Fish with Troy's Hana-Style Sauce, 135

VICTORIA ABBOTT RICCARDI | Sherried Mushrooms, 25; Japanese Chicken-Scallion Rice Bowl, 119; Wild Rice with Shiitakes & Toasted Almonds, 185

G. FRANCO ROMAGNOLI | Penne in Spicy Tomato Sauce, 81; Spaghetti with Tuna & Tomato Sauce, 144

MARIE SIMMONS | Melon, Tomato & Onion Salad with Goat Cheese, 63; Toasted Quinoa with Scallops & Snow Peas, 132

CORINNE TRANG | Grilled Pork Tenderloin Marinated in Spicy Soy Sauce, 170

LUCIA WATSON | Tuna Steaks Provençal, 142

BRUCE WEINSTEIN & MARK SCARBROUGH | Grapefruit Chicken Satay Salad, 68; Thai Beef Salad, 72; Flemish Beef Stew, 151; Chewy Chocolate Cookies, 197

VIRGINIA WILLIS | Chunky Peach Popsicles, 202

OTHER EATINGWELL BOOKS

AVAILABLE AT EATINGWELL.COM/SHOP

EatingWell in Season: The Farmers' Market Cookbook

(The Countryman Press, 2009)
ISBN: 978-0-88150-856-7 (hardcover)

EatingWell Comfort Foods Made Healthy: The Classic Makeover Cookbook

(The Countryman Press, 2008)
ISBN: 978-0-88150-829-1 (hardcover)
ISBN: 978-0-88150-887-1 (softcover, 2009)

EatingWell for a Healthy Heart Cookbook: A Cardiologist's Guide to Adding Years to Your Life

(The Countryman Press, 2008)
ISBN: 978-0-88150-724-9 (hardcover)

The EatingWell Diet: 7 Steps to a Healthy, Trimmer You 150+ Delicious, Healthy Recipes with Proven Results

(The Countryman Press, 2007)
ISBN: 978-0-88150-722-5 (hardcover)
ISBN: 978-0-88150-822-2 (softcover, 2008)

EatingWell Serves Two: 150 Healthy in a Hurry Suppers

(The Countryman Press, 2006)
ISBN: 978-0-88150-723-2 (hardcover)

The EatingWell Healthy in a Hurry Cookbook: 150 Delicious Recipes for Simple, Everyday Suppers in 45 Minutes or Less

(The Countryman Press, 2006)
ISBN: 978-0-88150-687-7 (hardcover)

The EatingWell Diabetes Cookbook: 275 Delicious Recipes and 100+ Tips for Simple, Everyday Carbohydrate Control

(The Countryman Press, 2005)
ISBN: 978-0-88150-633-4 (hardcover)
ISBN: 978-0-88150-778-2 (softcover, 2007)

The Essential EatingWell Cookbook: Good Carbs, Good Fats, Great Flavors

(The Countryman Press, 2004)
ISBN: 978-0-88150-630-3 (hardcover)
ISBN: 978-0-88150-701-0 (softcover, 2005)